Contemporary U.S. Latino/a Literary Criticism

AMERICAN LITERATURE READINGS IN THE 21ST CENTURY

Series Editor: Linda Wagner-Martin

American Literature Readings in the 21st Century publishes works by contemporary critics that help shape critical opinion regarding literature of the nineteenth and twentieth century in the United States.

Published by Palgrave Macmillan:

Freak Shows in Modern American Imagination: Constructing the Damaged Body from Willa Cather to Truman Capote
By Thomas Fahy

Arab American Literary Fictions, Cultures, and Politics
By Steven Salaita

Women & Race in Contemporary U.S. Writing: From Faulkner to Morrison
By Kelly Lynch Reames

American Political Poetry in the 21st Century
By Michael Dowdy

Science and Technology in the Age of Hawthorne, Melville, Twain, and James: Thinking and Writing Electricity
By Sam Halliday

F. Scott Fitzgerald's Racial Angles and the Business of Literary Greatness
By Michael Nowlin

Sex, Race, and Family in Contemporary American Short Stories
By Melissa Bostrom

Democracy in Contemporary U.S. Women's Poetry
By Nicky Marsh

James Merrill and W.H. Auden: Homosexuality and Poetic Influence
By Piotr K. Gwiazda

Contemporary U.S. Latino/a Literary Criticism
Edited by Lyn Di Iorio Sandín and Richard Perez

List of Previous Publications

Lyn Di Iorio Sandín. *Killing Spanish: Literary Essays on Ambivalent U.S. Latino/a Identity* (Palgrave Macmillan, 2004)

Contemporary U.S. Latino/a Literary Criticism

Edited by

*Lyn Di Iorio Sandín and
Richard Perez*

palgrave
macmillan

CONTEMPORARY U.S. LATINO/A LITERARY CRITICISM

Copyright © Lyn Di Iorio Sandín and Richard Perez, 2007.

First published in 2007 by
PALGRAVE MACMILLAN™
175 Fifth Avenue, New York, N.Y. 10010 and
Houndmills, Basingstoke, Hampshire, England RG21 6XS
Companies and representatives throughout the world.

PALGRAVE MACMILLAN is the global academic imprint of the Palgrave Macmillan division of St. Martin's Press, LLC and of Palgrave Macmillan Ltd. Macmillan® is a registered trademark in the United States, United Kingdom and other countries. Palgrave is a registered trademark in the European Union and other countries.

ISBN-13: 978–1–4039–7999–5
ISBN-10: 1–4039–7999–5

Library of Congress Cataloging-in-Publication Data

Contemporary U.S. Latino/a literary criticism / edited by Lyn Di Iorio Sandín and Richard Perez.
    p. cm.—(American literature readings in the 21st century)
    Includes bibliographical references.
    ISBN 1–4039–7999–5
    1. American literature—Hispanic American authors—History and criticism. 2. American literature—Hispanic American authors—History and criticism—Theory, etc. 3. American literature—20th century—History and criticism. 4. American literature—21st century—History and criticism. 5. Hispanic Americans—Intellectual life. 6. Hispanic Americans in literature. I. Sandín, Lyn Di Iorio II. Perez, Richard, 1969–

PS153.H56C67 2007
810.9'868073—dc22   2007003548

A catalogue record for this book is available from the British Library.

Design by Newgen Imaging Systems (P) Ltd., Chennai, India.

First edition: November 2007

10 9 8 7 6 5 4 3 2 1

Printed in the United States of America.

A mi endiablado Pitirre 51: que encuentres y derrotes a tu guaraguao
LDS

For my beloved father, Ricardo Perez:
advisor, friend, and best domino partner.
His spirit persists in my life.

And for my loving mother, Ana Cordero,
who taught me an ethics of hospitality.
RP

CONTENTS

ABOUT THE CONTRIBUTORS

Victoria A. Chevalier is an Assistant Professor of English literature at Furman University and the Director of the black cultures in the Americas Concentration. Her current project focuses on sexuality and materiality in the emplotment of the Moses and Caliban myths in African American and Caribbean literatures.

María DeGuzmán is Associate Professor of English and Director of Latina/o studies at the University of North Carolina at Chapel Hill. She is the author of the book *Spain's Long Shadow: The Black Legend, Off-Whiteness, and Anglo-American Empire* (University of Minnesota Press, 2005). She is also the author of published articles and essays on the work of Ana Castillo (in *Aztlán*), Graciela Limón (in *Revista Iberoamericana*), Rane Ramón Arroyo, John Rechy, and Floyd Salas. Currently, she is working on a second book project concerning Latina/o aesthetics of night and is continuing to produce photo–text work as Camera Query (http://www.cameraquery.com), both solo and in collaboration with colleagues and friends.

Román de la Campa is the Edwin B. and Leonore R. Williams Professor of Romance Languages at the University of Pennsylvania. His publications take a comparative view of Latin American, American, and Latino literatures, theory, and other cultural practices. They include nearly a hundred essays published in the United States, Latin America, and Europe, as well as the following recent books: *Late Imperial Cultures*, co-edited (Verso, 1995); *America Latina y sus comunidades discursivas: cultura y literature en la era global* (Caracas, 1999); *Latin Americanism* (Minnesota University Press, 2000); *Cuba on My Mind: Journeys to a Severed Nation* (Londres, Verso, 2001); *América Latina: Tres Interpretaciones actuales sobre su estudio, con Ignacio Sosa y Enrique Camacho* (Universidad Autónoma de México, Edición especial, 2004); *Nuevas cartografías latinoamericanas* (to appear in Letras Cubanas, Havana, 2006). His next book, *Split-States and Global Imaginaries*, is in progress and is scheduled to appear with Verso in 2007.

Lyn Di Iorio Sandín is the author of *Killing Spanish: Literary Essays on Ambivalent U.S. Latino/a Identity* (Palgrave Macmillan, 2004). She has just finished her first novel called *Outside the Bones*. Her short stories have been published in *The Bilingual Review, The Hogtown Creek Review*, and *The Texas Review*, and in other journals. Her short story "Queen of Colomer" was short-listed for the 2002 Pirates Alley William Faulkner Short Story Prize. She teaches at The City College of New York.

Margarite Fernández Olmos is Professor of Spanish at Brooklyn College of the City University of New York. She is the author/co-editor of numerous work on Caribbean and U.S. Latino literatures including *Sacred Possessions: Vodou, Santería, Obeah and the Caribbean* (Rutgers University Press, 1997), *Healing Cultures: Art and Religion as Curative Practices in the Caribbean and its Diaspora* (Palgrave Macmillan, 2001), and *Creole Religions of the Caribbean: An Introduction from Vodou and Santería to Obeah and Espiritismo* (New York University Press, 2003) with Lizabeth Paravisini-Gebert, *The Latino Reader: An American Literary Tradition from 1542 to the Present* (Mariner Books, 1997) and *U.S. Latino Literature: A Critical Guide for Students and Teachers* (Greenwood Press, 2000) with Harold Augenbraum.

Rodrigo Lazo is Associate Professor of English at the University of California, Irvine, and author of *Writing to Cuba: Filibustering and Cuban Exiles in the United States* (University of North Carolina Press, 2005). His articles have appeared in numerous journals and collections, including *American Literature* and *American Literary History*.

William Luis is the Chancellor's Professor of Spanish at Vanderbilt University. Luis has published twelve books and more than one hundred scholarly articles. His authored books include *Literary Bondage: Slavery in Cuban Narrative* (University of Texas Press, 1990), *Dance Between Two Cultures: Latino Caribbean Literature Written in the United States* (Vanderbilt University Press, 1997), *Culture and Customs of Cuba* (Greenwood Press, 2001), *Lunes de Revolución: Literatura y cultura en los primeros años de la Revolución Cubana* (Editorial Verbum, 2003), and *Del silencio a la escritura: Autobiografía del esclavo Juan Francisco Manzano y otros escritos* (2006). He is the editor of the *Afro-Hispanic Review*. Born and raised in New York City, Luis is widely regarded as a leading authority on Latin American, Caribbean, Afro-Hispanic, and Latino U.S. literatures.

Andrea O'Reilly Herrera is a Professor of Literature and Director of Ethnic Studies at the University of Colorado at Colorado Springs. O'Reilly Herrera is a published poet and the author of critical essays on writers ranging from Charlotte Brontë and Marguerite Duras to Cristina García and Sandra Cisneros. She has also edited anthologies including *Remembering Cuba: Legacy of a Diaspora* (University of Texas Press, 2001), which features a wide range of testimonials drawn from the Cuban exile community and their children residing in the United States. She is also the author of the novel *The Pearl of the Antilles* (Bilingual/Review Press, 2001), which was awarded the Golden Quill Book Award in 2005 and later transcribed into a play. Among her more recent work is a forthcoming edited collection of essays *Cuba: "Idea of a Nation" Displaced* (SUNY Press, 2007); a forthcoming co-edited textbook for McGraw Hill titled *The Matrix Reader: Examining the Dynamics of Oppression and Privilege*; and a monograph contracted by the University of Texas Press and tentatively titled *"Setting the Tent Against the House": Cuban Artists in the Diaspora*.

Mary Pat Brady is the author of *Extinct Lands, Temporal Geographies: Chicana Literature and the Urgency of Space* (Duke UP, 2002). She teaches at Cornell University.

Richard Perez is working towards his PhD in English and American literature at the City University of New York Graduate Center. He teaches U.S. Latino literature, Post-colonial literature and literary theory at Hunter College of the City University of New York. He is currently writing his dissertation on the specter in postcolonial, and trans-American literature. His work has appeared in *Centro: Journal of the Center for Puerto Rican Studies*. He also writes book reviews for *Tempo*, the Latino portion of the *New York Post*.

Kirsten Silva Gruesz teaches nineteenth- and twentieth-century literatures of the Americas, including Latino/a literature, at the University of California, Santa Cruz. Her 2002 book, *Ambassadors of Culture: The Transnational Origins of Latino Writing* (Princeton University Press, 2002), examined early U.S. periodicals in Spanish in the context of literary relations between the Americas. She has most recently written essays on the Gulf of Mexico as a border zone, on Latinos in post-Katrina New Orleans, and on Latino appropriations of Whitman, and is currently completing a book titled *Bad Lengua: A Cultural History of Spanish in the United States*.

Acknowledgments

A project such as this one is dependent on the collaborative effort of its esteemed contributors. To them we issue our first thanks. These essays showcase the extraordinary range and ingenuity at work in contemporary U.S. Latino/a literary studies. In many ways, the seeds for this book germinated close to a decade ago in conversations between the two of us about the apparent dearth of literary criticism in U.S. Latino/a Studies. Since then, our personal commitment to U.S. Latino/a literature has manifested itself in countless discussions sifting through the imaginative details of a literature we both love. This text is a testament to that persistent engagement.

The CUNY Graduate Center has fomented the kind of intellectual intersections this text demonstrates. In general, we want to thank the English Department. We are both grateful to Meena Alexander for her wonderful friendship and profoundly insightful guidance into the nuanced relationship between U.S. Latino/a literature and postcoloniality. Lyn in particular is indebted to Meena for an invitation to teach a graduate seminar in the spring of 2006 at The Graduate Center called "Latino Literary Textures," in which many of the ideas that led to the introduction and structuring of this book were incubated. Richard also wants to acknowledge Peter Hitchcock for imbuing the most complex theoretical questions with a sense of social urgency and pleasure; Barbara Webb for keeping his attention on the Pan-Caribbean aspects that suffuse the fictional writers of this study; and Juan Flores for his untiring commitment to Afro-Latino culture and identity. Moreover, for long-searching conversations that helped deepen and refine his thinking on U.S. Latino identity, Richard wants to thank colleagues: Maha Malik, Jonathan Grey, Nick Powers, Devin Zuber, John Rodriguez, and Una Chung.

Additionally, we would both like to thank the PSC-CUNY Research Foundation for a grant that got the book underway; the Center for Puerto Rican Studies; the Dominican Studies Institute; and the Institute for Research on the African Diaspora in the Americas and the Caribbean. It was Palgrave Macmillan's belief in the idea of this text that brought it to fruition. We are thankful for the patient efforts of our editors at Palgrave: Farideh Koohi-Kamali, Linda Wagner-Martin, and assistant editor Julia Cohen.

Lyn also wants to express her appreciation to her recent students at the CUNY Graduate Center, and most particularly to the hundreds of undergraduate and graduate students she has taught over the years at The City College of the City University of New York, whose enthusiasm and total involvement in the issues and polemics underlying U.S. Latino/a literary studies has always been nothing short of inspirational. Lyn's views of the relationship between Caribbean literature and U.S. Latino/a literatures have been enriched by discussions with Silvio Torres-Saillant, Director of Latino and Latin American studies at Syracuse University—one of the foremost thinkers in the field. She is also grateful to José David Saldívar for his support and insight into the relationship between Mexican American/Chicano and East Coast Latino literary studies. Her notion of the "Latino Scapegoat" also owes much to her City College colleague, the late Edward Rivera, with whom she often discussed the incommensurability of Latino/a assimilation. Last, and certainly not least, Lyn thanks her husband Pitirre 51 for his amazing editing skills, his insights, and support, and deep, infinitely wise, love.

Richard thanks his family for their support and patience: most importantly his loving wife Ana, and his children Jose, Kevin, and Laura; his beloved brothers Julio and Eric for their generous attention and comments; his uncle Pastor Edwin Cordero whose love of learning and language has served as an ongoing example in his life. Lastly, X, gracias for your invaluable help and friendship.

New Waves in U.S. Latino/a Literary Criticism

Lyn Di Iorio Sandín and Richard Perez

Over the last decade, U.S. Latino/a literary criticism has emerged as an innovative and invigorating theoretical presence, reflecting the similarly exciting and unprecedented literary production by Latino/a novelists, essayists, and poets. *Contemporary U.S. Latino/a Literary Criticism* brings to this milieu a series of distinguished essays demonstrating the diverse methodological trends currently at work in the field. The most immediate aim of this text is to address the literature itself: a literature that has grown progressively throughout the twentieth century, appearing after 1960 to dynamically document and reinvent Latino/a experience. A critical response must take into account rich narrative practices, which reshape, revise, and sometimes in their difference challenge Western literary traditions. Theorizing a literature that melds different languages, storytelling techniques, and memories of distant and diverse geographies is a daunting and exhilarating task.

Latino/a literature carries a foreign element, a newness that resists total incorporation into the culture at large. At the same time, it imaginatively carves out very particularized textures and spaces for its texts— from the startling bilingualism and genre-bending of Gloria Anzaldúa's *Borderlands/La Frontera* (1987) to the obsession with street life in writers ranging from Piri Thomas and Luis J. Rodriguez to Yxta Maya Murray and Junot Díaz. The critics in this anthology use varying methodologies with impressive skill and nuance to assess the imaginative directions U.S. Latino/a literature has charted. Side by side, these interdisciplinary essays create an interesting intellectual tension: at times converging seamlessly and at others existing uncomfortably in their methodological divergence. A consolidated U.S. Latino/a criticism would demonstrate a monolithic academic vision, a prescription much like that proffered by the critic Howard Bloom who prefers, to quote one of his titles, teaching Americans "how to read" literature. While these essays suggest a certain solidarity in their respect and fascination with U.S. Latino/a literature, they also present a widespread intellectual endeavor.

Part of what we wanted this anthology to exhibit is the extraordinary critical range U.S. Latino/a literature has elicited. How are Western theoretical practices applied to U.S. Latino/a literature and culture? What happens to the theory—Marxism, psychoanalysis, or feminism—in the exchange? What is this foreign or untranslatable kernel that exists in U.S. Latino/a literary theory? We are interested in the assimilative resistance evident in U.S. Latino/a literary theory even as it is suffused by Western analytic tools. In *The Location of Culture* (1994) Homi Bhabha argues that newness enters the world, usually the Western world, from a colony. By inserting in the new location an "agonistic supplement," namely, a racial, cultural, and linguistic difference, this colonial newness marks its "performance of cultural translation" with an "unstable" linking process.[1]

The "agency of foreignness" shifts the direction of the expected cultural transfer from the transformation of Latinos into "Americans."[2] The emphasis throws a different light on the forgetting, sacrificing, and implicit shame often entailed by such a becoming, to a radical transformation of the constitutive fabric of the United States into a place where Latino tastes and customs thrive, albeit with some alterations. In this sense the United States becomes, aesthetically and ontologically, "Latinized." Latino/a newcomers then not only inhabit a marginalized space, but also a creatively expansive location, stretching the borders and boundaries of a U.S. society they actively live in.

In this vein, U.S. Latino/a literary criticism uses traditional methodological theories—Marxism, psychoanalysis, feminism, to name only a few—but from an outside vantage point that reorganizes and revises its emphasis. Marxist theory, for instance, will be useless to U.S. Latino/a criticism unless the former also addresses questions of race, and language, and Latino/a sensibility. The U.S. Latino/a outside perspective extends the intellectual parameters of theory. It is a common mistake, a matter of ignorance and arrogance, to understand the U.S. Latino outside position as merely an excluded space. U.S. Latinos are not outsiders, despite the hyperbolic media images, but insiders who are pushing U.S. culture in a different direction, in order to change it and change with it. Herein lies the threat and the accompanying hysteria over Latino immigrants. U.S. Latinos, as the critics here demonstrate, do not shy away from Western cultural practices; they incorporate them into a dynamic and expansive mode of thinking and experiencing. A U.S. Latino party may include salsa, rap, and rock; a conversation will vacillate between English, Spanish, and English again; and a Latino/a literary criticism will reference psychoanalysis, Afro-Caribbean religions, Derrida, and spoken word poetry. The critics of this anthology write from this creative outside, cannily enlarging the theoretical panorama, while paying close attention to the specificities and tendencies of U.S. Latino/a literature.

U.S. Latino/a criticism, in its "agency of foreignness," functions outside the logic of the stereotype, or a reductive symbolic identification. Part of the resistance we are referring to here is a resistance to interpellation, wherein the U.S. Latino is called into existence by the assimilative demands of "American" culture. The analytic project of U.S. Latino criticism includes reissuing the terms with which it will enter into the national society. Latino literature narrates the questions and problems that such a facile offer implies. In this outside sense, the U.S. Latino/a critic must be an "initiated reader," to use Margarite Fernández Olmos's phrase from an essay in this anthology, interpreting the world from a creolized viewpoint. This implies a rhizomatic sensibility, with analytic roots that extend to Africa, Europe, Asia, and the Americas. For, as Žižek warns,

> the subject is always fastened, pinned, to a signifier which represents him for the other, and through this pinning he is loaded with a symbolic mandate, he is given a place in the inter-subjective network of symbolic relations. The point is that this mandate is ultimately arbitrary; since its nature is performative, it cannot be accounted for by reference to the "real" properties and capacities of the subject.[3]

U.S. Latino/a criticism posits a more entangled hermeneutics. If the "symbolic mandate" of the Latino is to become "Americanized" in a narrow sense, then the literature and criticism call for a new form of "Americanization" that creates the symbolic space for its complex cultural elements. The recognition that comes in an "intersubjective network" controlled in a relation of authority or, to use Lacan's phrase, the Big Other, is exposed by U.S. Latino/a criticism as a toxic form of belonging. Mimetic desire of this sort creates not only a docile subject but, ultimately, as Lyn Di Iorio Sandín argues in "The Latino Scapegoat" (chapter one), a socially dead one. Interestingly, in the prologue of Piri Thomas' *Down These Mean Streets* (1967), Piri stands on a rooftop and yells out to "anybody," "I'm here and I want recognition, whatever that mudder-fuckin word means."[4] The U.S. Latino critic speaks from the same platform: outside the "arbitrary" "symbolic relations" and in search of the more complex "properties and capacities" of Latino/a literary creation.

Can U.S. Latino literary criticism be figured as a welcome rather than an authoritative call? In her introduction to *Making Faces, Making Soul* (1990), Gloria Anzaldúa explains that Latina thought must work to uncover her interfaces:

> In sewing terms, "interfacing" means sewing a piece of material between two pieces of fabric to provide support and stability to collar, cuff, yoke. Between the masks we've internalized, one on top of another, are our interfaces. The masks are already steeped with self-hatred and other internalized oppressions. However, it is the place—the interface—between the masks that provides the space from which we can thrust out and crack the masks.[5]

What is the interface if not a call to the subject to welcome its own complexity and, by implication, the face to which it bears relation? For the U.S. Latino literary critic the interface is also an intertextual hermeneutics, where texts, theories, and traditions meet. The scene is an enriching and damaging one. Something is gained and lost. This is part of a creolized condition. However, the mask hardened by conformity, the subject interpellated by authority, allowing "self-hatred and other internalized oppressions" to stiffen into a stereotype, is in the hands of Latino literary criticism cracked, stretched, and expanded. The welcome in this sense is not a passive stance, but an emphasis on intellectual range, a creative playfulness, and an ethical attention to the ideology embedded in every aspect of our lives.

This notion of welcoming is not a passive position. Rather, this anthology attests to the intellectual detours in U.S. Latino/a literary criticism that create a relationality of converging and productively conflicting viewpoints. Hosts, as the etymology insinuates, can become hostile. The gesture of welcome, as a symbolic starting point for a critical approach, takes the faces that face us, and the faces we have "internalized," and weaves these relationships into a theory of literature. The literary construction of our identity, according to Anzaldúa, starts with symbolic attention to the face. The U.S. Latino/a literary critic must be hospitable to its presence.

Perhaps this sense of newness is the reason why U.S. Latino/a literary theory compilations have been so rarely produced, and none that is both intergroup and gender inclusive.[6] For the most part sociology, especially on the East Coast, has dominated U.S. Latino/a intellectual production. This sociological imperative is reflected in recently published anthologies, which, for the most part, ignore the literary altogether or give it a marginal placement. *The Latino Studies Reader: Culture, Politics and Society*[7] (1997) glaringly omits Latino/a literature; not one essay in this important text directly addresses literature, even though the book's title has "culture" as one of its analytical categories. Moreover, texts such as Agustín Laó-Montes and Arlene Dávila's *Mambo Montage* (2001), which traces the history of Latinidad in New York, only includes one of its fourteen essays on literature, despite the prolific history of U.S. Latino/a writers in New York.[8] *Latinos: Remaking America* (2002), a widely read compilation edited by Marcelo Suárez-Orozco and Mariela Páez, fails to overtly discuss the impact of U.S. Latino/a literature at all in its twenty-one essays, evidently not taking seriously the formative role writers play in our "remaking."[9] This demonstrates that, until recently, U.S. Latino/a literary theory was a subtle foreigner in the Latino/a scholarship taking place in the United States. This is not to downplay the groundbreaking work done by U.S. Latino/a sociologists; sociology is a field that continues to utilize various complex ways of apprehending and analyzing the U.S. Latino/a experience. Sociological scholarship informs this text and is an invaluable methodological tool in the reading of literature. The essays in this book, however, dare to venture outside the sociological field, adding other modes of analysis to its hermeneutic scope: psychoanalysis, aesthetics, and deconstruction. The essays expand on, and with, sociological scholarship that stands as an example and as an undeniable springboard.

Yet, when this emphasis on sociology is made primary, it becomes a limit in the study of literature. Again, Anzaldúa's interfacial principle instructs, enabling us to understand the vital importance of a varied intellectual approach to the U.S. Latino/a subject and U.S. Latino/a literature. Does U.S. Latino/a literature insist on or invite such an interdisciplinary response? Anzaldúa explains: "In our self-reflexivity and in our active participation with the issues that confront us, whether it be through writing, front-line activism, or individual development, we are also uncovering the inter-faces, the very spaces and places where our multiple-surfaced, colored, racially gendered bodies intersect and interconnect."[10] The "multiple-surfaced," intersecting, and interconnecting literary body that this anthology is concerned with actively elicits, in its narrative forms, in its diverse self-reflection, and in its voicing of spatial and psychic borders, an interdisciplinary logic. The critics of this anthology respond to a self-reflexive call from the literary terrain that is itself imaginatively negotiating a social presence. This anthology, then, is a text exhorted by, on the one hand, a political and aesthetic unconscious of a spectacularly growing U.S. Latino/a population, the largest immigrant and/or colonial groups of the last half-century, and now the largest minority group in the United States; and on the other hand, it is called forth by the dynamic literary production whose spirited explorations have left us with a significant body of fiction, a profound imaginary response to the complex psychic, cultural, and social relocations of U.S. Latino/a diasporas. Represented here is a new wave, a nascent trend and transfer emphasizing an interdisciplinary mode of reading, generated and welcomed by the prolific literary output of U.S. Latino/a poets and novelists of the last century.

This welcome that we are arguing is an underwritten principle in U.S. Latino/a literature and theory, also, paradoxically, becomes a resistance to what Frantz Fanon has called "thematization."[11] Is not the welcome a daring openness to the foreign, to the strange, to the outside? As Fanon observes, his desire was to "come lithe and young into a world that was ours and to help build it together."[12] The "lithe and young" foreign newness, which Fanon craves, is a state, this text illustrates, of inter-disciplinarity, where a "world" that is "ours" is built "together" not through a singular theme, but through an incessant and exemplary openness. Fanon understands that the act of building—a self, a home, a tradition—and ownership presupposes a world hospitable to difference.

But as Juan Flores warned in a talk given at Michigan State University in 2003, often categories that seem to suggest elasticity are in fact veiled attempts at hiding certain racial and class complexities. The "Hispanic" category in population reports, for example, "takes on the status of a 'race,' while at the same time its members 'may be of any race.'"[13] This kind of thematic (social, historic, psychic) obfuscation is the kind that the essayists in this anthology labor to "uncover" and rebuild. By taking into account the interface of U.S. Latino/a literature, through a theoretical gesture of interdisciplinary welcome, this anthology opens a space, new and young, foreign and at home, "foreign in a domestic sense," in which a community has imaginatively built itself. As Giorgio Agamben states: "The face is the only location of community, the only possible city."[14] The essays herein exhibit a brilliant sensitivity to the faces U.S. Latino/a literatures have created.

The essays in this text similarly evaluate these issues of relationality and welcome, and of a newness that opens out into a future community for Latino/a literary thought. The first section of the book, "Desire for the Other," examines epistemological issues raised by the relationship between self and other—specifically the Latino as produced by the gaze of the Other in Victoria Chevalier's essay, and U.S. Latino mimetic desire for the other in Lyn Di Iorio Sandín's essay—analyzing their violent consequences. In "The Latino Scapegoat: Knowledge through Death in Short Stories by Joyce Carol Oates and Junot Díaz," Di Iorio Sandín explores the complex development of mimetic desire, which for the Latino outsider leads to a real and symbolic death. Weaving René Girard's work on mimetic desire and the scapegoat, with Homi Bhabha's reflections on postcolonial mimicry, Di Iorio Sandín examines two stories that stage the toxic tensions between social belonging and exclusion. Interestingly, as Di Iorio Sandín points out, the element that constitutes the Latino scapegoat is not the fact that he is utterly alien, but that he is "not different enough." This paradoxical revelation drives Di Iorio Sandín's analysis as she unpacks the mimetic stages that progress from the impossibility of acceptance, to rivalry, and ultimately death. Di Iorio Sandín points out that these stories expose the assimilative fallacy that promises Latinos a place in the United States if only they would leave their cultural history behind. What they suggest, in the end, is that American Latinos feel that they cannot safely become American at all. Yet literary death also leads to knowledge and illumination in Di Iorio Sandín's analysis and the scapegoated Latino subject understands the fragile and mimetic nature of his or her relationship to others.

For Victoria Chevalier, ekphrasis serves as a conceptual tool that allows her to map the unsettling relationship between the visual image and the novelistic language of Dominican American writer Nelly Rosario. In her essay entitled "Alternative Visions and the Souvenir Collectible in Nelly Rosario's *Song of the Water Saints*," Chevalier argues that the "ekphrastic moments" in the text produce an alternative way of seeing, which opposes and revises traditional uses of ekphrasis. The representational mode ekphrasis has conventionally been used as a visual sign that rendered women as its "culturally produced other[s]." But as Chevalier's essay skillfully shows Rosario's novel subverts the gendered terms found in the historically fraught relationship between image and language.

The experience of race also plays a crucial role in a U.S. Latino/a imaginative present and future. "Afro-Latino/a Poetics," the second section of this anthology, examines Afro-Latino/a literary sensibilities. Margarite Fernández Olmos's "Spirited Identities: Creole Religions, Creole/U.S. Latina Literature, and the Initiated Reader" looks at a series of U.S. Latina writers and proposes a hermeneutics that takes a creolized viewpoint, emerging from Afro-diasporic religious traditions. The result is an "initiated reader," one who is linked to the symbolic language and magical practices of the Caribbean, having an "awareness of the spiritual layer(s) in an artistic work from the point of view of an 'insider,' an identity among multiple, complex and fluid paradigms." Richard Perez's essay, "Racial Spills and Disfigured Faces in Piri Thomas's *Down These Mean Streets* and Junot Díaz's 'Ysrael,'" explores the complex relationship between the face as both the façade of appearance and the locus of the struggle to exteriorize racial expression. Piri finds himself, according to Perez, caught in between two social and ontological options: one of either passive self-abnegation or a self-destructive street life. Perez concludes that Thomas's novel moves beyond these two restrictive options and offers a more active and creolized version of being and expression. His reading of Junot Díaz's story analyzes the mutilated face as a self-reflexive surface in which Rafa, one of the protagonists of "Ysrael," reads himself. The underlying trauma in Díaz's work, as Perez argues, is a paternal abandonment that internally damages the young Rafa, and that becomes metonymic of larger hemispheric, postcolonial relations.

The third section of this anthology is entitled "Archives, Histories, and Genealogies." The essays in this opening section simultaneously look backward and forward in articulating a present/presence. Time in this section is condensed into a dynamic "now," which intertwines past, present, and future into an inexorable constellation.[15] In the essay "The Once and Future Latino: Notes Toward a Literary History *todavía para llegar*," Kirsten Silva Gruesz confronts the complex problem of creating a U.S. Latino/a narrative history. For Gruesz, a literary history is not a survey that compartmentalizes time and space into a causal chronology, but into a Trans-American web that opens up unintended and unorthodox connections, revealing hidden continuities and connections. The implications are enormous because such a literary history would interlink the threads of past history with other cultural trajectories, establishing an ever unequal influence of these traditions upon any given set of writers and readers over time.

William Luis's essay "Hurricanes, Magic, and Politics in Cristina García's *The Agüero Sisters*" chooses as an analytical starting point, the end-of-century dates 1898 and 1998. For Luis, U.S. Latino literature invokes a historical mirroring reflected in the hurricane as event, which serves, in its continuous return, as an ominous reminder of repetition with some significant differences. Natural history recombines with imaginative production. Of course, the historical moment in 1898, which Luis alludes to, is the hurricane of invasion, war, and the restructuring of power and populations. In 1998, it is a reverse movement, wherein increased Latino populations are forcing the United States to recreate their customs into a Caribbeanized "synthesis," which Cristina García's novel and Latino literature represent.

Román de la Campa and Andrea O'Reilly Herrera analyze Latino/a literature in institutional terms and diasporic inheritances. While de la Campa's essay, "Latin Americans and Latinos: Terms of Engagement," does not explicitly look at Latino/a literature per se, it examines the discrepant intellectual exchange between Latin American and Latino/a scholars. What is important in this essay is the ideological and racialized undercurrents the author detects, which differentiate this relationship. Reading the work of literary critic Ilan Stavans, de la Campa finds that Stavans's playful studies of Spanglish and U.S. Latinidad overlook "the politics of culture in the shadows of capital," creating a breach between his Latin American and U.S. Latino critical concerns. He concludes with a reading of Juan Gonzalez's *Harvest of Empire*; *Latinos, Inc.* by Arlene Dávila, and *Living in Spanglish* by Ed Morales, exploring the relationship between disciplines such as history, media, and popular culture, as well as literary studies. On the other hand, the breach in O'Reilly Herrera's essay is a preoccupation with exile and a literary sensibility to which this expulsion gave birth. Exploring Cuban American literary trends and cultural expressions, O'Reilly Herrera finds that a multivalent past as well as the ongoing effects of historical trauma have "channeled across generations through a process of socialization and storytelling." The result is an aesthetic fascination with dislocation as a grounding literary experience. The condition of historical exile finds the terms of its psychic survival in literature.

In the last section of this compilation entitled "Ideology and Labor" the question of history is brought into a more specific focus. For Mary Pat Brady, Rodrigo Lazo, and Maria DeGuzmán, U.S. Latino/a literature takes a detailed look at the class conditions that pervade Latino/a life. For Brady it is politically urgent to attempt a "vernacular" examination of the economic and cultural shifts for U.S. Latinos, highlighting "the most vulnerable people in the U.S." Juxtaposing visual art with Esmeralda Santiago's *América's Dream* and Denise Chavez's *Face of an Angel*, Brady considers the "neo-feudal" working conditions demanded by a service economy. As her title " 'So Your Social is Real?': Vernacular Theorists and Economic Transformation" suggests, a service economy is accompanied and fortified by the invisibility of workers so that the identities of laborers find their "real" within a "circumscribed 'social.' " For Rodrigo Lazo, this question of labor, in the fiction of Oscar Hijuelos, is inscribed on the body, in the household, and in the act of textual production. According to Lazo, the fiction of Oscar Hijuelos—the only U.S. Latino writer to date to have won a Pulitzer for fiction for *The Mambo Kings Play Songs of Love*—offers a sustained contemplation of the working lives of the characters he breathes life into. Lazo's analysis explores work as a multidimensional concept, and he probes it on "physical and mental" as well as "material and literary" terms. In María DeGuzmán's "Mass Production of the Heartland: Cuban American Lesbian Camp in Achy Obejas's 'Wrecks'", the author details "the political or ideological" aesthetics showing the way repetition is used to manipulate the values embedded in cultural codes. For DeGuzmán objects are recycled by Obejas creating a dialectal relation between aesthetics and ideology, and in the process altering societal values that infringe upon concepts of citizenship and relations of desire. Repetition becomes a production of difference that unsettles heterosexist norms, national expectations, and nostalgic promises of a Cuban return. U.S. Latino/ a identity and literature find part of their present and future inexorably intertwined in a "queer lesbian–feminist" experience.

These sophisticated essays deploy a range of critical methodologies from psychoanalysis to Marxism, from comparative literary history to philosophy and anthropology, from feminism to social history, as well as cultural and queer studies and sociology, to elucidate a dynamic and exciting body of literature. One purpose in compiling this collection has been to showcase some of the best Latino literary critics writing today whose work focuses on creative writing from all the major Latino/a groups: Cuban American, Dominican American, Mexican American, and Puerto Rican American. More importantly our intention as critics is to theorize on the emergence, growth, and development of U.S. Latino fictions, noting how U.S. Latino writing ultimately informs and transforms American culture. U.S. Latino/a preoccupations with Trans-American relationships, origins, and genealogies expand the notion of what it means to be American. The U.S. Latino/a adds the "s" to America, compelling the United States not only to examine its relationship to the "Other" America but to understand itself as a territory within the Americas. These new waves of writing, theory, and literary imaginings reveal U.S. Latinos not as outside American society, but as insiders whose ability to summon outside perspectives can, and will, change the very notion of what constitutes it. To further Latinize the United States, then, is to make it truly American.

NOTES

1. Homi Bhabha, *The Location of Culture* (New York: Routledge, 1994), 227–228; hereafter cited as "LC."
2. Ibid., 228.
3. Slajov Žižek, *The Sublime Object of Ideology* (New York: Verso, 1989), 113.
4. Piri Thomas, *Down These Mean Streets* (New York: Vintage Books, 1967), ix; hereafter cited as "DTMS."
5. Gloria Anzaldúa, ed., *Making Face, Making Soul, Haciendo Caras: Creative and Critical Perspectives by Feminists of Color* (San Francisco: Aunt Lute Books, 1990), xv–xvi; hereafter cited as MFMS.
6. Ambitious in that it publishes a number of excellent essays on works by Latina writers, and by women critics, Alvina Quintana's *Reading U.S. Latina Writers: Remapping American Literature* (New York, London: Palgrave Macmillan, 2003) is the most recent intergroup anthology of U.S. Latino/a literary criticism. As the title reveals, however, it is not gender-inclusive in focus on either the literature or the critics.
7. Rodolfo Torres and Antonia Darder (eds.), *The Latino Studies Reader: Culture, Politics and Society* (Cambridge, MA: Blackwell Publishing, 1998).
8. Agustín Laó-Montes and Arlene Dávila (eds.), *Mambo Montage* (New York: Columbia University Press, 2001).
9. Marcelo Suárez-Orozco and Mariela Páez (eds.), *Latinos: Remaking America* (Berkeley: University of California Press, 2002).
10. *MFMS*, xvi.
11. Frantz Fanon, *Black Skin, White Masks* (New York: Grove Press, 1967), 112; hereafter cited as *BSWM*.
12. Ibid., 112–113.
13. Juan Flores, "Triple Consciousness? Afro-Latinos on the Color Line," paper presented at the Opening. Roundtable, "100 Years of W.E.B. Dubious' The Souls of Black Folk" of the conference "Race in the 21st Century," held at Michigan State University, April 2, 2003; hereafter, "Triple Consciousness."
14. Giorgio Agamben, trans. Vincenzo Binetti and Cesare Csarino, *Means Without End: Notes on Politics* (Minneapolis: University of Minnesota Press, 2000), 90.
15. Walter Benjamin, trans. Howard Eiland and Kevin McLaughlin, *The Arcades Project* (Cambridge: Harvard University Press, 1999), 463.

PART I

Desire for the Other

The Latino Scapegoat: Knowledge through Death in Short Stories by Joyce Carol Oates and Junot Díaz

Lyn Di Iorio Sandín

In *Killing Spanish: Literary Essays on Ambivalent U.S. Identity* (2004), a recent book of literary criticism, I suggest the idea that in many contemporary U.S. Latino/a works of fiction, the violent death of a double character, usually a woman, represents ambivalence about U.S. Latino/a identity, an ambivalence most often resolved through violence and the "killing" off of the character associated with the Hispanic origin.

The two stories that I analyze in this chapter augment this notion, but also offer a drastic deviation, and a disturbing spin, on it. The characters who die in these stories are not Latinos from the land of origin, but the American Latinos themselves. The ambivalence that in the previous novels and stories, resolved in favor of American identity and against the dangerous Latin American or Caribbean origin, in these two stories openly calls into question the notion that American Latinos feel they can safely become American at all, once they sacrifice language, affinity, and attachment to the origin.

My methodology in this examination of the "scapegoat" makes use of René Girard's ideas about mimetic desire, and incorporates references to Homi K. Bhabha's idea of mimicry, which has become a standard theoretical term in postcolonial literary studies. Girard sees mimetic behavior as the fundamental human dynamic in which subjects acquire being through imitation. Subjects desire objects not because of any inherent value in the object, or any genuine autonomous or unconscious drive within the subject, but because the "other" desires that object. And this other is perceived to possess the being that the subject lacks. Therefore objects desired by this other, whom Girard terms the model or mediator for the subject, are then mimetically desired by the subject. The contexts in which mimetic desire occurs create very specific dynamics. Subjects desire the objects that the models or mediators desire and these objects may change and thereby change the dynamics, which are also affected by external and internal mediation, variations of mimetic desire in which desire changes relative to the proximity of the mediator or model. In comparison, Bhabha's mimicry—which is both imitation and ambivalent resistance to domination—appears to be an inherent component of relations among colonizers and the colonized, or majority and minority subjects.

The texts I focus on in the discussion of this theme of the Latino scapegoat include a short story by the prolific American writer Joyce Carol Oates called "Landfill," and another by the Dominican American writer Junot Díaz called "The Brief Wondrous Life of Oscar Wao." Both are stories from *The New Yorker*, the former published recently in October 2006 and the latter in 2000. Inasmuch as they are both about the Latino scapegoat, one could say they are twenty-first-century representations of the hitherto inassimilable position of the U.S. Latino/a subject. In the stories Latinos seem to inhabit a contradictory subject position deemed by the majority to be different, but not different enough. Difference has to be such that the minority subject must both remain fixed as minority, and yet be deemed special or unique in some way. If the minority subject is too much like the majority one, s/he fills the latter with unease because s/he appears to be a mimic, a failed copy, and doesn't respect the distinctions in the majority subject's own cultural systems or codes of values. Both Bhabha's idea of mimicry and Girard's theory of mimetic desire meet on this point. Girard also indicates that the minority subject's failure to be different enough inserts him or her in the terrain inhabited by the scapegoat.[1] That Latinos inhabit the position of scapegoat in recent literature by mainstream Latino and non-Latino writers isn't surprising given the recent political debates and debacles in this country regarding anti-immigration policies targeting Latinos specifically among all immigrants, and most particularly Mexicans.

In each story that I examine, a young U.S. Latino man dies violently. Both stories focus on the "freakishness" or marginal status of the young men, their sense of feeling awkward in their bodies, and a rage in each character that is balanced by an odd and self-deprecating sense of humor. Additionally, each story highlights each young man's highly mimetic behavior. In both the stories, the young men, spurred forth by the desire to acquire the being of the model and therefore freedom from a life of nonbeing, are driven to near-death experiences that provide knowledge, and further propel them self-destructively on toward their deaths by scapegoating.

Mimetic Triangles and Mimicry

Girard began his analysis of mimetic desire in his groundbreaking study *Deceit, Desire and The Novel* (1965). The "great novelists," such as Cervantes, Flaubert, Stendhal, Dostoevsky, and Proust, Girard contended, unveiled the mimetic nature of desire: subjects desire objects not because of an inherent desire for the object, but because the object is desired by an other, a mediator or model. Subjects learn desire from models who are perceived to possess being, a quality the subject feels he or she lacks. The reason subjects feel such lack lies in the "false promise . . . of metaphysical autonomy" for modern man.[2] God is dead, man reigns supreme in his place, but this false promise is brutally exploded by everyday experience. Nonetheless, in modern times, pride has intensified in equal proportions to a sense of solitude.[3] It is an absurd existence, and, of course, such absurdity unveiled by writers such as Dostoevsky paves the way for the insights of later existentialist philosophers and fiction writers such as Camus and Sartre. People experience in their solitude and metaphysical loneliness that the promise is false, but paradoxically "the promise remains true for Others."[4] This perception of the superiority of the other seems to lie in the nature of social relations, in the physical and metaphysical reality that renders one a solitary being without access to the interiority of the other.

Girard, however, underlines the mimeticism and violence unleashed by such dynamics. The way mimetic rivalry leads to violence relates to the two types of mediation that Girard outlines: external and internal. In external mediation, there is a great deal of distance between the mediator and the subject. Girard regards this type of mediation as often beneficent, such as, for example, the imitation of Christ by the faithful, or Don Quixote's desire for and imitation of Amadis of Gaul, a great knight he reads about in chivalric novels. Neither Christ nor Amadis are physically accessible to their imitators and so their imitators do not become easily rivalrous with them. External mediation shows how mimetic behavior can produce salutary results. Models are admired, the behavior benefits society, and also allows the hierarchy to remain ordered with the models and subjects in their separate social positions, and not in rivalry with each other.

In internal mediation, on the other hand, the social distance between model or mediator, and subject, is telescoped, and the subject not only desires to be like the model, and desires what the model desires, but then frequently takes the model as a rival. This type of mimetic rivalry can obviously lead to violence in which the mediator is no longer perceived as a distant and distinct model. When all differences disappear and the model and mediator become similar, they are seen to be monstrous doubles.[5] They are similar in desire, in violent rivalry, and in a perception that they are different from each other when, in fact, the more they attack each other, the more similar they are.

In some of the "great" novels, Girard contends, transcendence is achieved by the protagonist at the end of the book through the renunciation of desire. Girard also suggests that such transcendence—achieved by heroes of novels such as *Don Quixote*, Stendhal's *The Red and the Black*, Dostoevsky's *Crime and Punishment*, and Marcel Proust's *The Past Recaptured*—implies the more detached vision of the author himself. The aesthetic creation is the author's own, cutting through the veil of mimetic desire.[6]

In his later, more anthropological works, *Violence and the Sacred* (1977), and *The Scapegoat* (1986), Girard suggests that in chaotic moments of social crisis the lack of differentiation caused by mimetic rivalries can be resolved by the selection of a scapegoat who bears sacred marks of both purity and pollution. The killing of the scapegoat can lead to a renewed sense of order. Girard's theory of violence and surrogation holds that it is at this point, when social chaos has erased difference and all are rivals, that a scapegoat is chosen, on whom the violence is blamed, and who afterward is also deemed to be savior of the social structure, so that differences and hierarchy, and the social order that follows, can return to society.

It is apparent that Girard's more philosophical notion of mimetic desire overlaps with the notion of mimicry, which has by now become a mainstay of both postcolonial and minority literary criticism. Homi Bhabha's notion of mimicry, for example, stresses that the failed imitation, the way in which the colonized are "almost the same but not quite" is a sign of agency and the ability to resist domination, even if that resistance may work at an unconscious level.[7] From the postcolonialist perspective it is agency that is important, even if it is just an offshoot of mimicry. From Girard's metaphysical perspective, though, the notion of agency would be deemed illusory.

If "being," the sense of having metaphysical certainty in the world, is what is at stake for the subject in Girard's theory of mimetic desire, power is what is at stake between the colonized and the colonizer in Bhabha's notion of mimicry. If in Girard failed imitation may lead to rivalry with the model, in Bhabha failed imitation is a way of resisting the power of the colonizer, and also showing up the ambivalence at play within the colonizing discourse itself.

The Latino boy—whose desire to become a frat boy leads to his ending up in the trash compactor—is a failed imitation if there ever was one. Is this ambivalent resistance? Is then ambivalent resistance purchased at the price of self-destruction?

The Latino in the Trash Can

What is a Latino boy, who's just arrived in college and who looks down on his own parents, supposed to want in life? Mimetic desire can lead to violence, but the rivalry and competition it generates can also save the desiring subject, who otherwise may feel lost, certainly in a metaphysical sense, if not practically. The disturbing story "Landfill" by Joyce Carol Oates is based on a real-life incident in which John Fiocco Jr., a student and fraternity pledge at The College of New Jersey, went missing and was later found in a Pennsylvania landfill.[8] Oates, however, changed the ethnic and racial markers from Italian American to Hispanic or Latino, of undisclosed group affiliation, obviously to register even more deeply the dead boy's difference from his fraternity brothers. She also changed the geographical location from Pennsylvania to Michigan, East Coast to Mid-West, again to deepen the chasm between a white majority and the Latino minorities among them. The narrator tells us outright that college freshman Hector Campos Jr. decides that he will want whatever his white fraternity brothers want:

> Hector, Jr. Called by school friends Heck or Scoot . . . At Grand Rapids [Michigan State University, at Grand Rapids, the college he attends], Hector, Jr., was called Hector by his professors, Scoot by his fellow-pledges at Phi Epsilon, and Campos by the older Phi Epsilons he so admired and wished to emulate.[9]

Hector's father is driven by the need to pay the bills, the increasing college bills and other expenses he doesn't quite understand the need for, such as the initiation fees Hector Jr. incurs at the fraternity house he has just been pledged into at Grand Rapids. Hector's mother is obsessed with her son, and disturbed by the way he is growing distant from the family. Neither parent understands the urgency of Hector Jr.'s need to fit in at school, and specifically his notion that if he can be a part of the fraternity, his metaphysical sense of emptiness will be filled:

> He'd once called his mother to say how crappy he felt, never having enough money—the other guys had money but he didn't. He'd told her . . . that if the fraternity dropped him, didn't initiate him with the other pledges, he'd kill himself, he would . . . And Mrs. Campos had pleaded, "Please don't say such terrible things!"[10]

Hector Jr. has become aware of mimetic desire, of how the world he lives in is run according to the power of the mediators—the white frat boys—who radiate a "being" that desiring subjects such as Hector wish to possess. Initiation into Phi Epsilon will put Hector Jr. on a par with the frat boys, conferring the being he lacks. His parents don't understand the truth of the situation. In fact, Hector has become a kind of mediator for his mother who desires him and tries to comfort him, and whom he spurns, ridicules, and tortures in favor of the more prestigious frat boys.

Hector practices being the model with his mother, as do many children of working-class and minority parents. A reading stemming from the perspective of mimicry and minority discourse would also suggest that Hector is imitating the white boys at the expense of his mother, who represents his Latino identity. The mimicry implies self-hatred. However, the inherent ambivalence in the idea of mimicry that Bhabha proposes also suggests that Hector's mimicry of the white boys resists their domination.

Both theories, Girard's regarding mimetic desire and Bhabha's regarding colonial mimicry, point to the ambivalence of imitation, but in different ways. Hector's "emulation" first of other boys in general, and later of the frat boys correlates with Girard's notion of internal mediation, since Hector is in close proximity with his models. This type of proximity breeds rivalry; rivalry is accompanied by resentment, envy, and rage:

> [Hector] was really happy when he got a bid from the Phi Eps . . . He was having kind of a meltdown with Intro. Electrical Engineering, also his computer course. He'd ask some of the guys on the floor for help, which was mostly O.K.—you had to feel sorry for him—but then Scoot would get kind of weird, and sarcastic . . . There were times Scoot wouldn't speak to us and stayed away form the room and over at the frat house . . .[11]

From Bhabha's perspective the mimicry—first of the other boys Hector rooms with who "help" him with his class, and later of the frat boys—is bound to also generate resistance. Although Hector is trying to be an engineer, the boys who actually study the subject treat him with condescension, and he responds by resisting them. Part of his Bhabhaian ambivalent resistance toward the engineers involves seeking a new mediator, and staying "over at the frat house." A frat boy mask helps ballast indifference toward the engineers. Hector experiments with trying to be what he assumes would impress or intimidate the engineers.

His mimicry of the frat boys involves not just joining the frat house, but also imitating the humor and general style of the boys. But he gets their humor and their style wrong. In not yet being those who seem to possess being, in the process merely of becoming the mediator, Hector bristles with an energy that makes him dangerous and ill at ease. He is trying hard and yet can't seem to finally "BE." And he becomes suffused with a rage that propels his binge drinking and reckless behavior.

Hector's immersion in violence alerts us to the intensity of his desire to be like the frat boys, to have what they have: women, an ease in manner, a sense of belonging, jokes that everyone laughs at. As Girard says:

> Whenever he sees himself closest to the supreme goal . . . [the desiring subject] comes into violent conflict with a rival. By a mental shortcut that is both eminently logical and self-defeating, he convinces himself that the violence itself is the most distinctive attribute of this supreme goal! Ever afterward, violence and desire will be linked in his mind, and the presence of violence will invariably awaken desire.[12]

Long before his final violent outburst and his death, Hector achieves lucidity about his situation at the frat house. He becomes drunk, passes out, vomits, is taken into a shower, and is left there: "he'd had to admit with the cruel clarity of stone-cold sobriety: They left me here on my back to puke and choke and die, the fuckers. His friends . . . And he thought, Never again . . . Meaning he'd de-pledge Phi Ep, and he'd stop drinking . . . "[13]

Violence and desire are linked however: "[T]he next weekend he'd come back, couldn't stay away. These guys are his friends, his only friends."[14] The lucidity that marks Hector's growing awareness seems like an important offshoot of the violent experience and his desire to be like his models. It's not that Hector forgets his lucid realization and goes back to the frat house out of habit. The growing awareness itself is important. Hector is starting to understand the mimetic nature of his own desire. He goes back to the frat house not just because he lacks any other friend, but because what he is learning is important, that is, he has no friend, now he really knows. And of course he is becoming addicted to the violence associated with this learning experience.

Oates brilliantly conveys through indirect free discourse the way Hector, also known as Scoot Campos, oscillates between insecurity— a sense of himself as inferior to his models—and a euphoric sense of himself as transforming into something other under the tutelage of his models. Transforming into them "Scoot Campos has fine honed a reputation at the Phi Ep house as a joker, funniest goddam pledge. The other pledges are losers, but Scoot Campos is a wrestler, he's witty and wired. And good-looking in that swarthy Hispanic way."[15]

His humor is as unsettled as his sense of himself. "Maybe it isn't funny, or is it?"[16] The uncertainty is telling. It is the uncertainty of Hector's situation. Is he or is he not? The recklessness and drinking— the violence—intensify his feelings of awareness in one way, allowing him to do things he wouldn't have done, say, among the engineers. But on the other hand the violence reveals what Girard calls the "reciprocity" among the frat boys. They are all the same in their drinking and recklessness.

In fact, it is quite possible that most of them are as gauche and unsettled as Hector himself. That the ease of being is only a mask— the mimetic mastery worn by the mediator whose being is as empty and uncertain as the subject's—is a truth that Hector senses, but does not yet know in the way that he knows he has no friends.

On his last night alive, he tries to pick up a girl who rejects him, he makes jokes again imitating the other boys who seem more at ease. He laughs to himself, climbs the stairs, and is so drunk he starts pissing uncontrollably. Eventually, he ends up surrounded by a guy or guys "stooping over him calling him names."[17] He doesn't distinguish among them. And in a way the reciprocity, the escalating violence between the boys and their victim Hector, makes them all indistinguishable from each other. The scapegoat is part of the crowd—in that the drunken, rollicking Hector is like the other drunks.

But at the point of victimage, the scapegoat has to be different too. Although they are all behaving in a disorderly way, Hector has called more attention to himself through his uncontrollable pissing on his way up the stairs, and his deranged laughter. He taunts the other boys who surround him. One of them, particularly violent, "giving off heat and the pungent smell of a male body in fighting mode" curses Hector, "calling him asshole, dickhead, fuckhead."[18]

The fact that Hector Campos is Latino might encourage readers to think that that constitutes the "difference" that makes him the scapegoat. And there are other indications in the story that certainly underline the anomalous situation of a Latino family living "in the gleaming-white Colonial" in a suburb in the Midwest.[19] We are told that none of the other working-class members of the Campos family own a house like that which Hector Campos, Sr. was able to purchase for his family.[20] This suggests the idea that if Hector feels inferior to his models in the dormitory and frat house at Grand Rapids, the Campos family itself is in the position of model for the other members of their own family, wholly Latino; although what kind of Latino is never specified by Oates, as if that were irrelevant. This underlines the fact that Hector's family has already attained a certain point of similarity; they are middle-class Americans living in a desirable house in a desirable suburb in Middle America.

It is his similarity to the other boys, not his radical difference, that sets the persecutors against him. Hector's roommates, presumably white, note that they are prepared to like him precisely because he is Latino, but then they become disenchanted with him:

> Me and Steve liked him O.K. at first, it's cool we got a Hispanic roommate, or what's it—Latino?—that's cool. But Campos he's just some guy, nothing special about him you could pick on, except he wanted to hang out with the frat guys.[21]

Girard notes in *The Scapegoat* that religious, ethnic, and national minorities are not actually criticized for their difference "but for not being as different as expected, and in the end for not differing at all."[22] Hector Campos is a "loser" to his dormmates, just "some guy" and in the end they admit they don't care he is dead, but they know they "can't tell any adult this."[23]

Girard notes that one of the primary features of the persecution of scapegoats is a social crisis of un-differentiation, a time of plague, warfare, or some other kind of crisis. Although there is no social crisis per se at the college, it is clear that the kind of uncertainty that plagues all the young men, whether they are earnest engineers like Hector's roommates or "cool" frat boys, is exacerbated through drunkenness and reckless behavior, the very type of behavior that the frat boys engage in on the weekends. The frat house is both a zone of a carnivalesque unleashing of repression, as well as a pressure cooker for the hostility that all the young people, particularly the boys as represented in Oates's story, feel toward each other.

At a campus that is desperately trying to recruit minorities, and at which minorities appear to have attained a certain prestige, Hector is in danger precisely because he is not Latino enough. Because he is not different enough, a notion that itself reveals bigotry in an unexpected texture. Hector's roommates express the notion, in the quote mentioned earlier, that the Latino can't be just "some guy"; he also has to be special in some way—perhaps a good student, good-looking, charming. Unfortunately for Hector the others—the engineer roommates and the more desirable frat boys—don't think he is any of these things. It is the fact that he is like them—just a regular guy, but also Latino—that ironically makes him a victim. Gawky, insecure, ill at ease, not really a good student—even though his interior voice tells him differently—he is too much like the crowd itself, which starts to persecute him.

According to Girard, a second stereotype that persecutors attach to the scapegoat is the commission of a crime, usually a heinous one such as incest, rape, parricide.[24] One recalls the accusations in the Middle Ages against the Jews that they would boil infants, or eat them. The persecutors never accuse Hector of committing a crime of this sort. However, his reckless behavior, which is not unlike that typical of the other frat boys, seems to worsen at the moment of crisis itself, helped by the fact that he is completely drunk. He pisses in his pants walking up the stairs. He feels shame at first but then he starts "laughing like a deranged little kid who's wet his diaper on purpose—hell the carpets at the Phi Ep house are already (piss?) stained, what's the big deal? 'Fuck you,' he's saying, defending himself against some guy, or guys, stooping over him, calling him names. Scoot Campos is wired tonight, he's laughing in their faces . . . ."[25]

Whether we want to call it the ambivalence of colonial mimicry, after Bhabha, or the love that turns to hatred of Girard's internal mediation, Hector has reached a point (even if he is drunk) where he not only recognizes his own ambivalence—as he had the first time he woke up from a drunken stupor with vomit all over him and realized that the frat boys had not helped him but had left him to die—but actually resists the domination of the others, in fact taunts them because the piss that they are saying is the stain that makes him different, actually covers the whole frat house.

This moment of resistance is also a moment of complete abjection in which he is pissing, and laughing, and in which he also seems to realize the sameness between him and the frat boys that so offends them. The piss coming from his body can hardly be an offense he reasons, when the whole frat house is "(piss?) stained." The interrogatory mark clearly symbolizes Hector's own uncertain state between confusion and lucidity, laughter and hysteria, understanding and misapprehension, and dominance and subjection, as well as between the mundane and the divine. This last binary of mundane/divine is most pertinent because after he laughs at the boys who are cursing him, Hector looks at the moon and it looks like an eye to him: "This is God's eye, Scoot thinks. (Or maybe a street light? . . .)."[26]

And the story adds a last rather shocking interrogatory: murder–suicide. Does Scoot get shoved down the trash chute by someone else or is it his own half-conscious and self-destructive act?:

> Scoot is being lifted, pushed into . . . the trash chute. Or maybe the drunken pledge is crawling head first into the chute of his own volition, and one of the guys grabs his ankle to pull him back . . . He's kicking like crazy, so whoever has hold of his ankles has to let go—Campos is goddamn dangerous when he's been drinking.[27]

It seems that the indeterminacy must come from drunken Hector's own perception of events; after all for most of this scene we are inside his head. But of course the indeterminacy of point of view at this juncture in the scene also emphasizes the fact that the other boys are just as drunk. That's why the narrator won't tell us whether Hector was pushed into the chute, or crawled into it on his own. Girard's mimetic reciprocity is clear at this moment. Earlier Hector might have wanted to "emulate" the frat boys, but now he is laughing at them. The fact that he is their rival is out in the open. It is just as clear that they now mean to harm him. This is a moment where Hector means to do things "of his own volition." He has finally learned to be like the mediator, whose autonomy of being, of course, is nothing but an illusion. This moment of seeming autonomy and freedom has disastrous consequences for him.

The moment of breakout from the double bind of mimicry underlines the idea that the scapegoat is the abject double of the model. Hector's derision of the frat boys elicits even greater derision from them: "'Fuck you,' he's saying, defending himself against some guy, or guys . . . calling him names."[28] In fact they are shouting at each other all at once in perfect reciprocity, all reduced to similarity in their violence.

And this story points to the self-destructiveness in Hector himself. His "ambivalent resistance" is liberating, but also ultimately undoes him. The violence that besets and finally resolves internal mediation leads to the transcendence of death.

The Power of Death

In Junot Díaz's short story "The Brief Wondrous History of Oscar Wao," the scapegoat is also as self-destructive as he is persecuted. Both the Díaz and Oates stories showcase young college-age Latino men who feel at odds with the other youth around them, and who are very concerned with their body images. Both stories feature humor. Hector Campos's humor is called "weird" by those around him, a result of the tacit judgment of the college boys that Hector's mimicry fails, that he doesn't get anything right, especially not his humor. Certainly, the reader doesn't find Hector's humor as funny as it is defensive. Right before he is attacked verbally by the frat boys, Hector laughs both at the fact that he is pissing "like a . . . little kid who's wet his diapers on purpose" and because the entire frat house is piss stained.[29] His humor is filled with his animus; it is part of his mimetic behavior and his ambivalent resistance. He pisses out of resentment for the purported models, and yet he is also imitating them, as the whole frat house is stained with piss, and it is literally a pissing match.

The humor in the Díaz story also has a mimetic root. From the time he is a small child to the time he dies in the pursuit of a prostitute in the Dominican Republic, the American-raised Oscar de León is involved in romantic triangles in which he always fails to achieve the desired object of love. The story is narrated by Oscar's friend, model, and double, the Yunior of Junot Díaz's acclaimed short story collection *Drown* (1997). The mimetic rivalry centers around the issue of what defines Latino manhood, be it among Americanized Latinos on the east coast of the United States or in the Dominican Republic. In the Oates story it is the being of the white boys that Hector desires, a desire that the story both recognizes and critiques. The ultimate fate of the Latino scapegoat follows a predictable pattern in terms of majority and minority discourse. Cultural and/or racial differences constitute one of the criteria categories through which scapegoats are selected.[30]

The Oates story focuses on internal mediation, rivalry between boys who are close to each other, and on the choosing of a minority as scapegoat by white boys. The Díaz story focuses on both internal and external mediation. Oscar de León, the obese American Latino who ends up murdered by a Dominican general whose prostitute girlfriend he falls in love with, has models that are accessible such as Yunior and other boys. He also has inaccessible models such as the Capitán, and the characters Oscar reads about in books, who are much like Don Quixote's idealized Amadis. Girard has pointed to Don Quixote's imitation of Amadis as one of the best examples of external mediation.[31]

The scapegoating in the Díaz story is the result of intra-Latino rivalry. The theme of the story is Oscar's romantic quest to find a woman when no woman, particularly no woman of his own cultural background, Dominican or Latina, from the United States or the island, will have him. The narrator tells us right off the bat at the start of the story that "Oscar de León was not one of those Dominican cats everybody's always going on about. He wasn't no player . . . he'd never had much luck with women."[32] In the course of the narrative, however, we learn that the narrator himself, to invert the terms of the quotation mentioned earlier, was very much one of those Dominican cats everybody's always going on about. He was a player.

"The Brief Wondrous Life of Oscar Wao" narrates Oscar's woes throughout his young life as an obese, earnest boy who is scapegoated by Dominicans and Latinos precisely because he isn't the player type. He rooms with Yunior, the narrator of the story, in college, and Yunior clearly feels that he is superior to Oscar, that he is the model: "You never met more opposite niggers in your life. He was a dork, totally into Dungeons and Dragons and comic books . . . I was into girls, weight lifting and Danocrine . . ."[33]

Yunior, however, narrates the story in some admiration of the way in which Oscar's role of scapegoat for Latinos who themselves feel marginal to the larger culture reaches its inexorable conclusion, but also a reversal, through Oscar's self-sacrificing death for the prostitute. The narration, which culminates in the account of the death of Oscar at the hands of the Capitán, shows how the process of scapegoating transforms the victim into the sacred. In Girard's theory, the subject or disciple once venerated the model or mediator, and was compelled to imitate the model's desire, thereby turning the model into a rival, but also becoming a model for the model, who was unaware or loath to acknowledge his or her own desire. The model ceased to be a model and became a monstrous double, and the rivalry grew more violent. Desire led to death. However, if the model could not confer being upon the subject, death through sacrifice conveyed a "plenitude of being."[34] The sacred then signifies the power of death. Death endows being upon the sacrificed subject. In the Oates story we saw how Hector seeks out the frat boys to "emulate" them, and keeps up his attentions even after they leave him to die after a drunk, and he feels he sees the eye of God just as they are about to set upon him before his death. Confused, desperate, about to die, the boy is touched by the sacred. Inherent in both violence and in death, the sacred is a kind of mystification.

The rivalry beset by mimetic desire that finally culminates in a victim marked by the sacred is even clearer in the Díaz story. Yunior starts out as Oscar's model, but at a certain point the distance between them breaks down when Yunior finds that Oscar is able to chat up La Yablesse, a gorgeous Rutgers student who had spurned Yunior. The two "opposite niggers," in Yunior's now suspect phrasing, start to resemble each other. Yunior protests that he and Oscar are different. It is the model's vain assumption of autonomy when in fact it is clear that in vital ways the young men are the same. They are both "dorks," again in Yunior's phrasing, in that they both write stories (Oscar is the author of an unpublished science fiction novel; Yunior is the author of the story we are reading); they both ardently pursue women (Oscar because he can't have them, and Yunior in the player mode to show mastery); and they both fail with women (Oscar because of his obesity, which is an exterior deformity, and Yunior because he can't be faithful, an interior deformity). Yunior is too cynical to be faithful and is also mimetic.

It becomes clear that Yunior is only interested in Oscar because he is like Oscar; something about Oscar reminds him of himself. Oscar, the nerd, wants to be a writer, but it is Yunior, the nerd who masquerades as a player, who really is the writer. Yunior is an Oscar who has lost all the weight through bodybuilding and who is unfaithful to all his girlfriends because he wants to protect his mask of model. He enjoys pretending he is Oscar's model. In fact, Yunior's behavior is what Oscar is told to imitate from the beginning of his life when parents and friends throw the little boy at girls, or later on when his uncle Rodolfo tells him that all he has to do is get a girl and 'stick it in her': "You have to grab a muchacha, broder, y méteselo."[35]

After death, Oscar becomes a model for Yunior because death creates the distance necessary for external mediation. In life, it was just the opposite. Yunior saw Oscar as ugly, obese, romantic, idealistic, hopeful, and depressed, whereas Yunior was a player, muscle bound, cynical, repressed. In death, Yunior admires Oscar for qualities that Oscar ultimately strengthened and that Yunior makes a show of not having. Oscar showed himself to believe in love, to be faithful, and to be willing to die for an ideal. But it is death that is the key. It is the transformative and sacred power of death that makes the live Oscar, seen by Yunior and other Latinos as a loser, a romantic hero. His passage through violence has made Oscar both victim of the worst values and assumptions of Latino culture—machismo and abuse of women—and hero, as if the sacrifice of his death throws into relief the Capitán's evil, and somehow also defeats it.

Yunior's drive to exalt Oscar reveals the former's guilt (that he is a player and a failure with women), a guilt that has to be projected onto Oscar and for which Oscar then pays in his self-destructive pursuit of the prostitute and in his death. Yunior feels guilty for having been unfaithful so many times to Oscar's beautiful sister Lola, another scapegoat in the story, raped as a child. Oscar's self-sacrificing death for love relieves Yunior's guilt, which is the guilt of all Latino and Latina players. That this may be a gender inclusive category is confirmed by Lola who says bitterly after her brother's death, and near the end of her relationship with Yunior: "Eight million Trujillos is all we are."[36] Interestingly it is Lola, raped by a pedophile, who identifies Dominicans from the island, male and female, as all guilty of the sins of Trujillo: rape, murder, the unleashing of violence, sins that are the deformation of qualities at one time worshipped in the dictator and father of the nation.

Instead of succumbing to imitation of the Latino macho model, throughout his adolescence and young manhood Oscar chooses characters in books as models: "He read Margaret Weis and Tracy Hickman novels (his favorite character was of course Raistlin) and became an early devotee of the End of the World . . . He didn't date no one. Didn't even come close. Inside, he was a passionate person who fell in love easily and deeply . . ."[37] He never states outright, nor does the narrator, his obsession with the role of the model.

But that may be because the author of the story, Junot Díaz, is not himself aware of the role of the model until near the end of the story. Girard points out that the focus on the object of desire reveals a lack of awareness of the true mimetic state of affairs and that this awareness of mimetic desire separates the great novelists from those who are merely romantic.[38] The conflict, between a "romantic" covering over of the role of mimetic desire and a "novelistic" revelation of it, certainly seems to be borne out by the trajectory of the Díaz story. When Oscar is actually involved with his objects of desire, we become aware of his rivals and possible models, first the little boy Nelson Pardo in the tragic–comic story of Oscar's childhood crush on Maritza, and then later we are given more details about Manny, Oscar's rival for the affection of Ana, his second major object of desire. When Oscar has his first, and last, consummated relationship with the prostitute Yvón Pimentel, her boyfriend, the Dominican Capitán, takes on a pivotal role in the story.

Oscar's relationship with this stereotype of evil, a Dominican military man used to murdering those who go against him, propels Oscar into both heroic and mimetic roles. The Capitán is driven by mimetic desire. He murders Oscar not because he cares much about the prostitute—one imagines that he probably has many such girlfriends—but because he simply doesn't want Oscar to have her. Oscar's pursuit of Yvón becomes more heated after he is beaten within an inch of his life by the Capitán's henchmen. The romantic surface nature of the story argues for Oscar's heroism. And in fact, the story remains romantic because the role of the mediator and the intensity of rivalry between the Capitán and Oscar are never explored in great detail. The author, and his narrator Yunior, take seriously Oscar's idea of romance.

But the importance of mimetic desire is clear. In desiring what the Capitán also desires, the prostitute who is incapable of leaving either the Capitán or a life of prostitution, Oscar shows that he is finally as misguided as any of the Latino macho role models he seemed to have rejected in the United States. His feelings for Yvón intensify after the Capitán stops him on a lonely road and has him beaten within an inch of death. This beating by his rival is revelatory. Oscar who has lusted after women to no avail for his twenty-five or so years thinks that his relationship with the prostitute must be "serious" because otherwise "the Capitán would probably never have fucked with him; proof positive that he and Yvón had a relationship."[39] There is a homosocial valence to the triangle. Oscar feels that the Capitán's desire validates his own. Yvón who is frequently described in the story as passing out or being on the point of passing out is an alienated character, which is not surprising, given her victimization. She lacks intensity. It is the Capitán's intensity that seems to provoke, even excite Oscar, and even fill him with the pleasure of having been "fucked with." One might say it is for the pleasure of being fucked with a second time that Oscar returns to the Dominican Republic, to a death that everyone has warned him about. Once Oscar self-destructively and masochistically returns to the island, he is pursuing the Capitán as both model and object. His interest in Yvón, who is still object, but also a rival, too, can only be maintained as long as the Capitán pursues them. Yvón finally deflowers Oscar because she, who is usually passive and indifferent, is provoked by Oscar's simultaneous flight from, and pursuit of, the Capitán.

If Oscar never got anywhere with his other two previous girlfriend possibilities, perhaps it was precisely because they were not prostitutes. Yvón uses sex, after all, as much as she is used by it, and she is the aggressor with Oscar. And perhaps in this sense what is "wondrous" about Oscar is that he is able to actualize the homosocial desire latent in machista Latino culture, a desire that is often a crucial element in Díaz's stories, and may explain why men like Yunior and the Capitán cannot be faithful to women, and in fact prefer prostitutes. It is because the prostitute, with whom many men sleep, has the function of providing a social bonding between the men, just as Yvón is able to link Oscar with his final model, the Capitán. Eve Kosofsky Sedgewick used Girard to argue that "between men" the desire for women as objects often serves as a conduit through which the homosocial desire for other men manifests.[40]

As in the Oates story, where Hector finds a kind of freedom in laughing at the frat boys before he dies, Oscar too seems to achieve freedom, as revealed in his final letter to his sister in the United States. And unlike Hector who is ambivalent to the end, Oscar loses his ambivalence with his virginity to the prostitute. Because he was able to finally achieve true intimacy with a woman, his final letter to his sister is ecstatic. This is a story rife with ironic allusions to postmodernism, Frantz Fanon, MLA panels, Aimé Césaire, and other literature and theory references. "'The beauty! The beauty!'" is Oscar's comment to his sister on his finally having sexual relations with Yvón, and also the last line in the story.[41] This ending is a wonderful piece of mimicry itself as it imitates, and subverts, the last words of one of the most important of texts for postcolonial critics, Joseph Conrad's late nineteenth century novel *Heart of Darkness*: "The horror! The horror!" In *Heart of Darkness*, Kurtz's last words are meant as self-critique of the darkness in his own soul. But he has of course been able to discover the darkness in his soul through contact with the dark other. It is his corrupt behavior in Africa that corrupts Kurtz's soul. The romantic inclination of the story is to describe for us an Oscar who has transcended corruption and mediation, having chivalrously pursued a prostitute to redeem her with his own innocence. Hence his final words are opposite to those of the corrupt Kurtz.

In fact Oscar's position vis-à-vis mimetic desire at the end of the Díaz story seems like Don Quixote's at the beginning of *Don Quixote*. Oscar is deluded, his discovery of the Capitán as rival for the prostitute's affections convinces him of the validity of his desire, and the importance of his object, the prostitute. "The Capitán was one of those tall, arrogant, handsome niggers that most of the planet feels inferior to."[42] The Capitán is all image and no substance; Yvón, who has fainting fits much of the time she spends with Oscar, is not all there either. Oscar wants what the Capitán wants, the Capitán also wants what Oscar wants, and Yvón ends up wanting what Oscar wants too. Oscar who perhaps wore his obesity all his life as a badge of a pure soul loses all the weight finally when he decides to go back to the Dominican Republic a second time and pursue Yvón until she becomes his girlfriend. He and the Capitán become doubles, rivals with the same desire, and so do he and Yvón. Desire is contagious, and so is violence. The three in the triangle play a game of musical chairs with object, subject, and model positions. One is an evil man, and the other has been an idealist and an innocent, and the third seems mostly indifferent, and yet they are all three driven and compelled by the violence attending Oscar's challenge of the Capitán and his pursuit of Yvón.

Oscar in "The Brief Wondrous History of Oscar Wao," and Hector in "Landfill" die because they are outsiders seduced by the promise of being unique, which really reduces them to sameness. Oscar is an outsider to the Latino notion of manhood, as well as to The Dominican Republic, and Hector is an outsider at both the Midwest college he attends, and even more so at the frat house. But they become scapegoats not just because they are the minority outsiders who must be sacrificed so that order can be regained (in the frat house) or so that a lie of order can be retained (in the Dominican Republic). They become scapegoats not just because they are outsiders, but because they are outsiders forcibly trying to attain the objects or being that they assume others, their models, possess. Even Hector's moments of awareness and lucidity only spur him onward toward the model who openly threatens death as he assures being through awareness of death. Oscar is the same way. Beaten almost to death by the Capitán, and dragged back to the States by his mother, he returns to the island a second time pursuing both being, and death. It seems that one is not possible without the other. The scapegoat achieves being only through the self-destructive pursuit of mimetic knowledge that ends in death.

NOTES

1. René Girard, *The Scapegoat* (Baltimore: The Johns Hopkins University Press, 1986), 22; hereafter cited as "*SG*."
2. René Girard, *Deceit, Desire and The Novel: Self and Other in Literary Structure*, trans. Yvonne Freccero (Baltimore and London: The Johns Hopkins University Press, 1965, 1961), 56; hereafter cited as "*DDN*."
3. Ibid., 56–57.
4. Ibid., 57.
5. René Girard, *Violence and The Sacred*, trans. Patrick Gregory (Baltimore and London: The Johns Hopkins University Press, 1977, 1972), 159; hereafter cited as "*VS*."
6. *DDN*, 288–314.

7. Homi Bhabha, *The Location of Culture* (New York: Routledge, 1994), 86.
8. "Joyce Carol Oates Criticized Over Story" (MSNBC/AP 10/11/06); Poets and Writers/From Inspiration to Publication; http://www.pw.org/mag/is_oates.htm.
9. Joyce Carol Oates, "Landfill," in *The New Yorker* (October 9, 2006), 69; hereafter cited as Oates.
10. Ibid., 71.
11. Ibid.
12. VS, 148.
13. Oates, 74.
14. Ibid.
15. Oates, 73.
16. Ibid.
17. Oates, 74.
18. Ibid.
19. Oates, 75.
20. Oates, 72.
21. Oates, 73.
22. SG, 22.
23. Oates, 73.
24. SG, 15.
25. Oates, 74.
26. Ibid.
27. Ibid.
28. Ibid.
29. Ibid.
30. SG, 17.
31. DDN, 1–26.
32. Junot Díaz, "The Brief Wondrous Life of Oscar Wao," in *The New Yorker* (December 25, 2000–January 1, 2001), 99; hereafter cited as "Díaz."
33. Ibid., 106.
34. Martha J. Reineke, *Sacrificed Lives: Kristeva on Women and Violence* (Bloomington and Indianapolis: Indiana University Press, 1997), 74.
35. Diaz, 100.
36. Ibid., 117.
37. Ibid.
38. DDN, 17. Girard uses the term "romantic" for works that reflect the presence of the model without revealing it, and the term "novelistic" for works that reveal the importance of the model and of mimetic desire.
39. Díaz, 115.
40. Eve Kosofsky Sedgewick, *Between Men: English Literature and Male Homosocial Desire* (New York: Columbia University Press, 1985).
41. Diaz, 117.
42. Ibid., 114.

CHAPTER 2

Alternative Visions and the Souvenir Collectible in Nelly Rosario's *Song of the Water Saints*

Victoria A. Chevalier

How to Read a Snapshot of a Soul

In the first page of Nelly Rosario's *Song of the Water Saints* (2002), the reviewer from *Time Out New York*, one voice in a long list of critical acclaim, celebrates the novel in telling language: "(l)ush and assured . . . each brief chapter reads like a snapshot of a soul."[1] In an overt reference to a dialectics of exteriority and interiority, the reviewer's accolade leads to the question: What would it mean to "read a snapshot of a soul"? How does one imagine, and image forth, an ineffable interiority? Apparently, through an image, photographic or otherwise, as opposed to words; it is through the image that a more immediate route to viewing an object is promised. As one theorist has noted, "an image brings forth a presence in a way words never do."[2]

The interpretation of a descriptive text through a representation of a visual image is precisely one of the projects Rosario's novel undertakes. *Song of the Water Saints* approaches this intersection of literary language and visual image through an initial use of ekphrasis that structures the entirety of the novel. W.J.T. Mitchell defines ekphrasis as "the verbal representation of visual representation" (p. 702). Etymologically the term literally means "giving voice to a mute art object" (p. 153). I will argue that Rosario's use of ekphrasis structures the epistemological foundations of her novel and, simultaneously, destabilizes those same foundations; if her work "reads like the snapshot of a soul," it does so by interrogating the rhetorical play produced by specific sorts of ekphrastically described visual media—specifically the photograph–postcard—in their relation to the function of the souvenir. My concern is to trace the ekphrastic moments in the novel that question a Western European epistemology of the visual; to read the oppositional spaces and revisions of ekphrasis produced by Rosario's structuring of those moments as both a recreation and a reference to different forms of "seeing" as historical knowledge. However, it is first necessary to explore the question begged by the *Song of the Water Saints*: What is the ekphrastic relation of the image to the word, and to what use is that relation put in the service of telling the story of the Caribbean on the island of the Dominican Republic during the course of the twentieth century?

Ekphrasis is described as a minority genre of literary figuration whose minor status has not prevented it from developing a formidable critical repertoire.[3] As a figure ekphrasis vexes the difference between text and image; in describing a visual object it figures forth that object as a presence. The object is not, of course, physically present; it is "made present to the mind's eye in its representation."[4] Since ekphrasis is so completely bound up with the visual and visual cultures, postcolonial and emergent literatures have taken it up as a field of inquiry into those specific forces of domination and disciplinary power organized by the visual.[5] As a literary figure that focuses on the exchange and circulation between the visual and textual modes of representation, ekphrasis functions as a "sign of the visual itself, whose production historically has often been put to the service of women's oppression," and, in addition, all those culturally produced as "other."[6]

Ekphrasis is also perhaps the literary figure that most obviously stages a literal conflict between self and other; it is "structured by the written word that produces, and enlists to its discursive power, a visual image."[7] Yet as others have theorized, the "dance between text and image is illusory, impossible, and seductive."[8] During his discussion of ekphrasis, Mitchell excavates the tension between "ekphastic hope" (in which the division between image and text is traversed and a verbal icon or image–text arises in its place) and "ekphrastic fear" (the moment marked by a realization that the difference between the verbal and visual representation might collapse, and the figurative, imaginary possibility of ekphrasis might be realized literally). As Mitchell states, if ekphrasis is constitutive of a social relation shot through with political, disciplinary, or cultural domination, it "takes on a full range of possible social relations inscribed within the field of verbal and visual representation embodied in an image–text. The 'self' (i.e., narration) is understood to be an active, speaking, seeing subject while the other is projected as passive, seen and usually silent object. Like the masses, the colonized, the powerless, and the voiceless everywhere, visual representation cannot represent itself; it must be represented by discourse."[9] Therefore, image–texts provide narrative ground through representation, and yet, simultaneously, "resist and elude narration."[10] As such, the image–text in *Song of the Water Saints* and all the souvenirs (visual and otherwise) collected in the novel by its protagonist Graciela function as metonyms for a specifically Caribbean encounter with Western "History." The ground of engagement both eludes a temporal "non-history" and produces the possibilities for experiencing alternative histories, thereby establishing a collective, historical consciousness.[11]

This exploration and revision of visual modes of representation pose a vexed problem for the author of emergent and postcolonial literatures. In the long history of representational and technological disciplinary strategies at the service of colonial and imperial Western powers, the project of the author who would destabilize such representative regimes runs the risk of reproducing the hierarchies already set in place.[12] However, it is precisely to the field of the visual in the form of ekphrasis to which Rosario returns. In her revision of the classical literary examples of the form, the image–text provides an oppositional way of seeing and reading the visual archives that produce the Caribbean black, feminine, colonized subject as other to the white, Western, imperial male gaze.[13] In so doing, oppositional forms of vision are advanced toward another reading of Caribbean histories.

EKPHRASTIC MODELS

Traditionally ekphrasis is characterized by an attenuated trajectory of famous examples that stretch from ancient epic poems, such as *The Iliad* and *The Aeneid*, to more modern novelistic and lyric examples such as Henry James's *Portrait of a Lady* and John Keats's *Ode on a Grecian Urn* and *My Last Duchess*.[14] What these celebrated moments of ekphrasis in Western literatures share in the first two examples is their role in "epic narratives of conquest and empire-building that construct masculine, nationalist identities"; and, in the latter two, the ways in which represented feminine images and bodies are objectified, circulated, and thereby marked as an object d'art whose status as property also constructs the masculine.[15] Both *The Iliad* and *The Aeneid* represent ekphrastic figures of foundational critical note: the description of

Achilles' shield in the former and Virgil's reproduction of Aeneas's own shield by Vulcan in the latter. In *Portrait of a Lady, Ode on a Grecian Urn*, and *My Last Duchess*, a mute, feminized object is made to speak, to varying degrees of success and through varying degrees of violence.[16]

My look, in particular, at one of the ekphrastic descriptions of *Song of the Water Saints* links it to the resulting narration that organizes the rest of the novel. The narrative begins in 1916, at the height of World War I in Santo Domingo, República Dominicana. Its chapter head entitled "Invasions" is meant to signify upon the U.S. occupation of the island at the height of U.S. imperial dominance in the Caribbean and South-East Asian theater of war. Prior to the beginning of the narrative, however, an "invasion" of another sort has already occurred. A description of a photograph precedes the formal narrative. Rosario arranges in the following fashion:

SCENE AND TYPE #E32
WHITE BORDER-STYLE POSTCARD
COUNTRY UNKNOWN, CA. 1900
PRINTED BY: PETER J. WEST & CO./ OTTO
NATHER CO. HAMBURG, GERMANY

They are naked. The boy cradles the girl. Their flesh is copper. They recline on a Victorian couch surrounded by cardboard Egyptian pottery; a stuffed wild tiger, a toy drum, and glazed coconut trees. An American prairie looms behind them in dull oils.

Shadows ink the muscles of the boy's arms, thighs and calves.

His penis lies flaccid. Cheekbones are high, as if the whittler of his bones was reveling when She carved him.

The girl lies against the boy. There is ocean in her eyes. Clouds of hair camouflage one breast. An orchid blooms on her cheek.

To begin a novel with a representation of a visual image is to cue the reader that the realm of the visual itself is under review. Ekphrasis is always political; it represents a field of contestation between the visual and verbal arts as to which can tell the more effective or more accurate story; it reflects a struggle for intellectual and material property.[17] As a poetic mode, ekphrasis is also the form that would "give voice to a mute object," literally, to make us see and hear through language. In using the photograph, the text introduces to the reader the subject of how an "effective story" is constructed. The initiating function of the image–text in the novel foregrounds the question of who controls the narrative. In this case, the audience is invited to consider how the presentation of a historical narrative is crucial to the mode of construction itself.[18]

In addition, the photograph rests in the margins of the novel. The description initiates and unofficially propels the audience into the "proper" narrative; in so doing, it raises the question of the relation between image and text, margin and center, improper and proper models of knowledge. The photo–postcard is parergonal in its marginal status to the rest of the novel. The notion of the margin as parergon, that which behaves as conventionally extrinsic, external, and supplementary to the "center," is also intrinsic to the entire body of the work; in as far as the association between margin and center is organized completely by their essential—and necessarily oppositional—relation to each other.[19] Occupying the margins, the image is simultaneously at the service of the narration, a metonym for the subjection of image to narrative, and constitutive of the force that propels the story. However, as Molly Hite argues, the "parergon also decenters what it appears to comprehend, shifting the story of the image to marginal status even as it contains and completes the story. Conventionally extrinsic, supplementary, and ostensibly inessential to that which it borders, a parergon is simultaneously intrinsic and essential, inasmuch as the priority of the center depends entirely on the oppositional relation of center to margin."[20] Yet "to call attention to this margin is to destroy its marginal status," for the parergon coheres by virtue of "disappearing, sinking into, and obliterating itself," just as it expends the greatest energy.[21] To call attention to the margin is to translate and destabilize the oppositional hierarchies "center" and "margin"; the parergon places the margin at the center of the text's questions, thus collapsing the categories that produce the interior and exterior.

In this way, the novel begins with a specific sort of a "lack," what has been named the illusory nature of the "natural" sign.[22] However, Mitchell challenges the "masquerade" of the "natural sign" in his suggestion that although the ekphrastic image behaves at a certain level like a "sort of unapproachable and un-representable 'black hole' in the verbal structure, entirely absent from it, but shaping and affecting it in different ways," it is all "a kind of a shams . . . the 'genre' of ekphrasis is distinguished . . . not by any disturbance or dissonance at the level of signifiers and representational media, but by a possible reference to or thematizing of this sort of dissonance."[23] However, the photographic image of the nude boy and girl on the Victorian couch is also superimposed on a postcard. As a photographic postcard, it is subject to transfers, exchange, and travel; the photo–postcard also bears a particular relation to memory in its proximity to the "souvenir." This photographic image refers at least doubly within its frame.

Since the novel begins with the chapter "Invasions," Rosario imagines the boy and girl pictured in the photograph to be subjects of a U.S.-occupied Dominican Republic. The photograph itself, whose country of origin is "unknown," operates as a metonym for the massive archive produced by the institutional structures of United States and other Western imperial and neo-imperial forms of domination. Exemplary as one among many of the sorts of photographs taken in regions dominated by the West at the turn of the century, the photo belongs to an archive of visual images produced with the Caribbean, Latin American, and the South Pacific peoples as subject. Although Rosario's novel is set at the beginning of the twentieth century, her use of the photo–postcard illuminates the role of both the archive and the staging of the primitive other whose production and circulation constitutes the transfer of global capital, rhetorical and fiduciary.[24] They provide a virtual library that tells a story of how imperial institutions produce their racialized others. That the actual photographer of the image Rosario uses to organize her narrative is named "Peter West" serves as a serendipitous nominative to solidify this point. Her ekphrastic description dramatizes the author of this visual production as "West"; the Western imagination that organizes this site of fantasy is singularly "West(ern)." At the same time, "peter," vernacular slang for "penis," is synonymous with the phallicism of the Western gaze, however challenged, that Rosario's text sets out to critique.[25]

Song of the Water Saints's use of the photo also showcases one of the primary difficulties postcolonial writers face when engaged with the processes of the imagination: How does one avoid reproducing the epistemologies, and attendant strategies of containment, that have produced the colonial/imperial other as "desired fantasy and interiorized scene of imaginative play?"[26] How does one avoid reproducing the hierarchies of the oppressive discourses through which one is constituted as a subject? Since colonial and neocolonial power replicate themselves with forceful authority through the realm of the visual and visual technologies, in which commoditized images of the colonized and neo-colonial national territories threaten to eliminate the inherent destabilizing forces of the imagination and putative oppositional strategies of the visual, writers of the postcolonies urgently turn their attention to the figurative devices through which vision is narrated. This turn in itself exposes the processes of identity and difference, and the relations of power organized by the colonialist/neo-colonialist imagination; in Rosario's example, the turn to the visual critiques hierarchies inherited from the West; and, in addition, *Song of the Water Saints* presents another imaginative space, another way of seeing, in an oppositional discourse of vision figured by the character La Gitana, the palm-reader.

The postcard, mailed through national governmental agencies of transfer and communication, also operates under the rubric of the souvenir, an object that again produces a history of the relation between self and the other. A postcard is sent from one person to another; usually the exotic location, site, or object possesses an "intimacy of distance." Susan Stewart theorizes the qualities of the souvenir in relation to the "primitive/exotic" and "civilization":

> In the cultivation of distance which we find in the uses of the souvenir . . .—the third facet is distance in space—the souvenir of the exotic. Just as authenticity and interiority are placed in the remote past, the exotic offers and authenticity of experience tied up with notions of the primitive as child and the primitive as an earlier and purer stage of contemporary civilization . . . *(t)o have a souvenir of the "exotic" is to possess both a specimen and a trophy,* on the one hand the object must be marked as exterior and foreign, on the other it must be marked as arising directly out of the immediate experience of its possessor. It is thus placed within an intimate distance; space is transformed into interiority, into "personal" space, just as time is transformed into interiority in the case of the antique object.[27]

The entire scope of the novel narrates the stories and the voices of these mute and anonymous immortals, the representation of two Caribbean children captured in the Western frame "circa 1900."

Although the photo is taken by Peter West, the phallic eye, Rosario's description of the image, incorporates the accoutrements one imagines West needs to produce a colonialist fantasy of the other. Simultaneously, she complicates how one should read the photographic scene. Although an "American" prairie looms behind the children, the mise-en-scene is littered with a hodgepodge of objects from other cultures and parts of the globe: "cardboard Egyptian pottery" and a "stuffed wild tiger." Drum and coconuts could easily belong to any one of several regions on the globe; the use of Egyptian pottery and the stuffed wild tiger implies the erasure of cultural, historical, and temporal difference among all the "others" who exist under imperial rule. In their inclusion, Egypt and the wild tiger also reference blackness and a specifically "African" and "Asian" primitive other. This conflation of the exotic as seen through Western eyes is meant to suggest several things. The Victorian couch upon which the children recline signifies the prop of empire. However, perhaps the most disturbing elements of the photograph's scene remains that the objects of this gaze are children. Ann Laura Stoler argues that the link between the savage other and childhood sexuality are constructs (and inheritances) of an eighteenth-century civilizing "custodial mission":

> [A] theory of degeneracy produced prescriptive definitions of race and class. Images of children and schools provide a surplus in U.S. imperial archives; part of the project was to produce the effect of modernization on the Caribbean islands that moved the populace further away from barbarity. This narrative of progress worked in circular fashion; occupation was necessary to lead people into modernity, also it deflected fears that the youth would grow up and become political agitators.[28]

In this example, the children are educated in a different way; their "barbarism" is highlighted by their nudity and the amateurish attempt at bordello surroundings. The education of their sexuality is framed, rather, by the pornographic photograph.[29]

These subjects of the imperial gaze look back at the viewer, however. All attempts at eroticism are undercut by the artificiality of the objects; they are toys: the cardboard pottery, the toy drum, and the stuffed animal. This is a staged scene in which "the children" are made to play a part, and yet no less importantly, the toys themselves function as material signifiers that are placed in a de-familiarized scene. Their sensuous character works against the objectifying intention of the image in that their displaced roles—that is, their displacement from the world of things into the world of visual and literary figure—frees them from the system's modes of definition.[30] And since the boy's penis "lies flaccid," we know that the scene, made apparent through the narrator's voice, titillating or not to the participants, is a constructed "eroticism" clearly for the pleasure of the viewer, both the eye behind the camera and the recipient of the postcard. Ultimately, the eroticism of the scene functions through the overt power relations represented, rather than any specific sexual titillation. Their "primitivism" is constructed by their context within the Western frame of the photo. Their "sexuality" is also staged as a "toy," a plaything, that which can be "set" and then remolded, much like the potter molds his or her clay, within the frame of the postcard photo.

In one deft move, the text's use of ekphrasis represents the internal workings, the meta-narrative of representation itself. Rosario's description of the photograph locates this image within an archive of visual markers, technologies, and cultures imposed through colonial and neo-colonial regimes of power both disciplinary and representational. She continues her critique of the exchange of the photo–postcard by narrating in the first chapter the actual staging of the scene with Graciela and Silvio in the warehouse, as well as the circulation of the image later in the narrative when its recipient, Eli Cavalier, travels to the Caribbean in search of a referent for his image, and a body upon which to enact his desire.

We now more precisely turn to the narrative content and representational dynamics of these "invasions."

THE STAGE AND THE SCENE

Chapter one of the text is devoted in some part to the profession and travels of Peter West and his encounter with Graciela and Silvio. It is primarily Graciela's journey that is traced through the novel; we are led through the experiences of the women in her family, daughter, granddaughter, and great-granddaughter whose own relation to the image–text and the souvenir continue to reconstitute a different "field of vision." During a make-out session on *El Malecón* in Santo Domingo, fifteen-year-old Graciela and Silvio find themselves the object of the "yanqui" gaze in more ways than one:

> Graciela and Silvio were too lost in their tangle of tongues to care that a few yards away, the yanqui was glad for a brief break from the brutal sun that tormented his skin . . . [w]ith her tongue tracing Silvio's neck, Graciela couldn't care less that Theodore Roosevelt's "soft voice and big stick" had dipped the yanqui the furthest south he had ever been from New York City. Silvio's hands crawled back into the rip in Graciela's skirt; she would not blush if she learned that the yanqui man spying on them had already photographed Marines stationed on her side of the island, who were there to "order and pacify," in all their debauchery; that dozens of her fellow Dominicans somberly populated the yanqui's photo negatives; and that the lush Dominican landscape had left marks on the legs of his tripod. Of no interest to a moaning Graciela were the picaresque postcard views that the yanqui planned on selling in New York and, he hoped, in France and Germany. And having always been poor and anonymous herself, Graciela would certainly not pity the yanqui because his still lifes, nature shots, images of battleships for the newspapers had not won him big money or recognition. (SWS, 8)

In no time they are approached by amateur photographer Peter West, whose photos of wartime occupation and "lush" landscapes of the Dominican Republic have not garnered him "big money or recognition." It is clear that neither "picaresque postcard views" nor the yanquis themselves, in "all their debauchery," are sufficient fodder for the West(ern) voyeuristic gaze that continues "spying on them." Peter West's concern is capital because his photos "still lifes, nature shots, [and] images of battleships" have not made a return on his investment; with the "moaning Graciela" in sight, he is about to embark on the production of an altogether different sort of image.

The linking of the imperial gaze represented by West's photography to the physical and cultural violence that the U.S. military occupation enacts upon the Dominican Republic reinforces the relation between vision and empire so thoroughly apparent in the photograph–postcard the audience encounters in the margins of the novel. In their construction, empires have been no less interested in the visual symbols that reproduce and sustain their authority in people's minds as they have been in the actual possession of land. As Patricia Mohammed remarks, "[s]ymbols are crucial to the ways in which empires are sustained in people's lives and minds."[31]

Graciela and Silvio are publicly caught in the act, "too lost in the tangle of tongues to care" who watches them. Lured to an empty warehouse owned by a "Galician vendor" with the promise of financial reward, the adolescents find themselves in a position similar to the one they occupied on the pier; and yet with different and far-reaching compromising results:

> When West lit the lamps Graciela and Silvio squealed. "Look, look how he brought the sun in here!—This yanqui man, he is a crazy . . ." The pink hand tugged at her skirt and pointed briskly to Silvio's pants. They turned to each other as the same hand dangled pesos before them . . . She unlaced her hair and folded her blouse and skirt. In turn, Silvio unbuttoned his mandarin shirt and untied the rope at his waist . . . In the dampness, they shivered while West kneaded their bodies as if molding stubborn clay . . . They struggled to mimic his pouts and sleepy eyes. Instead of wrestling under heavy trees by Rio Ozama . . . they were twisted about on a hard couch that stunk of old rags. Bewildered, they cocked their necks for minutes at a time in a sun more barbarous than the one outside. Their bodies shone like waxed fruit, so West wiped them with white powder. Too light. So he used, instead, mud from the previous day's rain. "Like this, you idiots." (SWS, 11)

The emphasis in the scene is brought to bear by the text's focus on the manipulation and the artificiality of Graciela and Silvio, literally, the staged direction of their "sexual" poses. The artificial light of the camera is mistaken for "the sun" by Graciela and Silvio, in this moment the barbaric side of enlightenment vision is foregrounded for it is a "sun more barbarous than the one outside." West is figured as the "artist" who photo-graphs (writes with light) the adolescents—he "knead(s) their bodies as if molding stubborn clay"; echoes of a pro-fane version of "the Creator" are inescapable. The physicality of their bodies is undercut by the "still life" metaphor in that they "shone like waxed fruit," and their limbs, racial identity, and human expressions are so clearly manipulated, and therefore produced, that the reader is not easily invited to participate in the voyeurism of the scene without first taking into account the details of its construction. There are no "natural savages" present here.[32] So clearly confused as to what the "crazy yanqui" demands of them, the teenagers are produced by and for the photographic gaze of West as natural "primitives," and it is all a piece of culture.

West continues in his attempts to elicit the grotesque facial expres-sions at which he imagines "the others" are so adept. Rosario recon-structs the scene that produces the photo as one wholly created by West himself. As a subject of mimicry, West "mocks his own power [to be] a model" when he literally models the animal poses and expres-sions he wants for his potentially lucrative production, his practices perform the obverse of their intention. My reading is here indebted to Homi Bhabha's theorization of mimicry. Constructed by the ambiva-lences of desire and identification, colonial mimicry necessarily pro-duces its own "slippage, its excess, its difference."[33]

> Where his Spanish failed, West made monkey faces . . . (t)hen Graciela and Silvio watched in complicit silence as West approached the couch and knelt in front of them. Graciela's leg prickled with the heat of his ragged breathing. One by one, West's fingers wrapped around Silvio's growing penis. He wedged the thumb of his other hand into the humid mound between Graciela's thighs. Neither moved while they watched his forehead glitter. And just as they could hear each other's own sucks of breath, they felt piercing slaps on their chins. West ran to the camera to capture the fire on their faces. (SWS, 11)

The Western gaze that produces the primitive other is thoroughly deconstructed by the end of this scene. West mimes "monkey faces" and physically manipulates the act of copulation for Graciela and Silvio. ("West's fingers wrapped around Silvio's growing penis. He wedged the thumb of his other hand into the humid mound between Graciela's thighs"); they are penetrated by the mechanics of West's invasive fantasies.

The violent pornography of the act is underscored by the slap on their faces meant to produce a simulation of eroticism and passion for both the future photo and for the very present, very aroused West. By handling Silvio, making him penetrate Graciela for his own fantasy, West completely produces both the fantasy and the Caribbean subjects' position within the historically mapped scene, the "American prairie." The text forces us to confront the unsubtle manipulations behind spectacular fashioning of the primitive other; it also suggests the power dynamics that link visual/sexual education and imperial imposition. In one way, Graciela and Silvio like being manipulated and watched; they are aroused by the scene they have been placed in by West; on the other hand, as subjects of the Western gaze, they are also ashamed at their pleasure in the manipulation.

Conversely, Rosario's scene also tellingly positions the children in perfect ignorance of how to pose for West's camera. Peter West has to maneuver them for the production of his fantasy not only because he can, but also because they are innocent of the pose required of them. As such, it is Peter West whose "peter" functions as the diminutive signifier of phallic power; the contortions to which he subjects himself in the fantasized pose belong solely to him, as does the image of the primitive he wants the children to model. Graciela and Silvio escape complete domination by the phallic gaze expressly through their marginalized position to Westernized forms of pornographic visual technologies; in fact, their marginalization acts precisely as the grounds of destabilization. The narrated scene that mirrors the photographic postcard as both narration and image is marginal: the postcard is formally marginalized in its placement at the margin of the text, and the content of the scene actually narrated in Rosario's representation is constitutive of the two Caribbean subjects' marginalization.

The fantasized and destructive scene imagined from the marginalized image–text correspondingly ends in destruction. Silvio's distraction over counting the money West pays them provides an opportunity for the photographer to proposition Graciela. Silvio knocks over the entire apparatus of camera and film plate so that they can escape without further indignity to Graciela's person. And although the adolescents prevent West from enjoying the scene in its photographic reproduction, (by destroying the camera and film plate), they are marked by the experience, their sexuality and desire reproduced in the public space at El Malécon. Back on the dock and in their own struggle over the money West paid Silvio, the "strange arousal they had felt in the warehouse pumped through them again."

The connection between sexual imposition, vision, and empire is again made when Graciela heads home after the incident in the warehouse. On her way, she encounters an anonymous islander, a "swan woman" who admonishes her to take care passing the "yanqui-men" on the road. Graciela watches to see how the "woman with the carriage of a swan and a bundle balanced on her head" would "move safely" past the armed soldiers. The sudden shooting and rape of the swan woman rewrites and de-romanticizes another poetic moment that theorizes colonial encounters: the "sudden blow" with which Leda is inflicted in William Butler Yeats's "Leda and the Swan." In Yeats' poem, Leda's "terrified vague fingers" push against the "white rush"; however, in this scene, the nameless swan woman, proleptically called to her fate by this poetic appellation, and that with which the soldiers' christen her immediately before taking aim, "Negro wench," only "thrashes in the grass" as the soldiers "milled about" the body. Many already "had their shirts pulled out of their pants."

In the acutely swift violence enacted upon the body of the anonymous swan woman the scene is instructional. In her anonymity, the swan woman functions as a placeholder for the obscured and anonymous histories of violence the island has experienced; that she is a black woman punctuates the vulnerability of black women in the Caribbean generally, and, in this case, the Dominican Republic, to the sexual appetites of the U.S. imperial mission. The only "knowledge" to be "put on" at the sight of such "power" is Graciela's; unlike Leda, this swan woman's rape ends in an ignominious, anonymous death, not the pregnancy that would bring forth a god. And what knowledge Graciela must take away from this scene reinforces the dangers for the black feminine subject reproduced as subordinate; the two scenes participate in the same logic, that the body is a site of power. Formerly effaced social groups (black, Latino/a-Caribbean subjects) are rewritten into historical and literary discourses at the site(s) of their production: at home, occupied, and in powerful contestation.

Graciela and Silvio get married soon thereafter and Silvio eventually becomes a fisherman, ultimately claimed by the imperial dangers of the sea he loves. In fact, the sea that takes his life is the same sea "whose depths contained jewelry unhooked from the wrists of the wealthy, whole bodies of metal sea animals with fractured waists, and hundreds of ball-and-chain bones trapped in white coral" (SWS, 30).[34] In this, one of the few overt references to the slave histories of the Dominican Republic and the Caribbean, the narrative links the complicated and obscured death of Silvio to the obscured histories of the island's inhabitants. It is intimated that Silvio was involved in resisting the yanqui occupation by running guns to another part of the island for the gavilleros who actively fought the U.S. soldiers.[35] Graciela, after having her daughter Mercedes (whose father is Silvio) remarries Casimiro, a light-hearted, sensitive thief. Fed up with the "smallness" and monotony of her world, five years after the "light-box" captures her with Silvio, Graciela one day grabs one of her few treasures, a hatbox with an image of a Victorian lady on the cover, and heads off for adventure to Santiago. It is there that the material, global effects of the circulation of West's photo-postcard are made apparent, in her encounter with Eli Cavalier, a European collector and vegetarian:

> Postmark: May 5, 1920
> Place Stamp Here
> This Space For Address Only:
> Eli Cavalier
> Hamburg, Germany
>
> This Space For Writing Messages:
>
> Dear Friend,
>
> As per your request, this is to acquaint you with the advantage being afforded by the Collector's Club for view card enthusiasts. We specialize in the exotique erotique beauty of racial types. Join us.
>
> Members receive a monthly catalogue during the term of their enrollment. Extra Special Offer—I will send you 10 dainty erotic views, excerpts from Carl Heinrich Stratz's stunning "The Racial Beauty of Women," plus a dictionary containing 30,000 words if you will send 25 cents for a year's trial membership in this popular club. Please do so before expiration date stamped hereon.
>
> Peter West, President
>
> New York, N.Y. (SWS, 65)

Peter West's photography business is a growing, global concern, and the circulation and exchange of "exotique erotique beauty of racial types" finds its way to Cavalier's Germany at the close of World War I. A collector of erotica, Cavalier flees war-torn Germany for the Dominican Republic, where he meets Graciela on a train bound for Santiago. Their encounter results in a sexual fling and it is intimated that Graciela contracts syphilis from Cavalier.[36] Eli and Graciela are mutually desirous of experience; one has the gendered, racial, social privilege, and capital to acquire racialized sexual pleasure, the other is bound to the island, despite her attempts to explore her own world. In this, their desires are mutually exclusive and yet construct each other. Eli's membership in West's club implies that he erotically collects and consumes the sexual, racial other (the "Racial Beauty of Women") visually, and that his visual consumption is directly connected to the sexual exploitation he plans for Graciela with La Pola, the prostitute whose house they visit in Santiago. That Eli Cavalier can purchase "erotic" images of black, Caribbean women from the distance of Germany is constitutive of their actual purchase as exploited sex-workers in their own country. As a souvenir mailed by West to Cavalier and other future, putative clients, to possess the photo postcard is "to have a souvenir of the exotic . . . to possess both a specimen and a trophy; on the one hand the object must be marked as exterior and foreign, on the other it must be marked as arising directly out of the experience of its possessor."[37]

However, while on this journey we learn that Graciela is herself a collector of sorts. She too acquires a series of objects through her journey that she keeps inside the hatbox. One of them is a photo she steals from the Álvaros, the family who hire her as a housekeeper after her brief tryst with Cavalier in La Pola's Santiago whorehouse.

The book of photographs the young bride Ana Álvaro shares with Graciela references another kind of photographic souvenir, different from West's compendium of images and Cavalier's collection of erotica, yet connected in its representation of its subjects and its relation to the production of sexuality and memory.

ALTERNATIVE MODES OF VISION

While in Santiago, Graciela escapes from La Pola's whorehouse and seeks refuge at a large house in town. There she meets a girl her own age, Ana, who is the young bride of Humberto Álvaro. The two young women, separated by social class, "race," and region, become closer during the viewing of a photograph album:

> Pasted on its pages were panels of various scenes. A man pushed a cart of sugarcane. A woman with voluminous curls tumbling from under a hat held the parasol that so haunted Graciela. There was an enormous house with many stairs and a blue, red, and white flag fluttering from a pole. A man and a woman smiled, their teeth unnaturally white.
>
> "¿And these people? Graciela asked, passing her hands over the panel to feel beyond the flatness of its scene."
>
> "Don't. You will ruin my wedding picture . . ."
>
> "¿Those are you?" Graciela said as she moved her head closer to the photograph. Then she sat back and laughed.

"Yes. Yes. That is us."

"Your teeth. Your teeth are so white, like horses'."

Graciela continued to laugh from behind her covered mouth. She could not understand why Ana was so proud of being inside that panel with such white teeth.

"We went to the studio in town after the wedding, and, ay, what a glorious day, but I had to ask them to touch up the flowers, ¿see?, and to lighten up Humberto a bit, and then they did the teeth . . ." (SWS, 90)

Ana and Humberto's wedding day is witnessed by the national flag; as proper, bourgeois, landowning, Dominican citizens they legitimate the island's national identity. The construction of identity is completed by the man pushing a cart of sugarcane, the national product one can assume composes the Álvaros's family capital, and the woman with "voluminous curls" holding a "parasol," a Western reference presumably used for fashionable protection from the sun. All the images in the photo work together to provide the simulacra of a wealthy, European, and "white" national identity, embodied in the young couple. As was the case with Silvio in the warehouse, when he and Graciela are physically manipulated by Peter West, it is clear that this wedding photo is also a doctored image–text. Ana "had to ask them to touch up the flowers . . . and to lighten up Humberto a bit, and then they did the teeth." It seems obvious that Humberto's darker skin had to be whitened, however, whitening the teeth suggests the nature of the couple as both a consumable and a labored product— literally "like horses," in Graciela's astute observation, and the possibility of forestalling the passage of time. To artificially lighten the skin and teeth constructs the image as an eternal present in which the couple are eternally, and artificially "youthful" and white.

It is telling that along with all the domestic objects Graciela steals (a saucer, teacup, and thimble), she also takes the Álvaros' wedding photograph. Photographic images haunt and attract Graciela since her experience in the warehouse with Silvio and Peter West. She tries to "feel beyond the flatness of the scene" in an attempt to experience the moment behind the artifice. This is Graciela's entire feminist quest throughout the novel, to "feel beyond" the limitations of her life and experience as she understands them to be. And yet the problem with her history, and her ability to experience it, remains its unknown or repressed character; stories told by El Viejo Cuco of Graciela's "maroon granpai" (SWS, 46–47), who she favors in temperament, suggest alternative and resistant, albeit suppressed, historical experiences. It is perhaps these sorts of experiences Graciela attempts to "feel beyond the flatness of the surface." Although many worlds coexist in Graciela, her ability to access them is crippled by the neo-colonial relationship of the Dominican Republic to the United States. This relationship of subordination is congruent to the emergence of visual technologies such as photography, which reproduce the relations of production, consumption, and power between the exploited island nation and its neo-colonial antagonists. The convergence of suppressed histories is, nevertheless, briefly revealed in Graciela's visit to La Gitana, the gypsy, whose alternative visions do not produce a flattened, artificial image, but something approximating a "snapshot of a soul."[38]

In her session with La Gitana, Graciela is told more about the particularities of her history than she appears to understand. The spirit work of the gypsy's visions of past and future directly oppose the photographic "flatness" Graciela struggles against throughout her life. If the photograph writes with light, the Caribbean subject writes with a subterranean and "submarine memory."[39] However, although La Gitana sees differently, and with another kind of vision than the one exploited by Peter West and Eli Cavalier, he does not fully understand the convergence of numerous lines and paths written upon Graciela's hand:

> Then La Gitana leaned in to examine the daunting system of lines. These lines were a tangled map of roads; some led to dead ends, others ran into each other, then swirled in opposite directions. One path led away toward from a road toward one of the mounts. The Venus, Mars, and Moon mounts melded. ¿What was what? La Gitana managed to find the mounts of Mercury, Sun, Saturn and Jupiter under their corresponding fingers. The major lines on the palm made him question his own gift of seeing beyond, a gift he had always flexed like a natural breath. The lines of the Sun and Fate and Affection contended with each other in a way he had never seen in a palm. Other, lesser lines crosshatched Graciela's palm like an unusual plaid. La Gitana traced and retraced the many lines, refusing to be dizzied by the labyrinth.— ¿You ever listen to your own language with strange ears? she asked. (SWS, 113)

La Gitana's confusion at the "major lines on the palm" causes him "to question his own gift of seeing." Graciela's history is itself illegible, at least upon first viewing, even to the seer's alternative mode of vision. The complicated process of cultural suppression experienced by the Caribbean finds expression in the lines of Graciela's hand. The cartographies of the past are mapped in their converging ways upon her palm—"(t)hese lines were a tangled map of roads; some led to dead ends, others ran into each other, then swirled in opposite directions."

Even La Gitana finds it difficult to "dig deep" into his memory and find adequate expression for Graciela's past and, presumably, her future.[40]

Although a seer from her own cultural context, La Gitana, like Graciela herself, must "listen to [their] own language with strange ears." In the project of understanding historical and cultural experiences erased or distorted by the long encounters with Western slave economies and neo-imperialism, both the seer and the seen find themselves initially at a loss. In this way, the text resists and problematizes a romanticized and essential alternative to Enlightenment vision potentially located in La Gitana's ontology. To "hear your own language with strange ears" is to decipher oneself from across the distance of translation that is temporal, and, therefore, linguistic. Such translation is necessarily vexed by the vagaries of textuality and, as important, what is missing for both Graciela and La Gitana at this historical moment in the history of the Dominican Republic: the material histories, documents, and institutionalized forms of knowing the past, in either oral or written form.

Eventually, La Gitana locates the Simian line written on Graciela's palm, "in which Head and Heart lines are one." In addition to the unity between reason and affect, the Simian line connotes the connection to past lives. These numerous and proliferating histories are part of what spurs Graciela's wandering quest for meaning; they operate as the "invisible presence" whose suppression and obscurity, which she never fully understands, spur her actions till her death. In response to the gypsy's question as to why she sought him out, Graciela answers, "To see how far I go. How far away I go." Her ability to "feel" and therefore "see" beyond the flatness of her present surface is characterized by Graciela's own alternative vision, subtly represented during the last days of her life when she sees into the future of her great-granddaughter, Leila, rebellious and to some degree reckless, like Graciela herself. Although Graciela dies before the age of thirty from complications due to syphilis contracted through Eli Cavalier, her particular gift for connecting past and future is inherited by her great-granddaughter, Leila. It is through Leila, in Washington Heights, New York City, in the 1980s–1990s that Graciela's questing for her history meets a similar spirit; indeed, a point of convergence. The words spoken to La Gitana in their spirit-session are made real: "(T)he future can be changed. Be not complacent."

Leila, Graciela's great-granddaughter, also possesses a vexed relationship to the visuality, history, and the image–text. Although Graciela never actually saw the photo produced by West in the warehouse, Leila is made the object and center of the family photo albums; every birthday is recorded with an image by her grandparents. However, after "her twelfth birthday, it seemed she disappeared. From then on she wanted no more birthday pictures." Leila's suspicion of the visual image emerges at the same age Graciela and Silvio encounter Peter West: sexual awakening. And when viewing her former, younger self in the photos, Leila experiences misrecognition:

> When she saw herself in pictures, it was as if she were looking at some-one else, not the person she remembers being at the time of the photo . . . Her fingers flipped through the twelve slices of her life. Back then, her stronger sense of self had allowed her to look straight into the camera. A toddler smiled in the opening frame where she reached toward a jeweled cake. Frame by frame, Leila stretched past Felíz Cumpleaños streamers (which became Happy Birthday by the sixth frame). With each frame, faces filled out, hairstyles flattened, and Mercedes and Andrés wrinkled, while the china cupboard behind them remained unchanged throughout Leila's growth and fading smiles. (SWS 211–212)

In the family album, constructed by Mercedes and Andrés, Leila's grandparents, otherness is also represented, albeit in a different way from Peter West's crude machinations with Graciela and Silvio eighty years before. As a younger child, Leila's "stronger sense of self allowed her to look straight into the camera." What is it that changes in Leila, and her experience of herself in images, through the years? The photograph does not offer a single, transparent truth; this ambiguity is part of its fascination and pleasure. However, for Leila, it is also a "document of unreadability"; she is illegible to her own self, "[w]hen she saw herself in pictures, it was as if she were looking at someone else, not the person she remembers being at the time of the photo."[41] Memory works through her experience of the image–text, to the detriment of her historical understanding. Like her great-grandmother, Leila wants to master her world. As she grows up, her "stronger sense of self" fades in relation to the camera; the photos do not provide a legible understanding of her history or her present surroundings in 1998 Washington Heights. Although the family album constructs Leila as part of the family, her history as the marginal outsider, so viscerally experienced by Graciela in the Dominican Republic seventy years before, hovers in her memory; she finds in the photos no lessons for how to understand her encounter (and her family's, since their 1980 emigration to New York) with the conflicts and contradictions of the United States, in Washington Heights or in the Dominican

Republic, at the site of both "home(s)" and "abroad." This opacity and illegibility will not be successfully transcended; neither by the image–text, nor by the alternative mode of vision Leila has also inherited from Graciela, the ability to "see how far she goes."

There is in this oppositional sight, however, a connection with the past from which Graciela herself could not benefit but could only bequeath. And this connection is not made available through the visual technologies that construct the family photo album. Leila is the recipient of the narratives told in the family about Graciela. Unlike her great-grandmother, who suffered from a lack of historical, collective memory, the novel's ending figures the beginnings of an access to memory that will hopefully gird Leila in her struggles in the United States. On her way home from a week of sexual adventure, fifteen-year-old Leila experiences "'the seed of an invisible presence' in the beating of her heart, [t]he Feeling had started up again. She smiled. It had been a while since she'd had it. The familiar flutter center-left of her chest got warmer" (SWS, 242). Graciela's voice emerges in the text in response to the narratives ("dirty tongues") about her with which Leila grows up:

> Waited on a long line to get born. Still, life dealt me a shit deal. Don't listen to whoever invents magics about me. Always tried to live what I wanted. Never pretended to be a good woman. Never tried to be a bad one. Just lived what I wanted. That's all my mystery. Forget dirty tongues. They're next door, in the soup, even in your own head. Some weak soul always trying to slip their tongue inside your mouth, clean as a baby's pit. You, listen. My life was more salt than goat. Lived between memory and wishes . . . but ¿how much can a foot do inside a tight shoe? Make something better of it than me. (SWS, 242)

Leila benefits from her ability to imagine Graciela's voice in response to dirty tongues, and "weak souls" who are "always trying to slip their tongue inside your mouth." In the late twentieth century from within the stronghold of empire, Leila's decolonizing imaginative narrative participates in the same work as does the text's historical reimagining of the lives of the "two immortals" framed by the souvenir–postcard. Graciela's life provides a historical model for Leila's nascent feminism and future understanding of her history. Her talent for ventriloquizing to herself Graciela's lessons: the maintenance of suspicion of master discourses such as photography, in all its forms, the souvenir photo–postcard and family album image–texts; the opposition to dirty tongues that would silence her voice in "trying to slip their tongue inside [her] mouth" will furnish her with the ability to access voices hitherto unheard, and images hitherto unread. All of this, however, will have to take place outside the frame of the discourses outlined in *Song of the Water Saints*.

Notes

1. Nelly Rosario, *Song of the Water Saints* (New York: Vintage, 2002), frontispiece; hereafter cited as SWS.
2. In a useful analysis of three "phases" of ekphrasis ("ekphrastic indifference," "ekphrastic hope," and "ekphrastic fear") W.J.T. Mitchell persuasively argues that the "indifferent" phase marked by the "impossibility" of ekphrasis must be circumvented, despite the fact that "(a) verbal representation cannot represent—that is, make present—its object in the same way a visual representation can. It may refer to an object, describe it, invoke it, but it can never bring its visual presence before us in the way pictures do. Words can 'cite' but never 'sight' their objects." *Picture Theory* (Chicago: University of Chicago Press, 1994), 152; hereafter cited as "PT."
3. A few examples of works that focus on ekphrasis as a literary genre include Murray Krieger's book-length study *Ekphrasis: The Illusion of the Natural Sign* (Baltimore: Johns Hopkins UP, 1992); W.J.T. Mitchell's *Iconology: Image, Text, Ideology* (Chicago: University of Chicago Press, 1986); and *Picture Theory*; Francoise Meltzer's *Salome and the Dance of Writing* (Chicago: University of Chicago Press, 1987); and Page DuBois's *History, Rhetorical Description and the Epic* (London: D.S. Brewer, 1982).
4. Mitchell, *Iconology*, 154.
5. Mary Lou Emery identifies the relationship between a "European epistemology of the visual" and "re-creation in postcolonial literatures of vision" in her essay "Refiguring the Postcolonial Imagination: Tropes of Visuality in Writing by Rhys, Kincaid, and Cliff." *Tulsa Studies in Women's Literature*, Volume 16, No. 2. (Autumn, 1997), 259–280. The logic of Emery's essay structures much of this chapter. Postcolonial examples of ekphrasis include, among others, Salman Rushdie's *Midnight's Children* (New York: Vintage, 2006) Jamaica Kincaid's *Lucy* (New York: Penguin, 1990), and Michelle Cliff's *No Telephone to Heaven* (New York: Penguin, 1996); African American novels that utilize ekphrasis include among the Harlem Renaissance authors, Jessie Fauset's *Plum Bun: A Novel Without A Moral* (Boston: Beacon Press, 1928), Nella Larsen's *Quicksand and Passing* (New Brunswick: Rutgers University Press, 1929, 1990), and Zora Neale Hurston's *Their Eyes Were Watching God* (New York: Harper Collins, 1937, 1990) as well as middle-to-late-twentieth-century texts such as James Baldwin's *Go Tell It On the Mountain* (New York: Random House, 1952), Toni Morrison's *The Bluest Eye* (New York: Holt, Rinehart and Winston,

1972), and David Bradley's *The Chaneysville Incident* (New York: Harper and Row, 1981), to name a few.

6. *PT*, 160.

7. Ibid., 159.

8. See Krieger's Introduction on the "illusory" nature of ekphrasis.

9. PT, 157, 162.

10. Marianne Hirsch, *Family Frames: Photography, Narrative and Postmemory* (Cambridge: Harvard UP, 1997), 271.

11. "'History' . . . [with a capital H] is a highly functional fantasy of the West, originating at precisely the time when it alone 'made' the history of the world. If Hegel relegated African peoples to the ahistorical, Amerindian peoples to the pre-historical, in order to reserve History for European peoples exclusively, it appears that it is not because these African or American peoples 'have entered History' that we can conclude today that such a hierarchical conception of the 'march of History' is no longer relevant." Edouard Glissant, *Caribbean Discourse: Selected Essays* (Virginia: University of Virginia, 1989); hereafter cited as "CD."

12. See Mary Lou Emery, "Refiguring the Postcolonial Imagination: Tropes of Visuality in Writing by Rhys, Kincaid, and Cliff" for an elaboration of this argument.

13. In this construction I am drawing on Mary Louise Pratt's notion of the "imperial gaze." *Imperial Eyes: Travel Writing and Transculturation* (London: Routledge, 1992).

14. Homer, *The Iliad* (Cambridge: Harvard University Press, 1999); Vergil, *The Aeneid* (Cambridge: Harvard University Press, 1990); Henry James, *Portrait of a Lady* (New York: Modern Library, 1936); John Keats, *Complete Poetry and Selected Prose* (New York: Modern Library, 1951); Robert Browning *The Poems of Browning* (Essex: Longman, 1991).

15. Emery, "Refiguring the Postcolonial Imagination," 262.

16. For a discussion of the gendered possession and dispossession of identity figured through ekphrasis in these examples, see ibid., 264.

17. PT, 153.

18. See Hirsch, chapter four.

19. The parergon comes against, beside, and in addition to the ergon, a work done [fait], the fact [le fait], the work, but it does not fall to one side; it touches and cooperates within the operation, from a certain outside. Neither simply outside nor simply inside. Jacques Derrida, *The Truth in Painting* (Chicago: University of Chicago Press, 1987), 54.

20. For a productive reading of the parergon in Zora Neale Hurston's *Their Eyes Were Watching God*, see Molly Hite, "Romance, Marginality and Matrilineage: The Color Purple and Their Eyes Were Watching God," in *Reading Black, Reading Feminist: A Critical Anthology.* Ed Henry Louis Gates, Jr. (New York: Meridian, 1990), 431–453.

21. Derrida, *Truth in Painting*, 59, Hite, 446.

22. "Not only do these objects not exist independently of their verbal depictions, but the narrative—the before/after character of their described images defies any attempt by the plastic artist to produce an object that is totally answerable to the words as their visual equivalent. From the first, then, to look at ekphrasis is to look into the illusionary representation of the un-representable, even while that representation is allowed to masquerade as a natural sign, as if it could be an adequate substitute for its object." Krieger, *Ekphrasis*, xv.

23. Mitchell, *PT*, 158. In Krieger's analysis, "the poem must convert the transparency of its verbal medium into the physical solidity of the medium of the spatial arts"; for Mitchell, this is to risk falling into the "misleading metaphor, 'the medium is the message.'" As Mitchell further states "[e]kphrastic poems speak for, to or about works of visual art in the way that texts in general speak about anything else . . . [e]kphrastic poetry may speak to, for, or about works of visual art, but there is nothing especially problematic or unique in this speech: no special conjuring acts of language are required . . . [s]ometimes we talk as if ekphrasis were a peculiar textual feature . . . but no special textual features can be assigned to ekphrasis . . . " Krieger, *Ekphrasis*, 107; Mitchell, *PT*, 158–157.

24. Javier Morillo-Alicea cites the role of the Caribbean subject in the U.S. colonial imagination in his exploration of photographs taken on the island of Puerto Rico post-1898. His argument follows Ann Stoler's call to "analyze carefully the functionings of the colonial archive, the manners and institutions through which colonial powers collected and created information about their possessions." In so doing he understands the "U.S. empire as integrated into the global history of modern empire . . . Puerto Rico (like the Dominican Republic, I would argue) and the United States should be thought of up against the European colonies and metropolis not because they are merely 'comparable' situations but rather because they are an integral part of the same kinds of global processes that created the modern Age of Empire." "Looking for Empire in the Colonial Archive," 129–144. In her essay on postcards from the South Pacific, Caroline Vercoe interrogates how, along with the other by-products of World War II, the establishment of the thriving photographic and sex work industries emerges. She theorizes the "staged . . . ironic faux reenactments" of photographic studios set up in order that servicemen have their photograph taken with "generic hula girls," whose mise-en-scene "worked to fix Islanders in a timeless paradigm, erasing any signs of acculturation or change." She states: "[b]y the mid-century, film and photography had allowed a form of virtual travel that blended fantasy and reality." "Where Truth Ends and Fantasy Begins: Postcards from the South Pacific," 371–379. Both essays in *Only Skin Deep: Changing Visions of the American Self* (New York: Harry N. Abrams, 2003).

25. For the seminal feminist critique of Jacques Lacan's phallic gaze (in which the mediating linguistic term of the human body in subjection should be male), see Jacqueline Rose's *Sexuality in the Field of Vision* (London: Verso, 1991), 49–81.

26. Emery, "Refiguring the Postcolonial Imagination," 261–262.

27. Susan Stewart, *On Longing: Narratives of the Miniature, the Gigantic, the Souvenir, the Collection* (Durham: Duke UP, 1993), 146–147; emphasis mine. One of the earliest interrogations of the savagery of Western modes of barbarism in relation to "others" is Michel De Montaigne's "Of Cannibals"; Michel de Certeau's essay "Montaigne's 'Of Cannibals': The Savage 'I'" argues that the place of the "Cannibals" is necessarily emptied by De Montaigne's own text's "meta-discourse that produces the space of the journey . . . which constitute(s) language in its relation to that which it is unable to appropriate." *Heterologies: Discourse on the Other* (Minneapolis: U of Minnesota Press, 1997), 67–79. For a comprehensive examination of the production of the primitive through discourses of modernity, see Marianna Torgovnick's *Gone Primitive: Savage Intellects, Modern Lives* (Chicago: Chicago UP, 1990).

28. Ann Laura Stoler, *Race and the Education of Desire: Foucault's History of Sexuality and the Colonial Order of Things* (Durham: Duke UP, 1995), 137–165.

29. Mitchell considers the pornographic element that underwrites ekphrasis as a genre, and as that which over-determines female otherness as an object of visual pleasure and fascination from a masculine perspective. "Ekphrastic poetry as a verbal conjuring up of the female image has overtones, then, of pornographic writing and masturbatory fantasy . . ." *PT*, 168.

30. See Stewart, *On Longing*, 147.

31. Patricia Mohammed, "Taking Possession: Symbols of Empire and Nationhood," in *Small Axe* (Bloomington: Indiana UP, 2002), 31–59.

32. In fact, West boasts to them before the photo session of his other images, "he had accumulated an especially piquant series of photographs: brother quadroons bathed in feathers, a Negro chambermaid naked to the waist, and, of course, he remembered with the silliest grin Graciela had ever seen, the drunken sailors with the sow." SWS, 9.

33. Homi K. Bhabha, "Of Mimicry and Man: The Ambivalence of Colonial Discourse" in *The Location of Culture* (London: Routledge, 1994), 85–92.

34. A concept of Caribbeaness is explored through the same metaphor by Glissant: "The unity is submarine. To my mind, this expression can only evoke all those Africans weighed down with ball and chain and thrown overboard whenever a slave ship was pursued by enemy vessels and felt too weak to put up a fight. They sowed in the depths the seeds of an invisible presence." *CD*, 66–67.

35. Rosario also links the early-twentieth-century oppression the Latino/ islanders experienced during the U.S. occupation to the terror of the Nadir in North America, visited upon African Americans in the form of lynching and rape. See SWS, 13–32.

36. Earlier in the narrative, it is also intimated that Silvio has contracted syphilis. Graicela's vulnerability to the disease, contracted through sexual contact with the men in her life, metaphorizes her social and political vulnerability as a black woman in the Dominican Republic.

37. Stewart, *On Longing*, 147.

38. In his discussion of "transversality," Glissant states: "The implosion of Caribbean history (of the converging histories of our peoples) relieves us of the linear, hierarchical vision of a single History that would run its unique course. It is not this History that has roared around the edge of the Caribbean, but actually a question of subterranean convergence of our histories. The depths are not only the abyss of neurosis but primarily a site of multiple converging paths." *CD*, 66.

39. Ibid., 65.

40. Because collective memory was too often wiped out, the Caribbean writer must "dig deep" into this memory, following the latent signs that he has picked up in the everyday world. Ibid., 64.

41. See Hirsch, Introduction.

PART II

Afro-Latino/a Poetics

Spirited Identities: Creole Religions, Creole/U.S. Latina Literature, and the Initiated Reader

Margarite Fernández Olmos

In nineteenth-century Caribbean, while the three major African-derived religions in Cuba—*La Regla de Ocha* (the Rule of the Orisha) or *Santería* (the way of the saints), *Regla de Palo*, and the *Abakuá* Secret Society—were undergoing a consolidation, Spiritualist and Spiritist practices of North America and Europe were making their way across the seas to the region and to Latin America for yet another spiritual transformation. The enthusiasm for Spiritist philosophical, religious, and healing notions were a response to several important factors in nineteenth- and twentieth-century Caribbean societies, among them the social upheaval created by the quest for democracy and the Diaspora of Caribbean peoples to the United States, a situation not unlike the present day. The Creolization process led to the creation of distinctly Cuban and Puerto Rican varieties of Spiritism—*Espiritismo*—and, in the Diaspora to the United States, the combination of Spiritism and *Santería*, often referred to as *Santerismo*.

A Creole spiritual healing practice with roots in the United States, Europe, Africa, and the indigenous *Taíno* Caribbean, *Espiritismo* amplified and transformed European Spiritism in its travels back and forth from the Old World to the New. It contributed as well to the creation of "spirited identities" that transcend traditional religious, social, and political boundaries, and appear on the pages of Caribbean literature and the writings of Creole U.S. Latina authors. The historical process that forged these Creole identities continues to evolve and develop a unique vision of Caribbean cultural identity in the region and in the Diaspora and, in some cases, a privileged initiated readership.

In our work *Creole Religions of the Caribbean: An Introduction from Vodou and Santería to Obeah and Espiritismo* (2003)[1] Lizabeth Paravisini-Gebert and I study the Creolization process in the Caribbean, the malleability and mutability of various beliefs and practices as they adapt to new understandings of class, race, gender, power, labor, and sexuality, one of the most significant phenomena in Caribbean religious history. Creole, of course, is a term first used in the Americas to refer to native-born persons of European ancestry and was later extended to other "transplanted" categories of interchange, from linguistic and literary to a wide range of cultural contexts—religious, musical, curative, and culinary. "There is, then, a vast range of examples of the Creolizing process, even without taking into account such areas of human activity as art, law, material culture, military organization, politics, or social structures . . ."[2] The term eventually evolved from a geographical to an ethnic label: New Word enslaved Africans were distinguished from African-born contemporaries by being labeled *criollos*.

For anthropologists and historians the concept of creolization has contested and supplanted assumptions regarding the "assimilation" and "acculturation" of subordinate peoples into a dominant "donor" European culture. Creolization therefore describes the ongoing and ever-changing process (not the static result) of new forms born or developed from the interaction of peoples and forces. The view of Creolization has expanded in recent years to become synonymous with "hybridity" and "syncretism," transforming and challenging the static and binary Western rhetorical oppositions of white/black, center/periphery, civilized/primitive, and so on. In an age of mass migrations and globalization, the concept is even more crucial to reframe notions of past and present transnational and Diaspora cultures and communities. Edouard Glissant has spoken of the "archipelagoization" of the Caribbean in its interaction with Africa and the United States and indeed in the "cultural Creolization" of the world.

> Europe is being "archipelagoized" in its turn and is splitting into regions. Florida is in the process of changing completely in response to its Cuban and Caribbean populations. It seems to me that these new dimensions of existence escape national realities which are trying to resist the forces of archipelagoization . . . We must accustom our minds to these new world structures, in which the relationship between the center and the periphery will be completely different. Everything will be central and everything will be peripheral.[3]

Literary Creolization created "spirited" identities and, in many cases, an "initiated" readership understood here as a reader with a familiarity and affinity with the magical realism of Caribbean everyday life based in great part on the African-diasporic religious traditions, a legacy of the region's colonial history. The initiated reader is not limited to the practitioner who has undergone initiation or the experience of sacred ritualized practice but is one with an awareness of the spiritual layer(s) in an artistic work from the point of view of an "insider," an identity among the multiple, complex and fluid paradigms discussed and celebrated in such sources as *Tropicalizations: Transcultural Representation of Latinidad* (1997) and *Mambo Montage: The Latinization of New York* (2001).[4] The initiated writer/artist has attained a certain degree or level of religious understanding from the most fundamental linguistic and cultural appreciation of the Creole religions, as in the writings of the Cuban author Leonardo Padura Fuentes and Cuban American Cristina García, to the more committed initiated level of the Cuban artist/ethnographer Lydia Cabrera or the Puerto Rican writer Marta Moreno Vega. The living dynamic of these religious practices has led to their continued Creolization in the islands of the Caribbean and in the Diaspora and, consequently, in the diasporic literature of Creole authors.

Spirited identities are not limited to the Caribbean and its Diaspora, of course. In his work examining the profound shifts in U.S. identity being forged by the ever-growing Latino communities of the country, *Defining a New American Identity in the Spanish-Speaking United States*, Héctor Tobar describes the divisions he observed as a child in South-Central Los Angeles between the "rational world of Yankee democracy" and the "antirational universe of catholic saints, of ointments and murmured prayers":

> When I was young, I thought this world was mine alone, but now I see that the latino supernatural hovers over most of the city . . . Over there, mystique is something created by makeup artists and special effects gurus . . . But on my side of the city we are ruled by the baroque, by angels who cure the sick, who relieve the suffering of wives with wayward husbands, and who sometimes take the souls of innocent children. My side of the metropolis is a round-the-clock Mass.[5]

A review of the works of the Chicano authors Rudolfo Anaya, Sandra Cisneros, and others validate Tobar's assertions; their works are imbued with the indigenous and Roman Catholic syncretized *mestizo* practices chiefly identified with the U.S. Southwest.[6] In the East Coast of the United States, however, the "latinization" of the culture is predominantly African based and reflects what Agustín Laó-Montes refers to as an

> inclusive, open-ended, contestatory and emancipatory project of identification . . . constructed as a montage and performed like a mambo. The principle of mambo in Congo cosmology as expressed in the Afro-Cuban and New York Afro-diasporic/Latino popular religion called Palo Monte implies a practice of community in terms of an interplay of identity and difference and the achievement of consensus based on individual freedom and fulfillment. In the final chant of a Palo ceremony, if there is no communal and individual self-expression and happiness, there is no mambo.[7]

LYDIA CABRERA AND THE INITIATED AUTHOR

The significance of the Afro-Caribbean religious/healing practices in the lives of Caribbean peoples is reflected in much of the literature on the islands and in the Diaspora. In Cuba, Lydia Cabrera was among the first to recognize their literary significance as emblematic of cultural identity, demonstrated initially in her short story collection *Cuentos Negros de Cuba* (*Afro-Cuban Tales;* 1940),[8] and in numerous subsequent works. Born at the turn of the twentieth century in Havana, Lydia Cabrera enjoyed the privileges of a Cuban upper-class life—travel, culture, the company of artists and intellectuals, as well as a household of black servants. The latter became Cabrera's entree to the complex world of Afro-Cuban culture, an interest she would pursue as a prolific ethnographer, oral historian, artist, and folklorist, leading her to ask, "What piece of our soil was not permeated with secret African influences?"

Often compared to the U.S. scholar/artist Zora Neale Hurston for her dogged defiance of gender and color prejudice in the pursuit of knowledge on underestimated cultures, Cabrera amassed a significant body of work during her lifetime. Her magnificent work, *El Monte: Igbo-Finda; Ewe Orisha, Vititi Nfinda. Notas sobre las religiones, la magia, las supersticiones y el folklore de los negros criollos y del pueblo de Cuba* (*The Sacred Wild: Igbo-Finda; Ewe Orisha, Vititi Nfinda. Notes on the Religions, the Magic, the Superstitions and the Folklore of Creole Blacks and the Cuban People;* 1954),[9] embodies the concept of transcultural Caribbeanness and is considered a fundamental text on *Santería* and the other African-based religious Cuban traditions.

Cabrera later amassed a significant body of ethnographic material elucidating the practices of the various Afro-Cuban religious traditions on the island, and linguistic research (classifications of popular sayings and compilations of diverse African dialects spoken by certain sectors of the Cuban population). Of her nonfictional work, *El Monte* is considered her most valuable, compared by one critic to the Judeo-Christian bible and the Mayan Popol-Vuh. *El Monte* transcribes the belief systems of New World African peoples in Cuba—their gods, their rituals, and their miracles. Cabrera claimed only one methodology and purpose, however: to allow Afro-Cuban people to express their spirituality in their own words, "they are truly the authors," permitting lapses, repetitions, omissions, and errors, as well as the occasional journey into genuinely artistic creativity. The first half of the nearly six-hundred-page work is organized according to several themes, including initiation rituals, the magical causes of illness, the utilization of herbs and specific prayers in spiritual healing, legends regarding religious and natural symbols, descriptions of secret societies, the African deities, and the traditions associated with the diverse religious systems in Cuba. This part of the book has attracted the most interest as it sheds light on practices considered taboo for centuries and therefore secretive; it has also become a useful tool for deciphering Cabrera's fiction as well as that of other Cuban writers.

The second half of *El Monte* contains an extensive list of medicinal plants utilized by *curanderos* (folk healers), the format of which generally follows a pattern. The plant is classified alphabetically according to its local, colloquial name in Cuba with the official Latin botanical nomenclature stated on the same line. The next category is spiritual: whenever possible Cabrera includes the Yoruba name used by followers of the *Santería* or *Regla de Ocha* religion as well as its classification in the Congo or Palo Monte tradition. Succeeding these is the plant's *dueño* or lord, that is, the deity associated with it. After this initial information the entries vary widely. Some are brief with several lines describing their medicinal usage, alternative names, and suggested medicinal recommendations, followed by a popular expression or anecdotal story related to the plant in quotations, indicating that the source is derived from an informant, occasionally contradicting a previous source and thus presenting an alternative or "second opinion."

Other entries are much more detailed. Several pages may be required to present more complex curative and ritual uses, historical background, and, on occasion, extensive and elaborate narrations (the entry for "Cotton," e.g., is fourteen pages long) akin to literary short stories with characters, plot, dialogue, and climax, the retelling of *patakís*, the *Santería* narratives that correspond to the Yoruba divination system. Cabrera's brand of ethno-botany is therefore neither the traditional format found in conventional botanical references nor that encountered in popular New Age herbal manuals. Although she initiates the data with systematic botanical terminology, she quickly shifts the focus beyond official scientific language; established Western authoritative codes and hierarchies fuse in a fantastic synthesis and on equal ranking with popular belief, personal anecdote, religion, spirituality, indigenous and folk healing traditions, official and oral history, testimony, fiction, and fantasy. Not limited to one religion or knowledge tradition, Cabrera presents several from within the Afro-Cuban contexts that complement rather than compete with the Euro-Western elements of Cuban culture. In most cases no attempt is made to interpret data or to translate African words or religious names used by sectors of the Cuban population thus privileging a local, initiated reader and providing an authentic tone and flavor while conveying a sense of community. But others are not discouraged; occasionally Cabrera will relate an African deity or belief with a Christian/Western counterpart, even extending to cultures beyond the Cuban historical tradition. This type of observation, however, is infrequent; *El Monte* is indisputably local and Cuban, only universalized when deemed essential to render its localized reality more human. *El Monte*, then, is a work that, like so much of Caribbean literature, must be read differently in order to discover the healing constructs of a discourse that incorporates the disempowered and alienated into the social corpus—the work of an ethnographer who was also a creative writer.

This approach is evident in Cabrera's short stories written prior to the ethnographic *El Monte*. *Cuentos negros de Cuba*, her first short-story collection, is frequently read solely in terms of local folkloric traditions and the author's skillful use of African languages; the stories should be recognized, however, as an example of the incorporation of the religious, cultural, and spiritual traditions into the body of Cuban and Cuban American twentieth-century literature in order to more accurately reflect Cuban identity since, as the author herself noted, "No se comprenderá a nuestro pueblo sin conocer al negro" (Our people cannot be understood without an understanding of our blacks).[10] Critics have emphasized the fact that Cabrera was a writer of fiction before she undertook her famous ethnographic work, although the latter has perhaps unfairly received more attention. According to Rosario Hiriart:

Subrayamos que esta mujer llega a los trabajos de investigación desde su condición de escritora de imaginación. Entre la publicaron de *Contes négres de Cuba* en París y *El monte* en La Habana, transcurren casi dos décadas. He dicho más de una vez que teniendo muy presente la importancia de sus estudios sobre la presencia negra en nuestra cultura, la mejor Lydia Cabrera, la narradora por excelencia, está en las páginas de su literatura de ficción.[11]

[We emphasize that this woman arrived at her research from her position as a creative writer. Almost two decades elapsed between the publication of *Contes négres de Cuba* in Paris and of *El Monte* in Havana. I have said on more than one occasion that keeping in mind the importance of her studies on the black presence in our culture, the best of Lydia Cabrera, the narrator *par excellence*, can be found on the pages of her fiction.]

In her study *Lydia Cabrera and the Construction of an Afro-Cuban Cultural Identity*, Edna Rodríguez-Mangual observes that Cabrera offers an "alternative to the standard, homogenous interpretations of Cuban identity . . . the black cosmogony re-created in her work becomes a place of enunciation of an alternative identity that exposes the limits of official discourse."[12]

The short story "El sapo guardiero" ("The Watchful Toad") from *Cuentos Negros* is one example of the author's foregrounding of a spirited identity within Cuban national culture. While it can be read as a mythical tale of twins "the size of bird feed" who are lost in the dark forest of an evil witch, the domain of which is guarded by a toad who "protected the woods and their secret," sleeps in a puddle of "dead water," and has not seen the light in many centuries, the "initiated" reader, aware of the ritual-specific language used in the story, will know that they are in a Palo Monte *Monte*, a sacred wild of religious spirits and rituals. The monte is for Afro-Cubans and for those familiar with the symbolic universe of the culture, the residence of the deities, the spirits of the ancestors, and supernatural beings.

Cocuyero, give me eyes so that I may see!
Horror of dreams, let all tremble! I knock over la Seiba[13]
angulo, the *seven Rays*, Mamma Louisa . . .
Sarabanda! Jump, wooden horse! Lightning Tornado!
Evil wind, carry it off, carry it off!

The woods were pressing against his back on tiptoes and watching him anxiously. From the dead branches, ears were hanging, listening to his heartbeat. Millions of invisible eyes, with sharp, furtive glances, pierced the compact darkness. And behind everything lay silence's inexorable claw.

The guardian toad left the twins lying on the ground.

"No matter who suffers, Sampunga wants some blood!
No matter who suffers, Sampunga wants some blood!"[14]

The forest is further described with ritualized expressions and language suggestive of the contents and rituals for the making of an *nganga* cauldron of the Palo Monte religion in Cuba:

In the muddy stomach.
Dust of the crossroads.
Earth from the cemetery, dug at night.
Black earth from an anthill, because ants have worked doggedly, thinking neither of pain nor pleasure, since the beginning of time. The *Bibijaguas*,[15] industrious and wise.

Stomach of Mama Téngue. She learned her mysterious work in the roots of the Grandmother Seiba, in the earth's womb for seven days. For seven days she learned the work of silence among the fish in the river's depths, Mama Téngue drank the moon.

With the hairy spider and the scorpion, the rotten rooster head and with owl-eye, eye of immovable night, blood yoke, the Word of the Shadows shone, "Evil Spirit! Evil Spirit! Mouth of darkness, worm's mouth, consuming life! Allá Kiriki, allai bosaikombo, allá kiriki!"

Flat on her stomach, the old woman spat alcohol along with dust and Chinese pepper in to the enchanted saucepan.

On the ground, *she drew arrows with ashes* and sleeping serpents with smoke. She made the seashells speak.[16]

For the uninitiated reader the story is a delightful example of folklore, similar to the naïve readings of Nicolas Guillen's well-known poem "Sensemayá,"[17] which ignored the ritualized language of the verses labeling them examples of *jitanjaforas*, invented poetic words created for their suggestive sounds rather than for their meanings. For the initiated or privileged reader, however, the references to "Evil Wind" in the Cabrera story and especially to "Sarabanda" (Zarabanda) are a clue to another—spiritual—reality: the Congo religious traditions in Cuba. While *La Regla de Ocha* or *Santería*, based on *Yoruba* practices, is commonly compared to a marriage with the deities—a *santo* or *orisha*—a dedicated, daily commitment to render worship in offerings, prayers, ritual ceremonies to keep the *orisha* contented and appeased, the religion of *Palo Monte* can be more accurately understood as a sacred pact with a spirit that is also binding but more occasional and intermittent, summoned when needed, a relationship with a reliable magical enforcer who will carry out one's will. The magical aspects of *Palo* are the most recognized parts of a practice that is less familiar to many inside and outside of Cuba but nevertheless plays an important role in Afro-Cuban religious culture.

Originally predominant in the eastern end of Cuba, the *Reglas Congas*, commonly called "Palo Monte" in Cuba, derive from the Congo religion of the *Bakongo* people, referred to as the "Conga" or "Bantu" culture in Cuba. More accurately, one should speak of Congo religions in Cuba as there are several branches contained under the general rubric of "Regla de Palo Monte Mayombe," including the *Regla Biyumba, Regla Musunde, Regla Quirimbaya, Regla Vrillumba,* and the *Regla* Kimbisa del Santo Cristo del Buen Viaje ("of the Holy Christ of the Good Journey"). Considered among the most syncretized of Afro-Cuban practices, Congo religions in Cuba derive elements from Yoruba and other African practices and Roman Catholicism, particularly in terms of religious structural organization, which has led to their being referred to as *religiones cruzadas* or "crossed." *Regla de Ocha/Santería* and the Congo practices, although different, are nevertheless complimentary. Many persons follow both religions and are both *santeros* and *paleros* or *mayomberos*, as followers of *Regla de Palo* are called. *Regla de Ocha* spirits have their counterparts in Palo Monte; Changó is *Siete Rayos* and Ogún is worshipped as *Zarabanda*, for example. Focused less on a pantheon of deities, however, the *Reglas Congas*, the religions of *Palo Monte* or *Palo Monte Mayome*, emphasize control of the spirits of the dead and healing with the use of fetishes, formulas, and spells.

The Congo element most carefully preserved and that which is most respected and feared is that of magic, and the main source of this magical power is the ability of the *Palero*, as the practitioners are called, to make contact with the spirit of a dead person and to control it and make it work for him. The spirit inhabits the *nganga*, a word that designates not only a spirit or supernatural force but also the recipient in which the spirit dwells, an iron pot or cauldron and its contents, the centering focus of Palo religious practice. Those used for good purposes are *cristianas* (Christian), those for evil ends, unbaptized or *judías*. The spirit protects the *palero* and is a source of power and support, bearing a name that identifies its owner as well, for example, names such as *Viento Malo* (Evil Wind) or *Remolino* (Whirlwind).

The making of an *nganga* is a complex, magical, and at times macabre process that has been recorded in several sources. It is an involved procedure that must take place at certain times of the day and of the month, and uses the spirits of nature in plants, insects (the *bibijaguas* ants mentioned in the story cited earlier), animal and human bones (if possible the *kiyumba* or human skull), blood, graveyard dirt, cane alcohol, and spices; the sticks and branches of special trees (*palos*) designate the sect and are a key ingredient in the *nganga*-making process. The pact with the spirit inside the cauldron takes place during a ceremony wherein the spirit is contacted through divination with gunpowder and trance. The receptacle is then buried for a period of time in the cemetery and in the *monte*, in nature, after which it is returned to remain with its owner for whom the *nganga* is a small spiritual world entirely dominated by him.

LEONARDO PADURA FUENTES AND THE INITIATED READER

The privileged or initiated reader of Cabrera's stories or of the literature by others referred to in this chapter as spirited writers are not necessarily everyone born and raised in Caribbean societies. In the course of our research for *Creole Religions* we noted that contemporary Cuban authors address such themes from the recognition that, though significant, they represent a spirituality or cultural identity not shared by all in Cuban society. In Leonardo Padura Fuentes' detective novel *Adiós Hemingway & La cola de la serpiente* (2001),[18] for example, the character of the *Palero* and his remarks are akin to those recorded by ethnographers, but the observations of the main character, the detective Mario Conde, on the unfamiliar nature of a world so identified with Cuban culture yet so distant from his everyday experiences as a Cuban living in the island today, reflect the comments of many who consider these spiritual practices as belonging to a world apart.

Mario Conde is involved in a murder investigation in which the main clues are an unusual symbol scratched on the victim's chest, which the detective is told is the sign of *Zarabanda*, and a missing finger from the victim, possibly to be used in the making of an *nganga*. *Zarabanda* (*Sarabanda* in Lydia Cabrera's short story) is in fact one of the Congo sacred drawings that are important elements of African Congo religions, a Congo mystic ground drawing that, Robert Farris Thompson reminds us, attracts spiritual power, "singing and drawing points of contact between worlds" invoked with the Congo chants referred to as *mambos* in Cuba (as in the earlier reference to the drawing of arrows in Cabrera's tale). The *Zarabanda* sign and the spirit conjured by it in Cuba is syncretic, identified with the *orisha Ogún* who in turn is identified with Saint Peter, combining the powers of *Regla de Ocha* and Congo practices. In the novel the detective, who is not intimately familiar with the Afro-Cuban religions, is told to visit a respected old man in Havana's neighboring town of *Regla*, the "Mecca of Cuban sorcery." The man is described as ancient, with eyes almost as black as his wrinkled skin. The grandson of African slaves, he was initiated into Palo and became a *Mayombero*, but "as if that weren't enough," he is also a *babalao* or Santería priest, a member and leader of an *Abakuá* chapter, and a Mason. "Speaking with him was like consulting an old tribal guru who guards all of the history and the traditions of his clan in his memory." The old man goes on to explain the construction of an *nganga* cauldron:

"The sign, Zarabanda, is traced on the bottom of the cauldron, which is the base for everything. Look here, the circle is the earth and the two arrows in a cross are the winds. The other crosses are the corners of the world, which are always four . . . Nowadays they use more arrows and adornments. But that's an old one from the colonial times."

"Is it true that they use human bones in an nganga?"

"Of course, if not, how are you going to control the dead person? The nganga has a thousand things, but it always has to have a man's bones, and better yet, the head, the *kiyumba*, where the bad thoughts lie. Then you add sticks from the forest, but not just any sticks, but those from powerful trees; then flint celts that have tasted blood, animal bones, the fiercer the better, cemetery dirt, quicksilver so that it will never be still, and holy water if you want it to do good. If not, it is unbaptized and remains Jewish . . . But if the nganga is Zarabanda, since he is the owner of all iron, a chain is placed around the pot and inside you have to put a key, a lock, a magnet, a hammer and on top of it all Ogún's machete . . . All of this you feed with the blood of a rooster and a goat, and then decorate it with many-colored feathers."

El Conde felt that he was losing himself in *a world in which he had always lived but from which he had been infinitely remote*. Those religions, eternally stigmatized by slave owners that considered them heretical and barbarous, then by the bourgeoisie who called them the stuff of brutish, dirty blacks, and lately marginalized by dialectical materialists who went so far as categorize them scientifically and politically as remnants of a past that atheism had to overcome, held for Mario Conde the lure of resistance . . .

"Does the owner of the nganga have to know the dead man he puts in the cauldron?"

The old man puffed on his cigar twice and smiled.

"That almost never happens, because people nowadays use any dead person . . . But if you know him, much better, because that way you can choose. Look, if you want to make an nganga judía to do evil, you should look for someone who had been very wicked in life . . . because his spirit will continue to be as bad as the live man was on earth. And sometimes worse . . . That's why the best bones come from crazy men, and better yet, Chinese men who are the angriest and most vengeful on the face of the earth . . . Mine I inherited from my father and it has the head of a Chinese man who committed suicide out of rage because he didn't want to be a slave, and you cannot imagine the things I have done with that nganga . . . may God forgive me."[19]

THE SPIRITED IDENTITY AND
U.S. LATINA AUTHORS

The *nganga* theme is also found outside of Cuban literature in Creole U.S. Latino writing. It is the basis of the short story "The Cauldron" (1998),[20] by U.S. Latina author Lyn Di Iorio Sandín. In the story a cauldron left behind in an abandoned hacienda, "made of iron blackened by fire and years of exposure, stands in the center of the ruins under the ceibas. Malodorous soil, flavored with blood and a human skull, is a sign that the cauldron is the prison of a fuiri a dead one." The author substitutes the word *fuiri* for the more commonly used words *nkisi* or *mpungo* for the Congo spirits as a more "poetic and evocative" choice of language, following the use of the word by the well-known writer of *Santería* literature Migene González Wippler.[21] History and spirituality converge in the story, along with the avenging of past injustices with regard to the enslaved Africans in Puerto Rico:

> La Margarita's owner was a *sinverguenza*, an upstart Corsican. He had a concubine, a slave who, according to the historical sources, had been a priestess among the Congos. The oral tradition tells us a little more about this woman. It says she got the man his property with her magic. After he had glutted himself on all the land he could get, he decided to marry the mayor's daughter and live happily after. The Congo woman killed herself out of grief. Or maybe the Corsican killed her. No one really knows. The rumor was that he learned her magic. He imprisoned her spirit in that cauldron you've been hearing so much about. It was after her death that strange things began to happen in the town . . .[22]

While Puerto Rican culture is not as closely identified with the Palo *Monte Mayombe* religious tradition as Cuba, Marta Moreno Vega claims that the Puerto Rican variant of *Espiritismo* is not a legacy of *Regla de Ocha* and the *Yoruban* tradition, but rather that of the ancestor worship of African Congo cultures brought to the island by enslaved Africans in the nineteenth century during the later phase of the slave trade in Puerto Rico.[23] The Congo practices and themes survive today in Puerto Rican literature on the island and in the Diaspora.

Other U.S. Latina authors also trace Creole spiritual themes in their writings, frequently in the creolized/diasporic variants of the practices, that is, *Santerismo*. U.S. Puerto Rican author Judith Ortiz Cofer in her novel *The Line of the Sun* (1989)[24] centers the spirit identity in a female character, the rebellious healer/witch "La Cabra," the town's most sought after medium who practices an *Espiritismo* combined with *Santería*, one of the "new ways" she had learned in New York. *La Cabra's* sexual fascination for the males is matched by the envy and fear she produces in the female population of the small Puerto Rican town, leading to her rejection and expulsion from the community. The protagonist's mother transports the family's *Espiritista* beliefs to their home in New Jersey, with disastrous results. In Cuban American Dolores Prida's play *Botánica*[25] the plot revolves around a young college-educated Cuban/Puerto Rican whose grandmother, Doña Geno, to the young woman's dismay, is the owner of a New York *botánica* or folk religious store and cures a variety of ills with healing modalities that combine *Espiritismo, Santería*, traditional and New Age herbalism, and folk psychology.

Both Ortiz Cofer's novel and Prida's play deal with a transplanted and blended Creole variant of *Santería* and *Espiritismo* begetting what some have called *Santerismo*, adopted by a significant non-Cuban population in the United States and Europe. In Puerto Rico this combination of *Espiritismo* with *Santería* or other African-based religions was intensified as a result of the immigration of Cuban exiles to the island subsequent to the Cuban Revolution of 1959. *Santería/ Regla de Ocha* gained in popularity, facilitating the syncretism process between popular Puerto Rican *Espiritismo* and *Santería*. The same phenomenon was observed among *Espiritistas* in Puerto Rican communities in the United States: the influence of Cuban exiles in the United States and a syncretized Spiritist practice from the island influenced by Cubans in Puerto Rico resulted in the establishment of syncretized Spiritist temples or *centros* (centers) in U.S. Puerto Rican communities. Andrés Pérez y Mena considers that the emergence of this variant, which he describes as one example of the "Afro-Latin" beliefs practiced in the United States and identified as "Puerto Rican Spiritualism," was tied to the search for ethnic and cultural identity in the Puerto Rican Diaspora. African worship became more acceptable in the "mainland" environment than it had been on the island based on several factors: the popularity in the 1950s of Cuban and Puerto Rican band music, which was influenced by *Santería* chants and instruments, and, more significantly, the social consciousness movements in the 1960s in the U.S. Puerto Rican community that identified with African American struggles motivating a positive reassessment of African cultural identity.

An additional observation by Alan Harwood with respect to the blurring of socioeconomic differences as migrants become a minority group in a new setting (observed in the Cuban exile community with regard to the participation of a range of races and classes in the Afro-Cuban religions outside of Cuba) is also a key factor in explaining the syncretism of the variety of Spiritism called *Mesa Blanca* ("White Table," a Europeanized variant based on the tradition as originated in France by Alan Kardec) with *Santería* traditions outside of the island: whereas in Puerto Rico Mesa Blanca and popular *Espiritismo* practitioners are divided along class lines, in New York City and in other areas of the Puerto Rican Diaspora in the United States, the demographic composition of *Espiritismo* practitioners is more heterogeneous, as is consistent with the socioeconomic realities of the Puerto Rican migration, contributing toward the blending of several traditions.

Since the extremes in class variation that obtain in Puerto Rico are by and large not present in New York, people in the narrower socioeconomic range in New York may, in the absence of the extremes, interact more readily and thus opt for either tradition. This homogenizing factor is further reinforced by the social organization of New York City, where the salient status for Puerto Ricans, regardless of class origin, is their ethnic identity, and sociocultural differences that are relevant on the island become much less important in this new context. Whatever the specific reasons behind the growing syncretism between Mesa Blanca and *Santería* in New York, however, its effect is that many New York Puerto Ricans are competent in performing the rites of either tradition, and cults that go under the name of either *Santería* or Mesa Blanca (or *Espiritismo*) in New York are usually a blend of the two traditions.[26]

According to the tenets of Spiritism, the primary purpose of life on earth is to master, through knowledge and participation, the lower nature and become guided and influenced by the higher aspects of the divine spirit within. Upon death the soul, or "vital fluid," leaves the body but the spirit remains and may be seen or heard by those in trance. It can grow morally and achieve enlightenment to approach perfection and the ultimate goal of becoming a pure spirit, or remain backward and malevolent, suffering and postponing evolution and causing physical and/or emotional problems for the living. Spiritism's goal, therefore, is the enlightenment of dark or "intranquil" spirits in need of light, redemption and progress through advancement toward spiritual perfection.

Espiritismo continues to be practiced in many U.S. Latino communities today as an alternative doctrine of beliefs and values, and a healing practice with widespread variations. *Espiritismo* may be practiced on an individual level for advice and healing, or in group sessions in a center or meeting place where the practice can serve as a community organization, a religion, and a cultural identity providing for many of the needs of urban Latino migrants. The healing is accomplished via the identification of a spirit as either a "protector" or, on the other hand, a *causa* (a spirit that causes or creates problems or misfortune) as determined during trance, the focus of the *Espiritista* ritual. In a typical meeting, the Head Medium (*Presidente*) with his/her assistant mediums and the developing mediums sit around a table covered with a white cloth upon which are typically placed a goblet of water and a candle in the presence of a number of believers. Through prayers (usually from Kardec's books) and concentration, the *Presidente* and the mediums summon the spirits to the table to aid the assembled congregation in their trials and in their relationship to the spirit world. As the spirits manifest in the trance mediums, the first stage of the healing process, *buscando la causa*, determining the cause of the problem, commences. Once the cause of the illness or predicament is discovered, the *Presidente* will interrogate and persuade the malevolent spirits to depart from their suffering victim, a process referred to as *trabajando la causa* "working the cause," to have the spirits lifted (*levantadas*), which is among the principal healing objectives of *Espiritismo*. In the final phase the spirit undergoes a *despojo* or purification wherein it is convinced that it is indeed a spirit and no longer a part of the world of the living and taught how to attain a more advanced level of spiritual evolution. In the variant of *Santerismo*, the African influence is clearly demonstrated in the connection to the spirit world via the *santos* or *orishas* of the Afro-Cuban religion, considered to be at an elevated spiritual level, as well as to African spirit guides or *congos*. *Santerismo* mediums communicate with lower ranking spirits as well but are possessed by the *orishas* in a ceremony that varies in many respects from that of the Mesa Blanca.

In Dolores Prida's play the *Santerismo* mix is evident in the characters and the spiritual *orishas*, and in the rituals and herbal solutions prescribed by the pharmacy/temple's healer. The references to what some critics describe as Prida's characteristic "ritual" humor is, in this work at least, true representation. For María Teresa Marrero, "The comic sense that Santa Bárbara *(Changó)* [the *orisha* of thunder] does not speak English and that people only think of her/him when there is thunder is a culturally coded insider joke."[27] Insiders will recognize the potions purchased for baths and spiritual cures or compounds created by the folk "pharmacist" in Prida's play as those of the type one can easily obtain in most botánicas: "follow-me potion" (*esencia sígueme*), "good-luck potion" (*esencia de la buena suerte*), "chain-breaking potion" (*esencia rompe cadenas*), "essence to tame tough guys" (*esencia amansa guapo*), "I-can-and-you-can't potion" (*esencia yo puedo y tú no puedes*), "essence of jealousy" (*esencia celitos*), "forget-me-not potion" (*esencia no me olvides*), "essence of mastery" (*esencia vencedor*), and "essence to subdue" (*esencia dominante*).[28]

From the perspective of language, the works by Ortiz Cofer and Prida share important characteristics. The authors of *The Line of the Sun* (in English but with *Espiritista* terminology in Spanish) and *Botánica* (presented in Spanish with English words and phrases interspersed throughout) both feel confident that their reader/audience does not require a translation of religious terms associated with either *Espiritismo* or *Santería*. These generally remain unexplained; a Latino public knows either firsthand or indirectly of the unusual spiritual spells or cures referred to in the works. Indeed it is unusual to encounter anyone from the Caribbean (and increasingly from the wider U.S. culture) who has not heard of such practices. But beyond the novel and the play's compassionate vision of ethic identity and generational conflicts of the type frequently found in U.S. Latino writing, poignant gender issues are also an important theme of their works: the spiritual leaders in these unorthodox practices as well as the nontraditional healers in both works are women. That females are the focus of this essay in the fictional characters of the authors and in the gender of the authors themselves is not remarkable. The gender of the proprietor and unofficial "therapist" of Prida's folk pharmacy/store/temple and of many who enter in search of such medical/spiritual advice and "ritual therapy" (men, of course, are not entirely absent) is authentic representation. Having played an important role in folk/spiritual healing for centuries, it is not unusual to encounter women presiding over such establishments or in comparable healing venues. Unfortunately, as portrayed in Ortiz Cofer's novel, they have endured an unequal share of the vilification and victimization traditionally associated with such practices. The women in these works are healers in the tradition of *curanderismo*, which is in fact a complex cultural healing system with common roots in healing modalities found throughout the Caribbean and Latin America, combining Hippocratic humoral (hot–cold) theories of disease with Amerindian herbal medicine and diverse spiritual traditions ranging from African-based systems to the Spiritist philosophy of Allan Kardec, which inspired the creation of spiritual healing centers throughout the Caribbean, Mexico, and Brazil, among other countries in Latin America—the "integrative" medical resource of the people.

Unorthodox medicine, like its religious counterpart, has been more accessible to women; there they can claim an authority denied them in mainstream institutions and are more at liberty to utilize female traditions of caretaking to alleviate their suffering communities. Joan Koss-Chioino notes that spirit-possession is "largely a feminine activity" with three to four women *Espiritistas* to every male and fewer men than women undergoing possession. Some describe the experience as a soothing and tranquil "coolness," although during healing work an intranquil spirit can be distressful and harsh. Others have described possession in a sexualized discourse as a "penetration" of their bodies, being filled up with heat or fluidity, expressing feelings akin to being "dominated, oppressed by a foreign force personified (for the sake of description) as an external being," leading some Puerto Rican feminists to retain ambivalent feelings toward the traditional healer role for women, which they believe reinforces the female subordinate role and lack of entitlement.[29]

"Guardian angels" and "protector spirits" steer human beings through life's "tests"; communication with these spirits is therefore fundamental. The dead are still considered important family members who can intervene in the affairs of the living and therefore communication with deceased family members consoles those who believe that a connection is still possible. Spirits can be elevated to a higher status in the otherworldly spirit hierarchy, thanks to the *misa espiritual,* the Spiritist mass. According to Jorge and Isabel Castellanos, the misa espiritual is nowadays a crucial part of Afro-Cuban religions; indeed, many practitioners and spiritual leaders of *Regla de Ocha, Regla de Palo,* and the other Cuban *Reglas* are also Spiritist mediums. As Lydia Cabrera's informants in *El Monte* declared: "*Ocha* or *Palo* . . . doesn't it come to the same thing? Spirits all! Doesn't one fall into trance with the saint as with the dead? In religion everything is to do with the dead. The dead become saints." According to Cabrera, "saints and spirits are daily visitors in the houses of the Cuban people."[30] Honoring the dead has always been an essential element of Afro-Cuban practices. During a *misa espiritual* the spirits who speak are not necessarily one's ancestors but any of a range of spirit guides and protectors. Food offerings reflect the syncretism of *egun* (the dead) veneration and Spiritism: "spiritual" items—incense, candles, tobacco smoke, cologne, and prayer—are offered to the spirits while food and other "material" offerings are made to the dead. The spiritual mass, observe Castellanos and Castellanos, while not a Spiritist session per se, merges *Espiritismo*, Catholicism, and the Afro-Cuban religions in its ritual, fusing the diverse elements of the Cuban cultural continuum.

The identification of a spirit as either a protector or a *causa* (a spirit that creates problems or misfortune) is revealed during trance, the focus of the *Espiritista* ritual (which is not limited to the mediums; everyone can join in calling the spirits). The *Espiritista* altar may exhibit a crucifix, flowers, candles, numerous and varied effigies, and chromolithographs (*estampas*) of Catholic saints (particularly of the patron saint of the centro). In addition one would probably find the stereotypic representations of various ethnic spirit protector guides of the mediums who offer advice, diagnose illnesses, witness events in the spirit world: the *Madama* dolls, a black "mammy" type, turbaned and rotund in a gingham dress, representing the *curandera* faith healer, akin to the West Indian Obeah woman; a North American Plains Indian, male and/or female, with typical headdress, representing a heightened warrior spirituality; the Hindu or Arab, a judicious philosopher spirit; the gypsy (*gitana* or *gitano*) who is in touch with the future; a Congo, a wise old African man or woman, familiar with nature, magic, and time-honored healing remedies. The mix of figures is undoubtedly based on healing cult practices from diverse earlier traditions, although one might also see representations of historical heroes.

Koss-Chioino and others consider that the spirits guides—the *Madamas* and gypsies, for example—serve the function of expressing repressed conflicts and represent a type of psychic resolution for women living in patriarchal cultures that allow most women only a constricted public space. This type of female spirit guide represents marginalized women, the sorceresses and witches feared and rejected by men and women, but are also a symbol of repressed feminine strength. They frequently express in possession the explicit sexual desires of women and repressed and unexpressed grievances, unavailable elements of the healer's self.

The fact that so many believers in *Espiritismo* are women is undoubtedly due to the spiritual possibilities it affords them that are difficult to find in mainstream religions; the spirit hierarchy is egalitarian, spiritual categories are not linked to age, race, class, or sex, and ascending in the spiritual pyramid is available to all. Female empowerment in the leadership role of *Espiritismo*, the position of a respected and admired medium-healer, is attainable if one has the strength of purpose to study the spirit world and strive to achieve its moral and spiritual principles. The status women can attain as healers does not require a formal education or rigid training, and the wide autonomy afforded for personal interpretation and approach to ritual practice as well as the absence of a centralized organizational authority (similar to other Creole religious practices) is appealing to women who discover there a sanctioned space.

The role of *Espiritismo* and the other Creole religious practices as a form of healing in the experience of exile is a theme frequently encountered in literature of Creole U.S. Latino authors. The various waves of Cuban exiles to the United States after the Cuban Revolution in 1959, called by some as the "second Diaspora" of Yoruba religion, has created challenges and served to inspire and create a "pan-Diaspora tradition of the *orishas*" beyond the borders of Cuba and beyond the Cuban exiles themselves: "there are hundred of thousands of Americans who participate in the tradition, ranging from relatively fewer committed 'godchildren' of a particular line of *orisha* initiation, to numberless 'clients' seeking consultations with priestesses and priests for help with critical problems. Nearly everyone of Caribbean background living in North American cities is touched by *Santería* in some way."[31] Exile and the displacement of the devotees of the *orishas* to a new foreign culture have once again tested the adaptability of an old tradition in a new environment. For Cuban exiles *Santería* has taken on a special meaning: an alternative medical system, a support system and coping mechanism for dealing with the stress of exile and immigration, eliminating the feelings of guilt resulting from such dramatic life changes, and a way of expressing cultural identity in a foreign society without the socioeconomic and racial restrictions they might have encountered in their homeland. "Outside of Cuba, *Santería's* function, as a social and economic network and as a supportive complementary health system, has been enhanced during the last thirty years. The people who frequent the house of a *santero* constitute a fictive extended family, who share economic and affection bonds."[32] The religion serves to substitute for lost kin, severed ties, and a missing sense of belonging.

The missing sense of belonging is an unmistakable theme in Cuban American Cristina García's first two novels, *Dreaming in Cuban* (1992) and *The Agüero Sisters* (1997),[33] which rely on the reader's familiarity with a tradition that began as a spiritual refuge for enslaved Africans in Cuba and has evolved into a religious practice bringing healing and hope to Cubans and non-Cubans alike. Family, diaspora, loss, and spiritual connections characterize her works. García's novels can be considered as following within the tradition of Lydia Cabrera's work in the recognition of the heritage of a spiritually identified community. Wherein Lydia Cabrera's writing served to introduce to her own Creole Cuban society in the early twentieth century a culture that, paraphrasing Padura Fuentes, was "a world in which they had always lived but from which they had been infinitely remote,"[34] Cristina García's novels likewise treat a subject that is marginally known to her English-speaking readership and is for some U.S. Latinos equally alien. The initiated readership, as we have noted, is not necessarily from the literary cultural group treated in a work and indeed, given the growing popularity of the practice outside the Cuban community, the contrary is increasingly a reality. *Santería* is more familiar to many U.S. Latino readers in English than the Congo tradition discussed earlier given that it has become more widespread and well-known, not only in the academic and religious community but also in U.S. popular culture, a fact that can be a burden as well as a blessing for the Creole U.S. Latino author.

The racist assumptions with which Cabrera and other Creole authors had to contend at the beginning of the twentieth century have been exacerbated by the myths and disinformation spread by manipulative filmmakers with such exploitation horror films as "*The Believers*" (1987) and "*The Serpent and the Rainbow*" (1988). In the years prior to the publication of *Dreaming in Cuban*, a spate of films that dealt with Vodou and what some mistakenly referred to as "Cuban Voodoo" or *Santería* were released; the importance of film and the dissemination of myths regarding Afro-Caribbean religious practices has been studied in many sources and cannot be overestimated.[35] Like "*The Serpent and the Rainbow*," "*The Believers*" is a loose fictionalization of a book that was a nonfiction study of the *Santería* religion. The plot revolves around a New York police officer in a state of hysteria believing himself to be the recipient of a *Santería* "curse," described in publicity for the film as a religion that is a "blend of voodoo and Catholicism." The film uses the killing of children and a distortion of the religion in order to falsely propose that *Santería* involves ritual human sacrifice. The World Wide Web is now increasingly also a source of misinformation. While it can be source of information and assistance for those who live outside of metropolitan areas with fewer opportunities to purchase the ritual items required for ceremonies, the Internet can also promote the type of distortions discussed here.

The theme of *Santería* was one that García worked into her well-known novel from a similar impulse to that found in Lydia Cabrera's fiction: the foregrounding of the ethno-religious as the locus of cultural identity. For María Teresa Marrero, "The practice of incorporating Santería in works of fiction by Cubans and Latinos in the United States, I believe, addresses more than literary tropicalization. More urgently, it suggests the creation and negotiation of a new cultural space for Latino self-identity."[36] The manner in which the religion is represented in *Dreaming in Cuban*, however, is problematic for some. The initiated reader will find the references to spirituality in *Dreaming in Cuban* both familiar and disconcerting. García acknowledges in early interviews that her experience of *Santería* was marginal having been raised in a Roman Catholic family disdainful and biased against the Afro-Cuban religion. Her knowledge when writing the novel was based on research that grew into a fascination with the religion: "It's part of our cultural landscape and, as Pilar [the protagonist/narrator in *Dreaming in Cuban*], says at one point, it makes a lot more sense than more abstract forms of worship."[37] The space for self-identity in the novel with reference to *Santería* is focused on the character of Felicia, a white Cuban who is mentally unstable due to syphilis contracted from a philandering black husband. Felicia dies due to her madness "and a mysterious *Santería*-inflected decline."[38] Felicia is one of the novel's most fully developed and intriguing characters and also the most complex. When she turns to *Santería* for salvation she is already past the stage where her physical problems can be resolved. For the protagonist Pilar, however, the connection to Cuba via *Santería* and the spiritual connection to her family in the Diaspora are life-affirming and confirm her cultural identity.

In part the image of *Santería* as a mysterious, "exotic," and powerful African tradition served the enslaved as an instrument of cultural survival . . . [Africanity's] current rearticulation by U.S. Cuban writers is not surprising, if their work is taken as part of a uniquely Cuban tradition which precedes immigration into the United States. As such, I believe, it forms part of a thrust towards a mediated and selective cultural retention. It signals a growing ethnic awareness by Cuban Americans to navigate through the lure of total "Americanization," the alienating impulse to perceive Self as an exotic Other.[39]

Critics consider García's second novel a more critical success. In Lyn Di Iorio Sandín's perceptive essay, "When *Papi* Killed *Mami*: Allegory's Magical Fragments in Cristina García's *The Agüero Sisters*," García's use of magic and religion as the elements of magical realism or, in Di Iorio Sandín's phrase, "magical allegory" differ from the Latin American literary style of Gabriel García Márquez and Alejo

Carpentier: rather than a communitarian reality with its political and spiritual implications for the societies they treat in their works, in García's novel "the magical always results from an alienated individual's repression or mystification of past events, and often through a projection of the beliefs and practices of Afro-Caribbean *Santería* onto misunderstood characters and situations."[40] The informed reader will note the authentic representation in the novel of *Santería* rituals of worship and in references to the characters and their ritual identification with the *orishas*; Di Iorio Sandín convincingly argues for an allegorical relationship among the human characters with their human and spiritual doubles.

The character of Reina (queen) is clearly a daughter of the *orisha* king *Changó*, for example, perhaps an inheritance from Reina's biological father who wears the *orisha* deity's red and white ritual beads, or a legacy from her mother whose love for the deity passes on to her child. The initiated reader will ascertain Reina's similarities to the *orisha* in her self-assured, androgynous, and hypersexual magnetism. Her endless conquests are what one would expect of the daughter of the most venerated and popular of the Cuban *orishas*, considered by many as the strongest and most important. Miguel Barnet's description of *Changó* applies equally to the character of Reina in García's novel: "a womanizer . . . quarrelsome, courageous, and daring; made for challenges and dares, proud of his masculine virtues, boastful of his strength and manly beauty, castigador (a heartbreaker)."[41] Both feared and venerated *Changó* rules over fire, thunder, and lightning and is believed to have been a historical figure, the fourth *Alafín* (a name *Changó* is also called in *Santería*) or king of *Oyó*. His attributes and symbols include the *piedras de rayo*, thunder or flintstones collected after lightning storms. The initiated reader will see in Reina's physical strength, her talent with her hands and with tools—the female electrician who lights up the Cuban countryside—and her forceful, magnetic power over men a spiritual inheritance and the source of her protection from harm. After miraculously surviving a lightning strike, Reina reflects in the hospital on the wonders of nature's powerful forces.

> Reina understands that lightning has its work to do. It's an atmospheric discharge, urgent between clouds or between clouds and the ground below. Many thousands of bolts strike the earth daily, searing their fatal messages. Yet Reina cannot accept a rational explanation. What she knows is this: that she was singled out to die but, instead, has survived.
>
> In Cuba, Reina has heard it whispered, *Changó* own the lightning, uses it to display his displeasure, his brazen force. *Oyá* his first and favorite

wife, also own the fire. She stole it from *Changó* once when he went off to battle. Reina asks a nurse to tie two ribbons for these fractious lovers—one red, one maroon—to the foot of her bead, just in case.[42]

Di Iorio Sandín correctly notes, however, that García's postmodernist magical realism is ambiguous, not as convinced or convincing as the world of the characters and narrator of Carpentier's Haitian creation in *The Kingdom of this World*.[43]

> Magical realism, when it appears momentarily and fragmentarily, in Garcías text implies the psychological return of a reality the characters do not consciously recognize. The reinvention of the past and the projection of spiritual or magical aspects onto the present in Garcías text underlines the partnership of desire with great doubt, an uneasy avatar of the deep faith that Carpentier describes as essential to the existence of *lo real maravilloso*.[44]

There is no ambiguity regarding the spirit world in Marta Moreno Vega's moving memoir, *When the Spirits Dance Mambo: Growing Up Nuyorican in El Barrio* (2004).[45] A "spirited bildungsroman," it differs from other growing-up texts by Nuyorican men and women in its celebration of the Afro/Puerto Rican diasporic culture and of *Espiritismo*, a practice that permeates life in El Barrio in the author's youth of the 1950s, the respect for which the author inherited from one of the major influences in her youth, her grandmother. The author of a prior work, *The Altar of My Soul* (2000),[46] a memoir of her journey from novice to *santera* or *Santería* priestess, Moreno Vega reveals in her spirited bildungsroman the youthful experiences of Afro-Caribbean spirituality that eventually forged her path to an adult spirited identity. The sacred mysteries of the religions are demystified and presented as a gift from Africa to the New World cultures of the Caribbean and Latin America, and to their diasporan communities in the United States. Whereas in *The Altar of My Soul* Moreno Vega narrates her trip to Cuba and her initiation in the *Regla de Ocha* religion, the subsequent memoir demonstrates that a trip to Africa or to the islands of the Caribbean were not required for her moral and ethnic development as a young girl: the spirits of her ancestors and of her spirit guides were located on the altar of her *abuela* in New York City and in the ritual contact with the spirit world during which her grandmother transformed spirit into matter.

The ancestors play an essential role in sanctioning everything that is done in the Afro-diasporic house and Moreno Vega clearly grew up in such a home. In a belief system in which death is simply one more step toward spiritual development, spirits and humans empower each other in *Espiritismo* rituals with the assistance of the medium. While the *orishas* of the *Regla de Ocha* religion will reside in the assigned cabinets or shelves within a room, ritual family ancestors are typically enshrined on the floor of the bathroom under the sink (the vertical pipes allow them to "travel" between worlds via their favorite medium, water) and other spirits of one's *cuadro espiritual* or spiritual cadre may be located on a table or *bóveda*—literally vault or crypt—an ancestor altar typically holding, among other things, an odd number of goblets filled with water, flowers, cigars, candles (all to appease the spirits), statues, photographs of deceased family members, rosary beads, bibles, and books of prayers.

When the Spirits Dance Mambo describes just such a space. African warrior gods are hidden from public view in her grandmother's home; the altar has fresh flowers and water for the Indian, Yoruba, and Congo spirits and, syncretically, shelves of the statues of Catholic saints who share the space with the representations of Africans and Native Americans. The memoir is filled with explanations for these practices in which the author gently takes her reader by the hand and translates both the words and the events. Titles are bilingual and are usually verses from the Cuban and Puerto Rican band music of the 1950s, which was influenced by *Santería* chants and instruments. The title of chapter seven is typical. "What Was Changó Doing at the Palladium?" is followed by a bilingual epigraph of song verses and the name of the composers or performers that popularized them. For chapter seven the song is "Changó ta veni" by Machito and his Afro-Cubans:

> *Changó ta veni. Changó ta veni, Changó ta veni, con el machete en la mano tierra va temblar.*
>
> *Changó is coming, Changó is coming, Changó is coming, with his machete in his hand the earth will tremble.*[47]

From the beginning of the work the reader is introduced to a spiritual realm in the Puerto Rican East Harlem neighborhood of *El Barrio* of the 1950s, a world in which emigrants formed close ties in order to survive the bias of the world outside of the cultural community. The late 1950s and early 1960s would see the fabric of the community being torn apart by the influx of drugs and violence on the streets, a reality clearly and brutally depicted in Piri Thomas's well-known 1967 bildungsroman *Down These Mean Streets*.[48] But whereas Thomas suffers even in his own Cuban/Puerto Rican home from racial prejudice and marginalization, Moreno Vega, while not ignoring the problem of racism in the community and in the general society, benefited from another experience; she was able to transcend these injustices based on the solid African self-identity she formed as a result of the spirituality of her grandmother, the spiritual center of her family and her community. Moreno Vega's experience of El Barrio was quite different from Thomas's despite their similar backgrounds. Why were earlier works of U.S. Latinos more ambivalent regarding spiritual issues? According to Moreno Vega, expressions of African-diasporic spirituality were neither condoned nor accepted leading to reluctance on the part of some to express their spirituality.[49] Following the reasoning presented in Zohar and Marshall's *SQ: Connecting with our Spiritual Intelligence*,[50] the "spiritual intelligence" she attained as a young girl allowed the young Moreno Vega to heal herself of society's bigotry and intolerance and avoid the pitfalls that earlier Nuyorican protagonists endured. Moreno Vega's work hopes to remedy that situation, a fact confirmed in the "Acknowledgements" of *When the Spirits Dance Mambo* dedicated to the young in hopes that "the stories of the past will help you to negotiate the wonders within out cultures" and in the appendix, "A Readers Group Guide," a didactic tool for readers and teachers.

Abuela Luisa, Moreno Vega's grandmother, was a healer and the community consulted her when in need; her ability to consult the spirits as an *Espiritista* medium solved their problems and those of her granddaughter's teenage emotional dilemmas. The scenes of spirit possession are introduced in an everyday fashion that the initiated reader will accept as a spiritual reality and the more skeptical as the psychological remedy of a wise old woman. When the family faces a problem they seek the advice of *Abuela* for solutions and she in turn invokes the spirit of *Juango*, a freed African Congo who speaks with the broken Spanish of the *bozal* or newly arrived enslaved African, whose manners and body movements transform the old woman. Spirit possession in the memoir recalls similar events in ethnographic literature where it has been described as an authentic experience of transformation. Though possession has been classified by some as a type of hysteria or madness, a control vehicle for repressed personalities, Eugene Genovese observes that contemporary anthropologists are skeptical of psychoanalytic explanations in the type of ritual possession involved in Afro-diasporic practices: "no genuine schizophrenic could possibly adjust to the firm system of control that the rituals demand. No matter how wild and disorderly they look to the uninitiated, they are in fact tightly controlled; certain things must be done and others not done [. . .] as Max Weber says, ecstasy may become an instrument of salvation or self-deification."[51] As demonstrated from the beginning of Moreno Vega's memoir, in a Spiritist Puerto Rican family the wife/mother's responsibilities are to tend to the spiritual as well as the material needs of the home: a periodic spiritual cleansing with a smoke purification or *sahumerio* followed by a washing or *riego* to prevent or dispel evil influences; the use of incense, flowers, or candles to attract the spirits; the maintenance of a home altar similar to those seen in *Espiritismo* centers. Glasses of water are regularly replaced on the altar and in other parts of the home. And in a manner analogous to other possession cults, *Espiritismo* confers a special status on mediums in the community.

The spirit of *Juango* speaks to the narrator through the host, the medium, who calms her granddaughter's anxieties regarding sex through the intervention of a spirit who understands her true dilemma: "Trying to understand *Juango* was difficult enough, but talking about sex with a spirit possessing my grandmother's body was startling." Consulting her grandmother initially to identify the identity of her spiritual protectors or guides, the fourteen-year-old *Cotito* ("Like our Catholic saints whose names disguised the ancient gods of Africa, many of us in El Barrio had nicknames that had replaced the names given by our parents at birth") receives a response from *Juango* in her grandmother's voice after *Abuela* had summoned the spirit to command her body:

> "*Sayita*, look at me." I looked up at Juango, who still had a mischievous glint in his eyes. "You came looking to know if this man is for you. Not about your own spirits." Juan laughed, again enjoying my shyness.
>
> "*Mi sayita*, you thought you could fool El Negro Juango." Abuela's mystic eyes, controlled by the spirit, blazed with intensity: "I am Juango, I see more than you can see and understand more than you can understand. Remember, I am spirit and I am everywhere. I have no boundaries."[52]

The girl will discover her spirit guides eventually and learn that the gypsy spirit, who solves problems through her movements, will cleanse her when she dances and the *orisha Obatalá*, as well as a warrior *cimarrona* or runaway slave spirit, will also protect her. In her 1999 essay "Espiritismo in the Puerto Rican Community," Moreno Vega observes that:

> Spiritualism, the belief in ancestor spirits, does not necessarily include the worship of the ancestor spirits manifested in the *Orishas*—gods and

goddesses—of the Yorubas. Spiritualists—mediums—in the Puerto Rican context can worship ancestor spirits (family members and other spirits of historical affinity) and be possessed by them without reference to the African gods or goddesses of the nature manifested in the Yoruba pantheon [. . .] the predominance of enslaved Africans from the Kongo region in the late-19th century into Puerto Rico suggest that their beliefs may have prevailed.[53]

The essay goes on to propose that spirits of Puerto Rican *Espiritimo* and the ancestor spirits in the Kongo region of Africa serve a similar function: they help to "establish a balance in the lives of believers" with messages of ancient healing remedies. The quest in Moreno Vega's spirited memoir is both a spiritual *and* musical journey as would follow from the identification of a gypsy spirit guide who cleanses her via the dance. The narrator's experience of music in the era of such performers as Tito Puentes and Celia Cruz at the Palladium nightclub affirms her ethnic–religious identity with a repertoire that "honored those warrior sprits that had traveled from Africa to Harlem" and "a beat that penetrated our hearts, calling spirits down and elevating or souls. Our *clave* rippled thorough our blood, creating kings and queens that soared beyond the limited borders of our neighborhoods."

"Cotito" or Marta Moreno Vega would go on to become the founder of the Caribbean Cultural Center and a Santería priestess, among other accomplishments, and the coproducer of the 2002 film documentary "Cuando los Espíritus Bailan Mambo"/"When the Spirits Dance Mambo," a celebration of the traditions of ancestor worship directed by Robert Shepard that traces the role of sacred African practices in the formation of Cuban culture, the spiritual journey that traveled from fifteenth-century West Africa to Cuba and New York. Her literary works as well as her research in the field will become a testament to a life harmonizing the secular worlds with the spiritual. In Moreno Vega's work, as in the fictional works discussed earlier and in so many texts of Creole U.S. Latina authors, spirits move across the pages of a writing that is distinctive in American letters and brings it own cultural "dance" to the site of the U.S. literary tradition. Always flexible, the Creole religions change with their travels, adapting to a new population and new environment, winning a new legitimacy for ancient practices that have not simply survived but flourish in a modern world, and the Creole/U.S. Latina authors are there to joyfully summon them to the pages of their writings.

NOTES

1. Margarite Fernández Olmos and Lizabeth Paravisini-Gebert, eds., *Creole Religions of the Caribbean: An Introduction from Vodou and Santería to Obeah and Espiritismo* (New York: New York University Press, 2003). The descriptions of the religious practices included in this chapter are based on those found in *Creole Religions* and in our prior works: *Healing Cultures: Art and Religion as Curative Practices in the Caribbean and Its Diaspora* (New York: Palgrave-St. Martin's Press, 2001) and *Sacred Possessions: Vodou, Santería, Obeah, and the Caribbean* (New Brunswick, NJ: Rutgers University Press, 1997).

2. David Buisseret and Steven G. Reinhardt, eds., *Creolization in the Americas.* "Introduction" by David Buisseret (College Station, TX: University of Texas Press, 2000), 12.

3. Edouard Glissant, "The Cultural 'Creolization' of the World: Interview with Edouard Glissant." *Label France* 38 (January 2000).

4. Frances R. Aparicio and Susana Chávez-Silverman, eds., *Tropicalizations: Transcultural Representations of* Latinidad (Hanover, NH: University Press of New England, 1997); Agustín Laó-Montes and Arlene Dávila, *Mambo Montage: The Latinization of New York* (New York: Columbia University Press, 2001).

5. Héctor Tobar, *Defining a New American Identity in the Spanish-Speaking United States* (New York: Riverhead Books, 2005), 17.

6. Rodolfo Anaya's *Bless Me, Ultima* (New York: Warner Books, 1994 [1972])can be considered a "spirited bildungsroman" in the context of the discussion of Marta Moreno Vega's memoir in this chapter.

7. Agustín Laó-Montes, "Introduction," in Laó-Montes and Dávila, *Mambo Montage*, 34.

8. Lydia Cabrera, *Cuentos negros de Cuba* (Barcelona: ICARIA, 1989). Rosario Hiriart, "Prólogo," 9–30.

9. Lydia Cabrera, *El monte. Igbo, finda, ewe orisha, vititi nfinda (Notas sobre las religiones, la magia, las supersticiones y el folklore de los negros criollos y el pueblo de Cuba)* (Miami: Ediciones Universal, 1983 [1954]).

10. Rosario Hiriart, "Prólogo," ibid., 18.

11. Ibid., 16; our translation.

12. Edna M. Rodríguez-Mangual, *Lydia Cabrera and the Construction of an Afro-Cuban Cultural Identity* (Chapel Hill: University of North Carolina Press, 2004), 20.

13. The tropical seiba (also written ceiba) trees are considered magical in many Caribbean cultures.

14. "El sapo guardiero" ("The Watchful Toad"), in *Afro-Cuban Tales. Cuentos negros de Cuba.* Trans. Alberto Hernández-Chiroldes and Lauren Poder (Lincoln, NE: University of Nebraska Press, 2004), 167; italics added.

15. Large ants.

16. Ibid., 167–168; italics added.
17. Nicolás Guillén, *Sóngoro cosongo* (Buenos Aires: Editorial Losada, 1952).
18. Leonardo Padura Fuentes, *Adiós Hemingway & La cola de la serpiente* (Havana: Ediciones Unión, 2001).
19. Fernández Olmos and Paravisini-Gebert, *Creole Religions of the Caribbean*, 83–84; italics added.
20. Lyn Di Iorio Sandín, "The Cauldron." *The Bilingual Review/Revista Bilingüe* 23.2 (May–August 1998).
21. Based on personal correspondence with the author.
22. Di Iorio Sandín, "The Cauldron," 159–160.
23. For Andrés Pérez y Mena, the Puerto Rican variant of Espiritismo is the historical equivalent of Brazilian Umbanda.
24. Judith Ortiz Cofer, *The Line of the Sun* (Athens, GA: The University of Georgia Press, 1989).
25. Dolores Prida, *Beautiful Señoritas & Other Plays* (Houston: Arte Publico Press, 1991).
26. Alan Harwood, *Rx, Spiritist as Needed: A Study of a Puerto Rican Community Mental Health Resource* (New York: John Wiley & Sons, 1977), 54.
27. María Teresa Marrero, "Historical and Literary Santería: Unveiling Gender and Identity in U.S. Cuban Literature," in Aparicio and Chávez-Silverman, *Tropicalizations*, 151.
28. Eduardo Seda, *Social Change and Personality in a Puerto Rican Agrarian Reform Community* (Evanston: Northwestern University Press, 1973), 119.
29. Joan Koss-Chioino, *Women as Healers, Women as Patients: Mental Health Care and Traditional Healing in Puerto Rico* (Boulder, CO: Westview Press, 1992), 82.
30. Cabrera, *El monte*, 31.
31. Joseph Murphy, *Working the Spirit: Ceremonies of the African Diaspora* (Boston: Beacon Press, 1994), 82.
32. Mercedes Cros Sandoval, "Santería as a Mental Health Care System: An Historical Overview." *Social Science and Medicine* 13B (1979): 94.
33. Cristina García, *The Agüero Sisters* (New York: Knopf, 1997); and *Dreaming in Cuban* (New York: Knopf, 1992).
34. Padura Fuentes, *Adiós Hemingway*.
35. See Lizabeth Paravisini-Gebert's essay in *Sacred Possessions*, "Women Possessed: Eroticism and Exoticism in the Representation of Women as Zombie," 37–58.
36. Marrero, "Historical and Literary Santería," 141.
37. Iraida H. López, "'. . . And There Is Only My Imagination Where Our History Should Be': An Interview with Cristina García." *Michigan Quarterly Review* 33.3 (Summer 1994): 610.
38. Lyn Di Iorio Sandín, *Killing Spanish: Literary Essays on Ambivalent U.S. Latino/a Identity* (New York: Palgrave Macmillan, 2004), 19; hereafter cited as "KS."

39. Marrero, "Historical and Literary Santería," 155.
40. *KS*, 17.
41. Miguel Barnet, "La Regla de Ocha: The Religious System of Santería." Trans. Lizabeth Paravisini-Gebert. In *Sacred Possessions*, 91.
42. García, *The Agüero Sisters*, 36.
43. Alejo Carpentier, *The Kingdom of This World*. Trans. Harriet de Onís (New York: Farrar, Straus and Giroux, 1989 [1957]).
44. *KS*, 32.
45. Marta Moreno Vega, *When the Spirits Dance Mambo: Growing Up Nuyorican in El Barrio* (New York: Three Rivers Press, 2004).
46. Marta Moreno Vega, *The Altar of My Soul: The Living Traditions of Santería* (New York: The Ballantine Publishing Group, 2000).
47. Ibid., 115; italics in the original.
48. Piri Thomas, *Down These Mean Streets* (New York: Alfred A. Knopf, 1967).
49. Telephone interview, 2005. Moreno Vega does not endorse the term Santerismo and has written that *Espiritismo*, as practiced by Puerto Ricans, is a form of Pan-African ancestor worship that was also practiced by indigenous peoples in the Caribbean, and combined herbalism and Native American healing practices; it was therefore not necessarily an import based on Kardecist practices.
50. Danah Zohar and Ian Marshall, *SQ: Connecting with our Spiritual Intelligence* (New York: Bloomsbury Publishing, 2000).
51. Eugene D. Genovese, *Roll, Jordan, Roll: The World the Slaves Made* (New York: Vintage Books, 1976), 239.
52. Moreno Vega, *When the Spirits*, 192.
53. Marta Moreno Vega, "Espiritismo in the Puerto Rican Community: A New World Recreation with the Elements of Kongo Ancestor Worship." *Journal of Black Studies* 19.3 (January 1999): 336.

CHAPTER 4

Racial Spills and Disfigured Faces in Piri Thomas's *Down These Mean Streets* and Junot Díaz's "Ysrael"

Richard Perez

THE EMERGING U.S. LATINO "I"

The face is a paradoxical figure of identification that pervades U.S. Latino literature. It oscillates, almost magically, between a truthful presence and a dissimulative mask. In a peculiar sense, the face communicates a promise of legibility followed by a realization that, in fact, it hides as much as it displays. This inability to deliver on the promise of itself gives the face a destabilizing aspect, combining, at once, an intentionality of appearance with an unwitting capacity to veil a complex internal life. The face, then, serves as the fleshy threshold to the extreme limits of being. In its simultaneous surface and depth there exists a relational interplay between opposing social realities. Thus the face uncannily invokes, conceals, and stands in for the conscious and unconscious; public and private; black and white; poor and rich. The static face is always on the verge of overflowing.

For U.S. Latino writers this ontological imbalance becomes a richly imaginative location for varying fictional explorations. In Latino street literature the simple contours of the face are charged with elaborate psychoanalytic, philosophic, and historic undercurrents, creating a thematic depth in a seemingly straightforward realist approach. This essay is directed by the intricacy of these currents or traces: imaginative routes that lead through the racialized mean streets of Piri

Thomas's Spanish Harlem, and the disfigured investigations of Junot Díaz's book of short stories *Drown* (1996).

If, as I will argue, the project of U.S. Latino street literature is to recompose a face or, in Anzaldúa's sense, make faces,[1] then this process of inscription must begin by taking into account a productive relation to the face of the other. The "I" of a narrative, Piri in *Down These Mean Streets* (1967) or Rafa and Yunior in *Drown*,[2] emerges in relation to a real and symbolic other that haunts them throughout their texts. In Thomas that other is a whiteness whose familial and societal potency forces Piri into a creative reevaluation of his face/race/being. His hermeneutic crisis is not just, as Lisa Sánchez González has it, a trouble of "articulation,"[3] but an ontological negotiation regarding the social and psychic difference indelibly marked by his blackness. Conversely, for Díaz, the face in its gruesome disfigurement represents a perplexing surface to be read: Rafa and Yunior hunt it compulsively, sensing the existential clues embedded in its outward mutilation.

What is it about this other's face that impels the story of oneself? How is the I dependent on the other in order to elicit a narration of itself? What kind of story is possible when the I is unwelcomed by another? Is hospitality an ethical precondition to this telling?

The U.S. Latino I constructs its story from a series of social injuries. In U.S. Latino street literature, the first-person narrator blurs the narrative distinction between an external realism that describes a story as it "happened," and a spectral interiority that attempts to make sense, however awkwardly, of the injurious conditions of those exterior experiences. The result is a tension, damaging and dynamic, as the I finds itself unable to translate a logic of identity imposed from the external world. The reaction to injury, in Thomas and Díaz, is to move inward. Interiority allows the I to hide from an aggressively rejecting reality; this painful withdrawal into the safety of its alienated body creates a distance from which the I is able to contemplate the implications of these violent encounters. Consequently, the first-person narrator shuttles in and out, from a hostile exterior to a safe and analytical inside, attempting to make sense of its apparent shortcomings.

It is in this violent process that the I reworks a story of itself emerging, ultimately, as a subject in the process. What is important here is how the I comes to know itself, develop, and, finally, respond as a result of these unsettling confrontations with another. As stated by Judith Butler:

> If I give an account of myself in response to such a query, I am implicated in a relation to the other before whom and to whom I speak.

> Thus, I come into being as a reflexive subject in the context of establishing a narrative account of myself when I am spoken to by someone and prompted to address myself to the one who addresses me.[4]

Integral to Butler's understanding of the beginning of self-narration is a catalytic relationship to another. U.S. Latino narrative then, following Butler's logic, can be characterized as the story of these estranging and familiarizing face to faces that elicit an imaginative rejoinder—a full-blown exteriorization in the form of fiction—to a disturbing set of social rejections.

Piri Thomas's *Down These Mean Streets* and Junot Díaz's *Drown* are the imaginative rejoinders that this essay centers on. Both authors narrate the difficult emergence of a U.S. Latino I. Imperative to their work is a fictional sensitivity to the face, from which this I symbolically materializes, that allows Thomas and Díaz to access an alternative or triple consciousness,[5] to use Juan Flores's provocative phrase, a language of identity that pierces through arbitrary social norms.

The intensely marginalized presence of the characters in this fiction calls attention to an ethical and ontological crisis that becomes an enabling dimension, opening up creative options for the exterior/interior growth of the U.S. Latino I. As Levinas puts it: "The face resists possession, resists my powers. In its epiphany, in expression, the sensible, still graspable, turns into total resistance to the grasp. This mutation can occur only by the opening of a new dimension."[6] U.S. Latino literature is epiphanic to the extent that it adumbrates a mutating face that resists the other's possession. Starting with a reading of Piri Thomas, this essay examines the fictional use of the face—its recompostion—as a site of ontological negotiation wherein an I willfully presents itself. This willful act of exteriorization, as these texts show, is a process fraught with social and psychic conflict. *Down These Mean Streets* maps, through the face, the assorted conflicts Piri must confront in order to be born as a social subject. The novel, in its most powerful sense, stands in narrative testimony to the struggle of Afro-Latino self-creation.

EXTERIORIZING BLACKNESS

Down these Mean Streets begins with what seems an innocuous scene: a "tired and sleepy"[7] father, who works nights and sleeps during the day, beats his restless son for knocking over a jar of coffee and a toaster in the kitchen, waking him up. Yet the quotidian nature of this opening scene inaugurates a deeper problem regarding race and its externalization. I want, before moving forward, to make a theoretical distinction between appearance, which Fanon maintains, over-determines blackness from without, rendering it a fixed surface, a monstrous object; and *exteriorization*, as fictionally portrayed in Thomas, an active, combative, and expressive manifestation of a racial self. My reading of Thomas will focus on the latter process. Piri makes clear in the prologue of the novel that his explict intention is to announce his presence—"I wanna tell ya I'm here"—and to assert his place as a subject—"I want recognition."[8] The opening scene between father and son is the first, and most primal, of a series of symbolic roadblocks Piri comes across.

It is interesting to think of Slajov Žižek's suggestion in *The Plague of Fantasies*: "The Unconscious is outside, not hidden in any unfathomable depths or, to quote the X files motto: 'The truth is out there.'"[9] For Žižek a hermeneutic emphasis on "material externality" reveals "the inherent antagonisms of an ideological edifice."[10] How does this familial scene between father and son instigate such a reading? Are the objects in Piri's kitchen charged with unconscious and ideological meanings? Thomas describes the emotional episode:

> I could feel my mouth making the motions of wanting to say something in my defense. Of how it wasn't my fault that José had almost knocked the toaster off the table, and how I had tried to save it from falling, and in trying had finished knocking it to the floor along with a large jar of black coffee. But I just couldn't get the words out. Poppa just stood there, eyes swollen and hurting from too much work, looking at a river of black coffee. He didn't give me a chance. Even before the first burning slap of his belt awakened tears of pain, I was still trying to get words out that would make everything all right again. The second whap of the belt brought words of pain to my lips, and my blind running retreat was a mixture of tears and "I hate you."[11]

The accident described is sparked by José, Piri's white brother, who in knocking over a toaster, precipitates Piri's futile attempt to "save it from falling," and instead knocks over a "large jar of black coffee" that spreads over the kitchen floor like a "river." While Piri's father's immediate response is due to his fatigue and the "racket"[12] that interrupts his sleep, the more complex antagonisms involve an unconscious reaction to the noise or co-motion[13] of blackness.

The "material externality," a toaster that darkens bread and a jar that contains black coffee, symbolically reinforce the omnipresent character of blackness, as well as its controlled placement on the kitchen "table," in the family, and in the culture at large. Significantly, the crisis is caused by the literal spilling out of a concealed blackness (coffee) that covers the kitchen floor expressing an undeniable racial presence struggling to display itself. The excess of blackness disturbs the father, himself an Afro-Latino, out of his own racialized sleep. He beats Piri, therefore, in order to reestablish a racial edict: blackness is to stay politely jarred. It is important that the darker skinned Piri, not his white brother who is neither beaten nor reprimanded, absorb the unspoken lesson.

The absence of his white mother from the scene further highlights the authority of whiteness. The power of her whiteness is evident by the feminine location of the dispute, making her absence all the more pronounced. Blackness, emblematized by father and son, is brought face to face, marking a race in conflict with itself. According to the beating then, blackness is disciplined into social confinement, literally beat in. The result, as the title of the chapter suggests, is a blackness that is cut out, castrated, and, as insinuated by the motherless kitchen, feminized.

The repressive punishment pays instant dividends: Piri is unable to compose an explanation, to "get the words out that would make everything all right" or white "again." Piri is left with a "hate" "awakened" by the "burning slap" eliciting a different liquid response, "tears of pain." As Aristotle argues in *Ethics* (1980), this rage can be thought of as a response aroused by "apparent injustice,"[14] while keeping in mind the "ideological edifice" that Piri will spend the rest of the novel trying to translate and creatively move against. How is this rage in search of justice, an anger that must be, at least to begin with, directed against the father?

Freud's 1909 case study on a patient he referred to as the "Rat Man" serves as a provocative analogy to Thomas's father-and-son conflict. The case describes a father who beats his son for an indiscretion. The angry son, unable to curse because "he had no bad language" responds nonetheless by calling his father "all the names of common objects he could think of," such as: "You lamp! You towel! You plate!"[15] Among other long-term effects, Freud notes that the Rat Man subsequently became fearful of any expression of rage; in Aristotle's notion, of justice; or in Žižek's, blind to an exposed "ideological edifice." Patricia Gherovici suggests that such a naming of his father transmogrifies him into "inanimate objects."[16]

The parallels to Piri's scene (the Black Man) are striking. The inanimate objects in Piri's kitchen are the toaster, coffee jar, and table that contain the restricted blackness. For Fanon the fact or face of blackness is caught in this process of objectification: "I came into the world imbued with the will to find a meaning in things, my spirit filled with the desire to attain to the source of the world, and then I found that I was an object in the midst of other objects."[17] Racial translation, Fanon observes, is from human to object. Piri's father has internalized this practice, standing guard against the tipping over of a racial identity that has been, if you will, neatly objectified and organized in his wife's kitchen. Piri, who like the Rat Man is outraged by his beating, has yet to learn how to curse and can only utter an inaudible "I hate you." The predicament Piri faces is to develop the ontological language that will allow him to recognize and combat the racially hidden transcripts lodged in these scenes of objectification.

Piri then attempts to punish and recover his father by leaving the apartment and roaming the streets, hoping his father will suffer because of his absence. It is interesting to remember that hysteria, the subject of Gherovici's analysis, has been called by psychoanalysts the wandering womb. Perhaps, in this vein, the hysteria and rage of blackness can be characterized as a wandering face in search of justice, in search of its own affirmation, and hungry, as the kitchen indicates, for social acceptance. Indeed, Michael Taussig, following Freud, speaks of the inextricable connection between the domestic, the genitalia, and the face, arguing that this strange interconnection is "an ineffable fusion of surges so conflicting and contradictory that they overburden language . . ."[18] Piri's muteness in this grounding scene is, in part, attributable to his youthful inability to understand the symbolic relation of the three, the rules of racial recognition. This is why Piri poignantly asks himself: "Pops, how come me and you is always on the outs? Is it something we don't know nothing about?"[19] Clearly, Piri's question suggests an ontological overburdening and confusion, a disjunction between a surface reasoning, a father who beats his son for waking him, and a deeper, unspoken knowledge hidden in the symbolic objects cited for the conflict. Is this question of concealed knowledge precisely why Piri's mother is absent from this opening scene? Does she represent the figure whose whiteness adds to the face value of her husband, a black skin jarred in white masks? The political submerged under a sign of cultural coupling?

In Antonio Gramsci's *Prison Notebooks* (1971), he warns against "political questions which are disguised as cultural ones."[20] Similarly, in Thomas, the domestic, which is metonymic of the cultural, veils the political dimensions of race. Is there an outside market force or political unconscious that drives this scene? This disciplinary episode between father and son is clearly a repetition of what the father faces at work everyday. For Thomas, class and race are tightly intertwined.

Notably, the father in this scene, and throughout the text, is overworked to the point of exhaustion: "I work my ass off and can't even sleep when I get home."[21] This beating then is metonymic of the daily abuse Piri's Afro-Latino father suffers in his jobs, in U.S. society, and throughout the Americas. To use Juan Flores' powerful phrase, he is socially diminished into a lowercase person. Piri's father marries a white Latina not just because of their cultural affinities but because of their racial difference. The ideological sway of difference is crucial for the father, since it is in difference that one becomes painfully aware of the distance between the social ideal and our own real and abject positions. Her whiteness draws him symbolically closer to this racial/class ideal. As Žižek argues: "The lesson is therefore clear: an ideological identification exerts a true hold on us precisely when we maintain an awareness that we are not fully identical to it . . ."[22] What is important here is to recognize how blackness in Thomas's text is ideologically enmeshed with psychic, social, and economic value.

Interestingly, Gherovici points out that the Rat Man's father married a woman who was considerably wealthier than he. She explains: "According to the family romance of the Rat Man's lineage, the father had married for money and not love; he had sold on his desire and was unworthy of her love. Because of the mother's deprecation of his father's desire . . ., the Rat Man found that this father had nothing worth appropriating."[23] The curses the Rat Man hurls at his father describe his commodification. The father's strength and "worth" are made proper by the social power of his mother. For the Rat Man then, his father is not a model "worth appropriating" since his value is strategically supplemented by his mother's wealth. Similarly, Piri's mother, who spends much of the novel trying to get Piri to "act like people," to be passive, polite, and nonthreatening; who loves her son despite the fact that he is "un negrito and ugly," "dirty and smelly"; and who orders him to "soak for a long time" in the bathtub to extract his ontological dirt: clearly is, in Piri's mind, the parent laden with value.[24]

Ultimately, the father's model of self-abnegation becomes an impossible position for the young Piri to occupy. If to appropriate whiteness means to make proper or clean, or to make one's own (property), then Piri refuses his father's racial adaptation. Unlike his father who works to keep his blackness contained, or his friend Dopey, a boy with a lopsided face who dies later in the novel from drinking dirty water (another iteration of coffee), Piri assertively develops and exteriorizes his Afro-Latino identity. He refuses to swallow or internalize his own blackness. *Down These Mean Streets* is an imaginative staging of these identificatory antagonisms through exteriorization.

This antagonistic black face that grounds and propels the narrative in *Down These Mean Streets* is forcefully dramatized in the chapter entitled "Brothers Under the Skin" in which Piri declares to his brother that he is black. It is the first time that Piri tries to speak openly to his family about race. The chapter begins with Piri "daydreaming" in the tub (masturbating), and his reverie is "splintered" into reality by José's banging on the door.[25] He spitefully keeps the door closed until José's "face has a pained look on it" and he urinates "all over"[26] his pants. Interestingly, Piri has transformed the bathtub from a place to wash off and symbolically manage his blackness, what Fanon describes as the condition of a "dirty nigger,"[27] to a closeted space where he secretly dreams, desires, and reflects. José's attempted entrance reminds Piri of the whiteness that stands outside, already ontologically cleaned, the splitting image of each other. Piri is pulled out of his desirous dream and back into the fact of his racial circumscription. Even though Piri tries to hurt and humiliate his brother here, to show him, if only for a moment, how it feels to hold something in, he can't reproduce for José the woundedness that pervades his racial being.

José's exclusion from the bathroom is an obstruction that causes, at best, a provisional discomfort. Is there, however, a way in which Piri is not only to trying to aggravate José, to transfer his pain, but in a more profound gesture, force insides out? Get something, once again, to spill? Extract an internal knowledge or truth? From José's face Piri's glance moves onto his penis noticing its phallic whiteness and sensing the uncanny relationship between face and penis, sacred and perverse. This sets off in Piri a need to discuss race: a yearning for release in conversation. Fanon describes this need for another's attention: "Sealed into that crushing objecthood, I turned beseechingly to others. Their attention was a liberation, running over my body suddenly abraded into nonbeing, endowing me once more with an agility that I had thought lost, and by taking me out of the world, restoring me to it."[28] However, the discussion Piri yearns for is short-lived, as José finds the suggestion he is black intolerable. Their discussion turns from talk into an impassioned argument; and from argument into a physical and figurative confrontation.

For José, like their mother, the family identity is fixed firmly in relation to a denial of blackness. When Piri tells his brother that he plans to go down South to "see what a moyeto's worth and the paddy's weight on him" because he is a "Negro," José, becomes outraged, understanding that, as Piri says, this means he too, at least in part, is black.[29] As Piri presents incontrovertible evidence of their blackness using himself and their father as powerful exhibits, José becomes filled with anxiety and then a patronizing anger. The evidence mounts and their argument progresses to a violent pitch: "I ain't black, damn you! . . . My motherfuckin lips are not like a baboon's ass. My skin is white. White Godddamit!"[30] José's exclamatory anger becomes a futile, if volatile, attempt to push away the Afro-Latino reflection that stands indisputably before him. Piri's fragmenting presence functions as a racial defacement, in Michael Taussigs sense, a desecration of a sacred white mask that feverishly conceals its own diversity. The uncooperative ambiguity or splitting of Piri's Afro-Latino image demands an acknowledgment of the racial complexity represented within their family. For as Taussig explains: "It is the cut of de/facement that releases this surplus, the cut into wholeness as holiness that, in surrendering, reveals as with a film montage, not only another view via another frame, but released flows of energy."[31]

The transgressive energy unfastened by Piri's assertive blackness forces his brother's whiteness outside of its idealized existence, confronted by "another frame" or face. Blackness represents the figurative difference or cut breaking the solidified form of the white face and externalizing insides that bring José in close proximity to his humanity. It is no accident that this scene and discussion take place in the bathroom, where internal excesses are released into view. However, José rigidly holds, despite the truth that stands before him, onto his sacred identification. His language reduces blackness to a state of irretrievable abjection. The irony being that as he fervently defends his whiteness, its beauty, its social rank, and value, he does so having urinated all over himself. "You can bow and kiss ass and clean shit bowls. But-I-am-white!"[32]

Interestingly, José's exclamatory refusals are reminiscent of the child who is startled by the fact/face of Fanon's blackness. "Look, a Negro! . . . Mama, see the Negro! I'm frightened."[33] For Fanon the child's response is a psychic and social "thematization" that obliterates his corporeal integrity: "What else could it be for me but an amputation, an excision, a hemorrhage that splattered my whole body with black blood?"[34] The generality of his blood, its humanity, is transmogrified into a confining "black blood," an unalterable "fact" that allows the child to make a purely reductive—"Negro!"—identification of him. The profoundly violent imagery— "amputation," "excision," and "hemorrhage"—recalling the brutal ghosts of slavery, describes the symbolic damage done by a racially infused assignation. The socially constructed gaze of the child performs an ontological tearing of identities into impossibly unpolluted beings. This exchange establishes a pure and negatively charged blackness, and, by extension, a pure positively charged whiteness. The child's comprehensive recognition of, not Fanon the (hu)man, but of the "Negro!" renders him a bloody abstraction, "dark and unarguable,"[35] diminishing him to an arbitrary physical characteristic, a "whole body" whose blackness becomes his only, over-determined, mode of classification. However, Fanon goes on to conclude that while the "Negro" is a societal demand, a need of whiteness to define itself absolutely against, the Negro must, as Piri does, "make myself known."[36] An active and imaginary rejoinder, for Fanon and Thomas, changes the ontological terms of engagement. Piri's dispute with José directly addresses the "dark and unarguable" themes that survive precisely because they go uncontested. A fight ensues: the "blurred confusion"[37] of violence is the only endpoint.

José finally admits the shame his brother's blackness has produced in him and, after the figurative blow, decides to walk away from the discussion with his whiteness intact. By contrast, Piri suffers a kind of short-circuit unable to absorb his brother's contempt: "Lights began to jump into my head and tears blurred out that this was my brother before me."[38] Piri beats his brother until his sacred white mask becomes a "blood-smeared face."[39] The violence here, the cut on José's de/faced face, his smashed skin, "beat beat beat"[40] like an African drum, draws out the blood that obfuscates the "wholeness as holiness" as whiteness. José's whiteness is displaced by a humanity that lies "under the skin."

If Fanon's symbolic blood hemorrhages to color him, irreversibly—a blackness that envelops his body, his psyche, his history—here José's despoiled blood collapses into a universal sign of humanity, a fluid face where black and white identities move in and out of each other, creating something new of something old each time they touch. Similar to the coffee that spills all over the kitchen at the start of the novel, Piri and José, also crash through the "bathroom door" overflowing into the living room. The private has become public; a living blackness, unabashed and unapologetic, exteriorizes itself. The coffee symbolism gives way to real bodies, injured and externalized, in a struggle for recognition. Piri emerges naked, from the dirty water of his bathtub, and is reborn into the *living* room for all to see. He has, as Fanon advised, made himself known.

For Piri, conflict would continue to follow him until, finally, he finds himself in a shootout with a cop after an attempted robbery—the act of shooting itself a form of rage-full exteriorization. He is subsequently shipped to prison, now openly and legally objectified. Feeling threatened and resentful Piri decides to try to play it cool. For Piri playing it cool or smooth is linked to an illegible outward appearance wherein his face becomes a "*cara palo,* " part poker face, part death mask. On the one hand, *Cara palo* aims to project strength and *corazón*, communicating to his street rivals a masculinity poised to defend its reputation at the slightest provocation, and on the other hand, a repressive mask that Piri hides behind covering his vulnerabilities beneath an unresponsive and unfeeling face. As Lyn Di Iorio Sandín argues: "*Cara palo* helps Piri mask both his anguish at having his humanity (his memory) taken from him, as well as take pleasure in the power (the hurt) he inflicts on others."[41] What *cara palo* does then is mark a mode of relation invested in dominance and violence: at once fearing its consequences and seeking its validation. It is, moreover, a logic with which Piri has learned how to mis/read his environment.

Soon after his arrival in prison, Piri sits "on top of a food locker in the recreation hall" when he is approached by three Afro-American inmates. Tense, analytical, and expressionless, he begins to interpret the intentions of the three strangers, assuming that they are going to test him. What ensues is an unusual request from the inmates followed by an uncanny response. "Hey mac can you draw?"[42] Piri nonchalantly volunteers to draw the face of one the inmates. After looking "at the cat, from side to side,"[43] Piri, inexplicably, hands Rocky, the inmate, a drawing of a "black cannibal, complete with a big bone through his nose."[44] The racial violation of the scene is exacerbated when Piri responds to Rocky's protest: "You're right *moreno . . .* you'll get a stiff dick up your ass."[45] Paradoxically, the drawing captures Rocky in the same racial language Piri has struggled against throughout the novel. Here, the racial roles are reversed. Is Piri distancing himself from his own blackness? Has he internalized the racial language and logic that have continually punished him? Piri later imagines how he is going to mutilate Rocky's face. "I'm gonna mess his shitty face up nice and easy, cut it *asi y asi.*"[46]

Piri, like his father, strikes out against an image of himself. He repeats the process of racial objectification he has experienced: fixing Rocky in a drawing; threatening him with rape/castration; and fantasizing his facial disfigurement. If exteriorizing blackness is the central struggle of this novel, then in prison Piri finds his blackness brutally turned back on itself. The prison is the logic of racism brought to its externalized end point. The self-internment Piri would not teach himself in order to exist as an Afro-Latino in society, symbolized in the novel by the objects, the coffee jar, the enclosed bathroom and bathtub, and the dirty water, is writ large in a prison, the monstrous "ideological edifice" of social death. Here he is an inmate trapped in rage and self-hatred. His drawing of Rocky is a mirror image of himself conveying a desire to destroy and exorcize the blackness that lies arbitrarily on his skin. A need for violent release speaks of the toxic pressure of internalization that ineluctably leads, to use a futile contemporary pharse, to Piri's "Black-on-Black" crime. Ultimately, the food locker Piri sits on to begin this scene represents a spiritual hunger that turns blackness into a social cannibal, eating away at itself in order to survive.

In the end, Piri, released from prison, reconfigures his face. "I grabbed my face with both hands and squeezed hard . . ."[47] Lisa Sanchez Gonzalez concludes that Piri's religious conversion is to a white father figure that "forecloses the quest to constitute an omniscient, self-authorizing narrative voice" taking "symbolic revenge on his father by rejecting him for an archetypal father figure who is as unquestionably white as his actual father wanted to be but never really could be."[48] On the other hand, Lyn Di Iorio Sandín concedes that while "he has acquired . . . a new mask of obedience," he also cannot simply let go of those "aspects" of the street that have constituted his life.[49] Perhaps his exit from prison, symbolic of his most extreme introjection, goes beyond the narcissistic need to self-authorize, and the suspended state that Di Iorio presents. Instead, the end of *Down These Mean Streets* forces Thomas to come to terms with an opacity of being that "cannot be reduced, which is the most perennial guarantee of participation and confluence."[50] Thomas becomes aware of a relational poetics and complexity of being that ruptures a racial form of existence that oscillated between subdued conformity, violent outbreaks, and other self-destructive patterns. His novel testifies to a nonviolent insertion of a face, of an Afro-Latino being, dynamically opening out onto a future. He describes a transfigurative moment: the most dramatic example of spilling I have so far described:

> I pulled away from the mirror and sat on the edge of my bed. My head was still full of pot, and I felt scared. I couldn't stop trembling inside. I felt as though I had found a hole in my face and out were pouring all the different masks that my *cara-palo* face had fought so hard to keep hidden. I thought, *I ain't going back to what I was.*[51]

Here Piri's face opens up "pouring" out the strategic and violent identities he had accumulated. He does not renounce his past, but "*what I was,*" a reductive ontology of race that made him choose between a passive self-abnegation and a self-destructive street life. When confronted with himself Piri finds a "hole in my face" that counters the *cara-palo* that had served as a hardened defense, keeping "hidden" and repressed a more expansive sense of his humanity. As Levinas reminds us, "the epiphany of the face is ethical."[52] For Thomas justice is located in an unabashed widening of experience; an exteriorization that makes us tremble inside. In another sense, it is an ethics of hospitality wherein one opens to the stranger in oneself and thus to the world before us. What we are moved by in *Down These Mean Streets* is this struggle with dislocation, with a yearning for hospitality that finds its most vulnerable and resilient expression of humanity in the other's face. As stated by Derrida: "Perhaps only the one who endures the experience of being deprived of a home can offer hospitality."[53]

THE DISFIGURED STRANGER

This notion of hospitality and the other's face as the staging of the ethical is an overriding concern in Junot Díaz's book of short stories *Drown*. Similar to *Down These Mean Streets, Drown* is driven by poverty and a fraught relationship to a father. While Piri's father is emotionally detached, presenting an unviable example of blackness for his son, Yunior's father exists in painful absentia. Rafa and Yunior, throughout the stories, finds themselves dealing with the material and psychic effects of his father's abandonment.

My reading of *Drown* focuses on the first story "Ysrael," in which two brothers become obsessed with seeing a boy's face that was eaten by a pig when he was an infant. Their fascination with Ysrael's face becomes a curious and passionate quest. Several questions shape my reading of the story. What is it in Ysrael's mutilated face they need to see? What are the possibilities and conditions of hospitality in such a forced encounter? And how does the father's absent presence figure in the children's restless need to see Ysrael?

"Ysrael" begins with an innocent "errand" to the "colmado" to buy a "beer" for their uncle.[54] The beer, loud music, and "drunken voices" exhibit a community engaged in the festive interaction elicited by the summer.[55] Established, both as part of the community and in isolated contradistinction, are the young narrator Yunior, nine, and his twelve-year-old brother Rafa. Yunior serves as the ambivalent participant and witness to his brother's rageful musings. This communal sense of the *colmado* stands in the background to Rafa's solemn withdrawal, "as if listening to a message I couldn't hear,"[56] distracted by an internal pre-occupation that is yet unclear but has, from the very beginning, an ominous feel. What is this inaudible message, seemingly "beamed in from afar"[57] that Yunior intuits, but can't translate? The errand to the *colmado*, filled with Latino men reminders of Rafa's absent father, ignites a desire in Rafa to make a symbolic trip to "pay that kid a visit."[58] As Yunior tells us, it was Rafa who "wanted to see Ysrael."[59] Interestingly, to see, hear, and touch are important conduits of knowledge that the story becomes increasingly aware of.

In many ways, Yunior and Rafa are orphaned in the story. Not only has their father been in the United States for most of their lives, but their mother works inordinate hours at a "chocolate factory"[60] making it impossible for her to take care of them during the summer. They are sent to the campo every summer, bereft of parental affection, as their mother makes sweets for other children. Rafa's angry behavior is symptomatic of this parental distance: precipitated by the aftereffects of a Caribbean economy brutalized by postcolonial relations wherein life's sweets are unevenly distributed to others. When he looks out at the beautiful country landscape, "the mountains, at the mists that gathered like water, at the brucal trees that blazed like fires on the mountain,"[61] his response, as if resisting the seduction and harmony of its beauty, is to coldly say this is all shit. He goes on to exchange the image of a peaceful landscape for an aggressive yearning to "go crazy" and "chinga all my girls" and "everyone else's" and to "dance four or five days straight."[62] It is easy to attribute his response to the boredom of a young boy who needs more activity and stimulation. However, the manic quality of his response suggests a hostile energy, an unspoken and unspeakable aggression masked as masculinity that crosses over the border of mere fun for a twelve-year-old boy. Moreover, the manic feel to his desire exposes a disturbingly disconnected affect. His energy is not an attempt to make human contact, but has a deeper symbolic purpose.

In Robert Karen's gripping analysis in *Becoming Attached: First Relationships and How They Shape Our Capacity to Love*, Karen explains that a boy often separated from his parents "act[s] out his aggression in symbolic ways, like theft, which may simultaneously enact his wish for love."[63] Rafa's rejection of the *campo* landscape, unable to conjure the feelings of pleasure or respect that such a sight normally elicits, bespeaks the discomforts he feels with positive sensations. His subsequent desire to *chinga* any anonymous girl is an attempt to actively dissociate from an idealized landscape that instead of making him feel connected to his surroundings, reminds him of the parental neglect that pervades his life. To *chinga* here, or to write *chocha* and *toto* on the wall is to make sure that his activity secures a safe and antagonistic distance, while also enacting "his wish for love." It is, moreover, the expression of a sadistic impulse that repeats his father's violence of abandonment. As Deleuze points out not only does the "sadistic fantasy ultimately rests on the theme of the father destroying his own family" but more specifically, "sadism is in every sense an act of negation of the mother and an exaltation of the father who is beyond all laws."[64] The words *choca* and *toto* publically inscribe this erotic negation of the maternal.

This sense of antagonistic distance and wishful connection is clearer in his perverse longing to see Ysrael's face. Again, his longing is not to make a friend, but to see, first hand, Ysrael's gory disfigurement. Rafa's most in-depth conversation with Yunior, part speculation, part fantasy, is concerned with the condition Ysrael's face might be in. "I wonder how much of Ysrael's face is gone,"[65] Rafa asks, not really looking for an answer, but the chance to detail the damage. The fact that Ysrael has his eyes is surprising, Rafa explains, because eyes "are soft" and "salty," a good target for a hungry pig.[66] He continues, almost like a serial killer planning a murder, "maybe his ears" or "his nose" since it "sticks out."[67] His obsession with Ysrael's facial dismemberment is further emphasized by his uncle's concomitant discussion taking place right outside their bedroom window. Their uncle had just won "big" in a cock fight and was reporting the day's events. Interestingly, the cock fight prefigures the confrontation Rafa will have with Ysrael at the climax of the story.

While Yunior is clearly drawn to their uncle's voice outside, splitting his attention between Tio and Rafa, Rafa makes no gesture toward the celebratory noise, immersed completely on the negative potential of Ysrael's face. To cite Karen again, "Unable to tolerate his hateful wishes toward his parent, he may displace these feelings unto a sibling or a pet and torment them with sadistic behavior."[68] Rafa, following this logic, displaces his rage for his parents, especially his father, onto Ysrael's brutal scars. His scars function as a release of Rafa's angry tension. Unlike Piri, who spends much of the novel trying to find a way out, trying to carve a space for communication and contact, Rafa's "sadistic behavior" is a result of his staying lodged inside, while projecting his pain onto an apparent unrelated party. Even the cock fight could not symbolically compete with Ysrael's gruesome wounds. The face in Díaz is not linked to the genitals the way it is in Thomas, but to a psychic state hiding or reflecting a deeper internal damage. It is not about power, as his machismo suggests, but failed attachment. "My brother kept pinching my face during the night, like I was a mango. The cheeks, he said. And the Chin. But the forehead would be a lot harder."[69] The textures of the face signify for Rafa the corporeal site of identfication where hidden pockets hold traumatic secrets.

His urge is not merely to witness the scars but participate in their creation. It is at night that demonic obsessions are lived and spoken.[70]

The next day Rafa and Yunior go off to find the elusive Ysrael. In order to get on the bus that will take them to Barbacoa, Rafa helps people board in an attempt to distract the driver and get a free ride. Yunior furtively moves to the back and sits near an older man. A *pastelito* that Yunior had put in his pocket starts to "stain" his pocket and the strange man next to him offers to "help." "He spit in his fingers and started to rub at the stain but then he was pinching at the tip of my *pinga* through the fabric of my shorts. He was smiling."[71] What for Thomas are excessive spills, in Díaz are calculated spits. Spitting comes at the moment when speech or desire can no longer be withheld.

The man takes advantage of the fatherless boy, his stain a sign of vulnerability. What is interesting here is Rafa's response, which addresses his own feelings and not Yuniors. Should not Rafa have acted as his brother's keeper? After they get off the bus and Rafa notices that Yunior is crying, he "spits" and inexplicably yells at him: "You have to get tougher. Crying all the time. Do you think our papi is crying?"[72] Out of nowhere, the father, the spectral presence of the narrative who has not been mentioned once, emerges in this moment of crisis. If the man spits on his finger as a precursor and suggestion of his strange desire, Rafa spits as if to let something out, a congested unconscious of repressed feelings, that have been building beyond his power to hold them in. Without even asking Yunior what happened, he assumes that his little brother's pain is the same as his. Clearly, then, Rafa's quest for Ysrael is tied, as his abrupt reaction to Yunior shows, to his father's abandonment and the mirroring Ysrael's disfigured face promises.

When they finally reach Ysrael, what stands out are his optimism symbolized by his love for kites and wrestling; his new clothes that come from the United States; and his voice "full of spit" and an excess of "saliva that trickled down his neck."[73] While Rafa measures every word, rigidly closed and ungenerous, Ysrael, on the other hand, talks and relates freely with the confidence of a child secure in his expression. Ironically, the spit that spills from his cheek is a sign, as it is in Thomas, of extroversion. It stands in opposition to the stain that marks Yunior's shorts and Rafa's personality, precisely because a stain is a dried residue that soils and discolors. Is not spit here symbolic of a spiritual generosity, an emblem of hospitality itself? Is Rafa's failure to be hospitable to the landscape, his brother, and Ysrael, symptomatic of his being a foreigner to himself, to his father? Is the stain a sign of his inability or unwillingness to share himself and be vulnerable once again? If the Other or foreigner puts the I into question,[74] as Levinas tells us, then what is Rafa looking for in Ysrael?

After an extended discussion in which Ysrael confesses to his belief that American doctors will reconfigure his face, Rafa, smashes a bottle over his head. The blow comes unexpected to the reader, to Yunior, and to Ysrael. His violent anger has materialized, the blow reverberating with the stains and scars of his own life. We are struck by his rage that has deadened all sense of consequence or responsibility to the other. Yet his rage is impelled and directed at his absent father, whose shadowy presence leaves Rafa psychically mutilated. What is shocking about this scene is that Rafa's violence, which has lain dormant throughout the story, reveals itself without forewaring or provocation. We are shocked precisely because Rafa now exposes the impulsive violence that lies within. Interestingly, his sadistic pleasure is expressed in this volatile unpredictability. Ysrael unconscious on the ground allows Rafa to take off his mask. The result is horrific:

> "His left ear was a nub and you could see the thick veined slab of his tongue through a hole in his cheek. He had no lips. His head was tipped back and his eyes had gone white and the cords were out on his neck. He'd been an infant when the pig had come into the house. The damage looked old but I still jumped back and said, Please Rafa, let's go! Rafa crouched and using only two of his fingers, turned Ysrael's head from side to side."[75]

The elaborate scars of Ysrael's face represent the internal damage that Rafa carries from his father's abandonment. His father is the ruthless pig, a cannibal, leaving his devoured children to meet the world alone. Like Ysrael, Rafa's senses—ears, nose, lips, cheeks—have been dulled. What is extraordinary here is the patience and peace with which Rafa moves Ysrael's head "from side to side" to examine and absorb the wounds as if finally seeing himself for the first time. Rafa is confronted with a vision of his interiority and monstrousness. Ysrael's disfigured face gives him a second sight, the ability to see beyond the visible, to look at the foreigner within. As Žižek puts it: "The subject is the nonsubstance; he exists only as a nonsubstantial self-relating subject that maintains its distance toward inner-worldly objects. Only in monsters does this subject encounter the Thing that is his impossible equivalent—*the monster is the subject himself, conceived as Thing*."[76]

Hospitality, then, begins, as we saw with Thomas, with the other of the home, namely a Father's child, and with an internalized relationship to one's own strangeness. Hospitality, the foundation of the ethical, transmogrifies into hostility for Rafa because attachment turned into abandonment. Abandoned, Rafa looks for himself in the scars of a face, understanding that the mask he wears can only be removed in relation to the face of another. The epiphany of the face reveals that beneath the mask lies—individual, familial, and colonial— mutilatons, forcing one into new dimensions with oneself and with the world.

NOTES

1. Gloria Anzaldúa, ed., *Making Face, Making Soul, Haciendo Caras: Creative and Critical Perspectives by Feminists of Color* (San Francisco: Aunt Lute Books, 1990), xv–xxviii.
2. Piri Thomas, *Down These Mean Streets* (New York: Vintage Books [Random House], 1997, 1967); Junot Díaz, *Drown* (New York: Riverhead Books, 1996); hereafter cited as "DTMS" and "D," respectively.
3. Lisa Sánchez González, *Boricua Literature: A Literary History of the Puerto Rican Diaspora* (New York: New York University Press, 2001), 107–119; hereafter cited "BL." Articulation is one component in Thomas's fictional project that is preoccupied, in a larger sense, with Afro-Latino being. While the face is concerned with speech it also takes into account a series of differing internal/external aspects of identity.
4. Judith Butler, *Giving an Account of Oneself* (New York: Fordham University Press, 2005), 15.
5. Juan Flores's "Triple-Consciousness? Afro-Latinos on the Color Line" was a talk given at the Opening Roundtable of "100 Years of W.E.B. Dubois' The Souls of Black Folk," held at Michigan State University, April 2, 2003.
6. Emmanuel Levinas, trans. Alphonso Lingis. *Totality and Infinity: An Essay on Exteriority* (Pittsburgh: Duquesne University Press, 1969), 197.
7. *DTMS*, 3.
8. Ibid., xi.
9. Slavoj Žižek, *Plague of Fantasies* (New York: Verso, 1997), 3; hereafter cited as "PF."
10. Ibid., 3.
11. *DTMS*, 3–4.
12. Ibid., 3.
13. *BL*, 13.
14. Aristotle, trans. David Ross, *The Nichomachean Ethics* (Oxford and New York: Oxford University Press, 1980), 127.
15. Sigmund Freud, "Notes Upon a Case of Obsessional Neurosis," Standard Edition, 1909, 10: 205–206.

16. Patricia Gherovici, *The Puerto Rican Syndrome* (New York: Other Press, 2003), 97; hereafter cited as "PS." This essay owes much to Gherovici's brilliantly detailed analysis of the Puerto Rican Syndrome and hysteria.
17. Frantz Fanon, trans. Charles Lam Markmann, *Black Skin, White Masks* (New York: Grove Press, 1967, 1952), 109; hereafter cited as "BSWM."
18. Michael Taussig, *Defacement: Public Secrecy and the Labor of the Negative* (Stanford: Stanford University Press, 1999), 50; hereafter cited as "D."
19. *DTMS*, 1.
20. Antonio Gramsci, trans. Quintin Hoare and Geoffrey Nowell Smith, *Selections from the Prison Notebooks* (New York: International Publishers, 1971), 149.
21. *DTMS*, 3.
22. *PF*, 21.
23. *PS*, 100.
24. *DTMS*, 18–19.
25. Ibid., 142.
26. Ibid.
27. *BSWM*, 109.
28. Ibid.
29. *DTMS*, 143.
30. Ibid., 144.
31. *D*, 3.
32. *DTMS*, 145.
33. *BSWM*, 112.
34. Ibid.
35. Ibid., 117.
36. Ibid., 115.
37. *DTMS*, 146.
38. Ibid.
39. Ibid.
40. Ibid.
41. Lyn Di Iorio Sandín, *Killing Spanish: Literary Essays on Ambivalent U.S. Latino/a Identity* (New York: Palgrave Macmillan, 2004), 114.
42. *DTMS*, 251.
43. Ibid., 252.
44. Ibid.
45. Ibid.
46. Ibid., 253.
47. Ibid., 322.
48. *BL*, 118.
49. *KS*, 114–116.
50. Edouard Glissant, trans. Betsy Wing, *Poetics of Relation* (Ann Arbor: University of Michigan, 1997, 1990), 191.

51. *DTMS*, 321.
52. *TI*, 199.
53. Anne Dufourmantelle and Jacques Derrida, trans. Rachel Bowlby, *Of Hospitality* (Stanford: Stanford University Press, 2000), 56; hereafter cited as "OH."
54. *D*, 3.
55. Ibid.
56. Ibid.
57. Ibid.
58. Ibid.
59. Ibid.
60. Ibid.
61. Ibid., 4.
62. Ibid.
63. Robert Karen, *Becoming Attached: First Relationships and How They Shape Our Capacity to Love* (New York: Oxford University Press, 1998), 49; hereafter cited as "BA."
64. Gilles Deleuze, *Masochism* (New York: Zone Books, 1989), 59–60.
65. *D*, 8.
66. Ibid.
67. Ibid., 8–9.
68. *BA*, 49.
69. Ibid.
70. *OH*, 50.
71. *D*, 12.
72. Ibid., 14.
73. Ibid., 15.
74. *TI*, 195.
75. *D*, 18–19.
76. Slavoj Žižek, "Grimaces of the Real, or When the Phallus Appears," *October* vol. 58 (Autumn 1991), 66.

PART III

Archives, Histories, and Genealogies

CHAPTER 5

The Once and Future Latino: Notes
Toward a Literary History
todavía para llegar

Kirsten Silva Gruesz

Alfredo Véa's exhilaratingly strange novel *Gods Go Begging* (1999)[1] is structured around an extensive analogy between soldiers in battle and urban gang members. Both have effectively been left to perish, whether on a hill in Viet Nam or in the housing projects of San Francisco—the settings of its retrospective and forward action. One character muses, "these kids have no future and no cultural memory . . . they are forced to live in the eternal now": for urban youth as for soldiers under fire, "everything in their lives is physical and in the immediate present" (170). *Gods Go Begging* keeps returning to this notion of temporal trauma—the idea that losing access to the whole range of past and future brings about spiritual and social death. The path to healing, even to simple survival, requires that the main characters revisit and work through the past in a way that trauma theory has made familiar. Beyond that, however, recovery also requires a restoration of the lost horizon of *futurity* foreclosed by a power structure that (as Véa suggests) promotes both urban and foreign warfare as a way to maintain a perpetual underclass. The past and the future matter vitally in *Gods Go Begging*, but not in the way prescribed by most appeals to ethno-cultural preservation. While the worldview of its shell-shocked veteran, Jesse Pasadoble, is indisputably informed by the historical revisionism prompted by the Civil Rights movement (he offers a seriocomic lesson in U.S. Latino history to his platoon in Viet Nam), Jesse is too much of a cosmopolitan to embrace any particular version of "cultural memory" as an antidote for the disease of living in the "eternal now."

Gods Go Begging provocatively opens up a number of related questions about the place of history—and time in general—in Latino literature. In marked contrast to other Latino novels that narrate world-historical events as they touch on the lives of a particular family (bestsellers such as Victor Villaseñor's 1991 *Rain of Gold* or Julia Alvarez's 1994 *In the Time of the Butterflies,* for instance), Véa does not suggest parallels between a family's story and that of an ethnic community or nation across time.[2] The genealogical analogy is a standard historical-novel tactic to frame the impossible largeness of history with reference to individuals; it reinforces values such as legacy, tradition, and descent. But Jesse has no children, and we learn virtually nothing about his family of origin. Culture, not genealogy, is his way of situating himself in relation to a past and future: access to the full experience of human temporality comes through the mediation of certain powerful cultural texts, from Euripides to traditional Ladino prayers to Robert Frost's poetry and (especially) to jazz. These are Jesse's weapons against forgetting, against the "Tourette's gas" that has seeped into modern life. He is, in short, a literary and cultural historian: his assignment of African American literary classics to a young man charged with murder changes the boy's life. But his view does not square with the conservative, Arnoldian vision of western culture as a set of sacred artifacts from an ossified past; rather, his canon is made up of a set of living practices in flux, practices whose potential for constant reinvention over the course of time gives them their power to humanize and to heal.

But if Jesse can be seen as a cultural historian, what is particularly "Latino" about his practice?[3] To see his work as a character in this way, as an analogue to our own as literary critics, raises again that vexed question at the heart of the endeavor of Latino studies: what are the outer limits of Latino identity? That identitarian problem, as I want to suggest in this essay, needs to be addressed within a temporal framework that is generally either taken for granted or undertheorized. Jesse Pasadoble's idiosyncratic vision of tradition underscores the difficulty of composing a narrative of Latino literary history—though, as I will argue, it does not obviate the need for one. For to speak of Latino literary history is to describe an absence: despite a proliferation of scholarly reference works such as biographical dictionaries, chronologies, and encyclopedias, as well as annotated anthologies designed to be used both in and out of academic settings, no one has yet ventured to build a comprehensive narrative around the tens of thousands of texts produced over time by Latinos living in what is now the United States.

There are, indeed, literary histories of Latino subgroups—particularly in the Chicana/o and Puerto Rican traditions—but their specificity makes the lack of an interlinked history all the more palpable. Without challenging the indisputable value of such group-focused developmental narratives, it seems to me that if "Latino" is to have any long-term conceptual staying power, it must grapple with the construction of a usable past that would be, if not *common* to all Latinos (what historical stories are?), intelligible and meaningful to that constituency. This dilemma applies to Latino history in general as well as to literary history in particular, but it has a specific impact upon the practice of Latino literary criticism even when that practice seems directed at "contemporary" texts. For the genre of the literary history has traditionally served to cement the institutional presence of emergent fields of writing, although the present situation of Latino cultural studies as an institutional "free radical" that floats between various university departments complicates this pattern. If a Latino literary history existed, what might it look like, and what role might it play in the ongoing struggle to legitimate Latino studies? Given that present-day attention to Latino issues tends to be oriented toward the future—that is, to be hyper-conscious of demographic projections in which Latinos will become ever more dominant in the United States—we must consider more broadly not just the meaning of the past, but the overall conception of *temporality* that shapes our work.

Anticipating a Latino Future: The Politics of Temporality

If "Latino" is a fiction—a term of "government fiat," in Suzanne Oboler's influential phrasing—it is a fiction with an increasingly broad cultural momentum, not just a bureaucratic one. Most discussions of Latino identity draw on spatialized images of group boundaries: concentric circles, or umbrellas that shelter a multitude of constituent groups. Where does this leave time, as a self-locating term equally as important as space? Juan Flores distinguishes between "two 'levels' or kinds of ethnic affiliation" that can be expressed by the same term, Latino: "the single-group and the pan-ethnic."[4] When "Latino" serves as a pan-ethnic or "umbrella" term, one that has meaning only as the coalescence of its affiliated subgroups, the past is likewise divided by subgroup, according to the national framework of its place of origin. In this usage, the notion of the Latino past (whether narrativized by official history or communal memory) seems to register impassable difference. Indeed, it seems self-evident that the Chicano tendency to dwell on the wound of Mexico's mid-nineteenth-century loss of territory to the United States ("we didn't cross the border; the border crossed us") produces a different vision of the present's relation to the past than, say, the severing of Cuban American time around the milepost of 1959, or the paradoxical time-space experienced by a Maya-Kich'é speaker recently relocated from the Guatemalan highlands to the global city of Houston. These distinct identities may begin to converge when individuals begin to be constructed as Latino in the U.S. cultural and state apparatus, but their pasts remain separated and even severed from each other.

What would happen if we imagined the Latino past outside the pan-ethnic frame, as something other than the sum total of its composite ethno-national histories? Recent theorists of Latino identity have come to embrace the single-group usage of the term despite its suspect legacy as a term of governmental power.[5] History or past experience serves for many of them as an antidote to essentialist or bloodline-based concepts of Latino identity: Oboler, for instance, locates the common ground of *latinidad* in the manifold U.S. expansionisms of the nineteenth century, concluding that because of this hemispheric historical legacy, "Latinos have been racialized such that they experience the effects of invisibility in social and political institutions" in the United States.[6] In more elaborate fashion, Jorge Gracia argues that what joins Hispanics or Latinos together is "not a unity of commonality; it is *a historical unity founded on relations* . . . There is no need to find properties common to all Hispanics in order to classify them as Hispanics. What ties us is the same kind of thing that ties the members of a family."[7] As he resolutely rejects any genealogical or descent-based component to the family metaphor, Gracia concludes, "There is no essence here; there is only a complex historical reality."[8] Flores's even more developed discussion of the "imagined community" of *latinidad* also includes a significant temporal component: "From a Latino perspective . . . analysis is guided above all by lived experience and historical memory, factors that tend to be relegated by prevailing sociological approaches as either inaccessible or inconsequential."[9] Like Paula Moya's "post-realist" approach to identity, Flores's reclamation of the Latino identity question from the quantitative methodologies of social science involves *the experience of the past* in a crucial way.[10] Within the growing body of work on transnational frames for Latino studies, as well, a historical component to identity is presumed, if not fully described. Juan Poblete writes in the introduction to his influential *Critical Latin American and Latino Studies*, "In this new configuration [of globalization], while preserving the historical structural inequities that have character- ized most of its long history in the hemisphere, the U.S. and Latin America are intertwined in inextricable ways by the new flows of people, capital, goods, and communications."[11]

Despite this widespread acknowledgment that temporal experience is a crucial component of Latino identity in its single-group sense, narratives of the Latino past still tend to be framed on the pan-ethnic, umbrella level, with the experience of each subgroup recounted sepa- rately rather than intersectionally. The default structure for most works labeled "Latino history" thus remains nation-time, which str- uctures the text according to each component group's nation of provenance—even when (as in the case of longstanding *tejano* and *nuevomexicano* communities) the connection to that "national ori- gin" is distant or tenuous.[12] What, though, would comprise the field for a coherent single-group narrative of the Latino past? It might be located in the whole of *post-conquista* Spanish America (as Gracia argues), or in the history of Anglo-Spanish colonial and national ten- sions in the hemisphere (as Flores and others suggest)—but to some readers, those canvases are too broad to use as meaningful compo- nents of identity.[13] In keeping with recent trends in the historical dis- cipline itself—where the grand narratives of history have given way to communal memory, peripheral knowledge, and noncontinuous lived experience—literary critics keep gesturing away from the centers of power toward the particular, the communal, and the local. The very genre of a "history of the people," some would argue, seems staid and overly authoritative—a relic of a discarded, Romantic way of compre- hending the past.

But this postmodern hesitation to generalize is not the only position literary history, in the present moment, can take. Rather than seeing history (like the very term Latino) as an abstraction imposed from above upon unwilling subjects, we might consider what forms of *rela- tion* to the past are fostered by specific social, political, and economic structures: to think, in other words, about temporality as it is lived, performed, and textualized, as Véa's novel suggests. Any given "his- torical sense," any way of orienting oneself to specific origin-points one shares with others in a community, also contains within it an implied relation to the future, and assigns a shape to time itself. Certain visions of origins and ends, certain teleologies both religious and secular, get promoted by specific group experiences and reinforced by textual prac- tices. Flores gestures beautifully at this question in closing: "Memory fuels desire: the past as imagined from a Latino perspective awakens an anticipatory sense of what is, or might be, in store."[14] In exploring the underdeveloped *temporal* axis of what has been so far a primarily *spatial* approach to Latino identity, we must begin where his gesture leaves off. What exactly is the status of Flores's "desire"—a synonym, presumably, for both futurity and hope?

Another, more pointedly literary, example may help to situate the question of Latino temporality. John Christie and José González end the editorial comments in their recent anthology *Latino Boom* this way: "There is a sense that the Latino writer, perhaps more than most writers, now contemplates the past with an eye toward what is to come. In the end, what can be expected from Latino writers in the future is the unexpected itself."[15] Tautology aside, the comment hints at some *distinctively Latino* relation to temporality—again, understood as a whole range of relations between past, present, and future—without actually spelling it out. Christie and González's piece, like Flores's, implies that the truest forms of *latinidad* have yet to appear. The future will reveal new, utopian forms of the single-group meaning of the term, as Latinos reverse the initial intentions of the "government fiat" and expend it as political capital, as Oboler suggests hopefully; and as hybrid forms of Latino subjectivity, like Angie Chabrám-Dernersesian's much-cited *chicana-riqueña*, proliferate. But what are the consequences of imagining the temporal dimension of Latino identity with a particularly intense orientation toward the future?

Both state apparatuses such as the U.S. Census Bureau and the many unofficial think tanks that deal in demographic projection have associated Latinos very powerfully with *futurity*. An exceptional degree of prolepsis informs discussions of Latinos, both from without and from within: the magazine *Latino Future*, which boasts of being "Latino owned and operated," suggests in its very title an orientation toward a different moment than this one.[16] Such an acute stress on the projected "Latino future" in turn promotes different temporal relations: where the future looms large (and, by definition, unknown), there is a new pressure to scrutinize the arcane signs of the present moment in hopes they might reveal themselves as crucial turning points in some larger historical process. In the spirit of Johannes Fabian's classic *Time and the Other*, we need to interrogate the ideology of temporality at work here, for "*geopolitics* has its ideological foundations in *chronopolitics*."[17]

Fabian's work indicted the discipline of anthropology for its "persistent and systematic tendency to place the referent(s) of anthropology in a Time other than the present of the producer of anthropological discourse" (31). He called this temporal inequity a "denial of coevalness" (a phrase later adapted by Walter Mignolo, among others): just as visions of center and periphery use space to reinforce conditions of social inequality, dyads such as civilized/primitive and modern/premodern divide and police human time. While there are certainly tendencies in U.S. popular culture to portray Latinos as "backward," the denial of coevalness works in an even more complex way here: Latinos are so overpoweringly identified with the conditions of the present and the promise/threat of the future that we are denied a *past*. Or, more precisely, we are denied *the common occupation of past time* with other U.S. Americans. The assimilationist paradigm of the United States is a nationalist ideology with geopolitical ramifications, and it implicitly contains a temporal vision. The difficulty with assimilationism is not only that it forces the immigrant to discard his or her past at the border, to be hauled out for costumed parades of "ethnic pride" once a year, but that it imposes an adopted national past that does not *intersect* with the immigrant's own. Scholarly movements such as the Recovering the U.S. Hispanic Literary Heritage Project, which I will discuss later in this essay, work against this denial of coevalness, and indeed many of the critical works to emerge from that loosely constituted group have made powerful disavowals of the dominant idea that all Latinos are "recent arrivals" in the United States. But such projects, too, are products of their own historical moment and its particular "chronopolitics."

Political analyst Samuel P. Huntington's *Who Are We? The Challenges to America's National Identity* (2004), whose vital center is his polemic against "Hispanic" immigration, provides an illustrative example of those contemporary politics of time at work. Huntington begins by intoning the demographic projection that the United States will become a Latin-majority nation by 2050, extrapolating backward from it to form a corresponding vision of the crisis of the *present* in a way that exemplifies what Anne McClintock calls "imperial paranoia."[18] But Huntington presents this dark vision of the disunited nation of the future as the result of longer-term historical trends. He appears to have even read a bit in Chicano history, acknowledging that current Mexican immigration is different from prior immigrant waves in part because of the "historical presence" of Mexicans on this side of the border: "Mexico is the only country that the United States has invaded, occupied its capital—placing the Marines in the 'halls of Montezuma'—and then annexed half its territory. Mexicans do not forget these events. Quite understandably, they feel that they have special rights in these territories" (229–230). He goes on, paraphrasing Jorge Castañeda, to affirm that Latinos have distinct "concepts of time epitomized in the *mañana* syndrome" as well as different "attitudes toward history," meaning that Mexicans do not, in his view, share the American vision of a perfected future (254). Huntington's own obsession with the future is expressed within the rhetorical tradition of Puritan eschatology: a self-appointed prophet in the tradition of Sewall and Edwards, he wants to read and interpret the signs of the present crisis—a nation of two languages and two cultures—in order to spur salvational action A version of these chapters that appeared in *Foreign Policy* just before the book's publication includes two telling sentences not included in *Who Are We?:* "The transformation of the United States into a country like [bicultural Canada or Belgium] would not necessarily be the end of the world; it would, however, be *the end of the America we have known* for more than three centuries. Americans should not let that change happen unless they are convinced that this new nation would be a better one."[19] The message of the jeremiad is clear, at least to the implied "us": change your ways or be damned.

Huntington does not, like some less-informed conservative commentators, deny the historical presence of Spanish-speaking people in what is now the United States. Instead, since his mention of a three-century-old tradition presumes an unbroken continuity between Puritan New England and the present-day United States (itself a highly contestable claim), his denial of "past-ness" stems from an unwillingness to reconceive the *national* temporal frame as one in which Puritans and *indios* and Spaniards occupied the same past moment. Latinos are "othered" in a complex way in his analysis: we are, on the one hand, too backward and un-modern, clinging too hard to language and cultural traditions in a way that makes us unsuccessful assimilators; but also too oriented toward the *future* (the so-called mañana syndrome, as well as the separate threat of Latina fertility). Yet Huntington's book is not the only example of the way that an ideologically freighted vision of time informs discussions of Latino life: the rhetoric of novelty and futurology appears in works across the ideological spectrum, from Victor Davis Hanson's *Mexifornia: A State of Becoming* (2003) to Ilan Stavans's *Spanglish: The Making of a New American Language* (2004).[20]

The overwhelming association of Latinos with futurity, with the supersaturatedness of the crisis moment of the present, and the corresponding denial of coevalness with regard to the past are not only imposed from the outside. David Hayes-Bautista's recent regional study *La Nueva California: Latinos in the Golden State* (2004) also falls into the rhetoric of present crisis: it opens with the question, "Whither California?" (xv), and ends with two vivid descriptions of "best-case" and "worst-case" scenarios of the state's future (208–228). But what's most original in the book is its penultimate chapter, titled "Creating a Regional American Identity: 2020–2040," which, despite the chronological fantasy of its subtitle, begins by going *backward* to describe the origins of what Hayes-Bautista calls "Latino civil society," articulating with far more precision than Huntington what distinguishes it from the "Atlantic American" civil society that has not a single Puritan, but multiple Anglophone origins. On the other hand, Hayes-Bautista's history—like most of the rest of the book—assumes that Latino is more or less coextensive with "Mexican." And it is the *Mexican* roots of California that Hayes-Bautista references in his history of *latinidad* in California, regardless of the presence of (for instance) Chilean miners working during the Gold Rush, Puerto Ricans picking in the orange groves at the turn of the century, or Salvadoran refugees organizing a distinct community subculture in Los Angeles of the 1980s.[21] (Huntington, incidentally, commits the same metonymic error: he cites *Mexican* emotional investment in the U.S. Southwest, but conflates that with the attitude toward the past of Latinos *as a whole.*) While Hayes-Bautista's social–scientific study is exceptional in the way that it links present issues to the deep past rather than merely summarizing the past decade or two as introductory background, he seems unsure about how to conceptualize the Latino past in the broader sense and thus falls back on the well-established bibliography on the rise and fall of the *californios.*

To return to Flores's distinction between "levels" of Latino affiliation, then, when the single-group usage of the "Latino past" does surface, it does so problematically, by conflating the experience of one subgroup with the whole. There is sometimes a tendency as well to suggest a progressivist vision of the development of Latino identity in which the separate histories of long ago are now in the process of melding into one (better, finer) *latinidad.* At the same time, though, a retreat into the safer methodology of composing separate histories of different ethno-national subgroups tends to foreclose the methodologies of *comparison* and *interconnection.* What's more, when we avoid thinking about the Latino past in a holistic fashion, we cede ground to the wider tendency of U.S. popular culture to deny temporal coevalness to Latinos. This brings us, at last, back to our original inquiry into literary history. For in literary criticism, too, a respectful separatism is the norm: there are far more studies of Puerto/NuyoRican, Chicano, and to a lesser extent Cuban and Dominican American literature than comparative Latino works, and most of the latter take a thematic rather than a developmental approach, often segregating authors according to national-origin groups in their chapter arrangements as well.

ANTHOLOGIZING LATINO LITERATURE: TAXONOMIES OF UNITY AND DIVERSITY

This timidity in conceiving *latinidad* in a broader way may well stem from the historically determined divide between West Coast/ Southwestern academic institutions, with their stronger roots and interests in Chicano/a culture, and Midwestern and East Coast Latino/a studies that focus more on the Latin Caribbean.[22] The fact that all of these iterations of Latino cultural studies ultimately owe their institutional presence to minoritarian political pressures, whether during the later years of the Civil Rights Movement or during the multiculturalist movement of the 1980s, binds them together in another respect. One of the major agendas of Latino history (and thus of literary history as well) was initially *to help create the very group whose consciousness it presumes.* As a textual rather than an oral form of access to the past, history used the tools of imagined community defined so successfully during the nineteenth century: to isolate powerful mythic structures that would place readers in a synchronous, imagined relation to other members of that (nationally defined) community, as well as to their non-genealogical "ancestors" who had occupied it earlier.[23]

Following the challenges posed by Foucault, Hayden White, and other theorists loosely described as "postmodern," both history in the broad sense and literary history in particular took pains to repudiate what remained of this Romantic legacy. The very title of David Perkins's *Is Literary History Possible?* (1992)[24] indicates the degree to which the combination of postmodernism and the politically charged critique launched by civil rights and anticolonial movements, occurring roughly at the same time, seemed to render the master narratives of literary history obsolete. Perkins's defense of the genre selectively embraced postmodernism while rejecting multiculturalism outright. He was skeptical about using ethnic experience as a taxonomical category to organize literary expression, concluding that the political events that produced the *demand* to use ethnicity this way would magnify the already-existing tendency of literary history to distort the past according to present-day needs: "The movements for liberation of women, blacks, and gays produce literary histories for the same motives, essentially, that inspired the national and regional literary histories of the nineteenth century. These groups turn to the past in search of identity, tradition, and self-understanding. Their histories do not usually stress discontinuity but rather the opposite. They find their own situation reflected in the past and partly explained by it . . . because the same situation of suppression of marginalization continues from the past into the present. To see it this way is part of their protest" (10). Perkins implies that *non*-minoritarian literary tax-onomies are somehow outside ideology, somehow less likely to fall prey to present-day political exigencies and therefore commit the sin of anachronism.

But if that is the case, what accounts for the impressive *resurgence* of the grand literary history as a genre in the past two decades—and for the fact that these recent entries into the field are so concerned to adopt ethnicity, in addition to nationality, as a legitimate taxonomical category? Both of the major disciplines that generally claim Latino writing as part of their curricular and research mission, English/ American and Spanish/Romance/Latin American literature, have seen at least two major new volumes appear in that period: the *Columbia Literary History of the United States* (1988), the *Cambridge History of American Literature* (1994–2005), alongside the *Cambridge History of Latin American Literature* (1996) and *Literary Cultures of Latin America* (2004).[25] Taking the Anglophone and Hispanophone tradi-tions separately, the one-volume *Columbia History* appends Latino writing along with other multicultural "challenges" to the canon in its closing pages; less forgivably, so does the nine-volume *Cambridge History*, composed a dozen years afterward and with far more space to roam. In his half-book-length closing essay, Cyrus K. Patell adopts from Raymond Williams the temporally rich notion of "emergent lit-eratures" to speak about three very different bodies of writing: queer, Native American, Asian American, and Chicano/ Latino. While Patell's attention to earlier Chicano texts does do something to combat the denial of historical coevalness to Latinos, his characterization of all Latino writing as "emergent" leads to a deterministic prediction that Latino writing will continue to occupy a perpetually marginal place: "When the next multivolume literary history of the US is written sometime during the next century, it will no doubt still need to include a section or set of sections on emergent literatures, because it seems unlikely that American culture will, in the intervening years, cease to marginalize nonwhiteness and nonheterosexuals."[26] Marginality and resistance may well categorize a number of Latino literary produc-tions, but not all of them, and certainly not atemporally; nor does the *Cambridge History* project allow room for those pre-contemporary

Latino texts to enter into revisionist dialogue with the periods and canons of the earlier volumes.[27]

Given the increasing enthusiasm for transnational approaches to Latin American and Latino studies—not to mention the inherent comparatism of the field itself—the two Latin American projects seem more promising. While the *Cambridge History* makes a few (mostly proleptic) remarks about the literary production of U.S. Latinos, the first two volumes of *Literary Cultures of Latin America* deliberately foreground it: two differently conceived essays approach the U.S.–Mexican border as a distinct cultural system, while another focuses on New York as a "center and transit point for Hispanic cultural nomadism." These three essays exemplify the virtues of thinking transnationally, even though they shy away from considering English-language and Spanglish works. Curiously, it is in the third volume's separate section on "Hispanic Cultures in the United States: Diversity, Hybridism, and Constant Transformation" that the project falls short of the integrative goal it meets so intelligently elsewhere: the seven essays are distributed unevenly among the three traditional ethnic subgroups (Mexican American, Cuban American, and Puerto Rican) and thus effectively discourage the very sort of analysis of "Latino" as a complex cultural category that the *Literary Cultures* project as a whole was designed to foster. Not only does this separate section fail as a mini-history of Latino literature, but it suggests that Latino writing can *only* be seen as fragmented by national-origin group, and further isolates the whole of this production to the peripheries of Latin American literary culture "proper."[28]

It may be cynical to suggest that it is precisely because of the increasing demographic and political clout of historically marginalized groups that the disciplines of U.S. American and Latin American literature have felt compelled to return to the task of reinventing their literary past, again and again—as if desperate to assimilate Latino writing to their larger paradigms. As Raymond Williams himself suggested, it is generally in the dominant culture's interest to incorporate emergent cultural forms in order to retrench its own power. It is further suggestive to see English and Spanish departments, in whatever shape they take in particular institutions, engaged in a kind of contest to stake a claim on this body of work. A broadly conceived Latino literary history, then, would arise in part as a reaction-formation against the "additive" approaches that both U.S. and Latin American literature have taken toward it. One may well ask whether Latinos need a coherent literary history. But since the work of it is already being done *for* us, by other interested parties with other agendas (not least of which has to do with consolidating institutional power in the form of enrollments and the faculty lines that stem from them), the question of need seems moot.

Although there is as yet no single work has dared to call itself a Latino literary history, the work of constructing temporal paradigms for Latino textual expression is in effect being done by anthologies, textbooks, and encyclopedic reference works. Because of the currently intense demand for curricular materials on Latinos,[29] the traditional division of labor between the mainstream press anthology and the higher-education textbook has to some extent dissolved: teachers of contemporary literature frequently assign popular anthologies, and academic publishers cannily market themselves for use outside the classroom by encouraging adoption by book groups and establishing webpages, as Pearson/Longman has done for *Latino Boom*. These accessory or teaching texts do not generally foreground their methodological assumptions self-reflectively, as the recent literary histories just mentioned feel obliged to do. But like a literary history, an anthology's structure contains an apparatus for reducing the multitude of potential beginning and ending points to a single one in each direction, as the very structure of narrative dictates; it thereby frames a *telos*. As Agnes Lugo-Ortiz has pointed out, the case of Latino literature has reversed the usual temporal order by which an already-existing archive is distilled into an anthology: "ante la debilidad de la tradición institucional . . . la antología es el archivo."[30] This manipulation of past, present, and future into a shaped relation with one another helps determine the way that the individual selections in an anthology are read, just as its manner of chapter arrangement identifies certain thematics or socioeconomic factors as more creatively generative than others. These implicitly ideological structures are often reinforced by biographical introductions, headnotes, and classroom prompts.

Clearly, such multi-audience texts privilege "contemporary" content over "historical" textual selections in homage to market demands, but in light of the denial of coevalness that haunts the Latino past, these temporal structures demand closer scrutiny. How are the demands that the present makes upon the past influenced by the general tendency to over-identify Latinos with the future? The introduction to *Daughters Of The Fifth Sun*, to take one such anthology, mentions recently recovered works by turn-of-the-century New Mexican women as further evidence of "the diverse identity of all Latinas" that is now coming to maturity; the anthology constitutes as a kind of celebration of this fact, a textual *quinceañera*.[31] A more in-depth examination of those earlier works—taking them on their own terms, with their more unattractive racial and class ideologies intact—would surely undermine that alleged feminist unity, as José Aranda's discussion of the political uses of Maria Amparo Ruíz de Burton suggests. The frequently assigned anthology *Currents from the Dancing River*, likewise, erects a subterranean temporal structure of eventual completion and perfection that recalls Christian eschatology: addressing the diversity among the backgrounds of the writers it includes (from fourth-generation Chicanos to immigrant Peruvian Americans), editor Ray Gonzalez writes, "Although cultural differences remain . . . Latino writers are *coming together* in a cohesive yet exciting and unpredictable whole."[32] The present progressive tense signals readers to scrutinize this supersaturated present moment for signs that Latinos have outgrown the past—a past apparently tainted by those ominous "cultural differences"—and are moving toward the erasure of intra-Latino difference. Again, the single-group model of *latinidad* is foreclosed from the past, while the present moment of "contemporary" literature flattens out the historical differences among, say, 1970, 1980, 1990, 2000, and 2010.

When a contemporary anthology limits itself historically, as does Ray Gonzalez's *After Aztlán: Latino Poets of the Nineties*,[33] that historical consciousness tends to be constrained by giving contextual information that is more spatial than temporal—with biographical headnotes attending to the author's regional location but not her or his inscription within history. The "Nineties," in this work, gets marked as a distinct period only by virtue of its emergence from the (presumably boring) prelude of "history"—meaning the Civil Rights era, the "origin" of Latino consciousness, as the editor notes "the powerful development of Latina writers since those exciting times" (xvi). The comment makes little sense given the very distinctive trajectory of Puerto Rican and Chicano empowerment rhetorics and events during the early 1970s, and the virtual absence of Cuban Americans and other Latinos from this dialogue; but more vitally, it locates this politicized writing as "early" and thus suggests that *apolitical* writing is somehow more complete, more finished, and truly "literary." As in *Currents*, this contemporary writing is cast as more evolved to the degree that it reflects a more unified Latino consciousness.[34] Even the admirable *Latino Boom*, which grounds its focus on contemporary literature with introductory maps and chronologies, leaves the actual work of situating works and authors within this spatiotemporal grid to the classroom or to the individual reader.[35]

Herencia: The Anthology of Hispanic Literature of the United States (2001), and *En otra voz: Antología de literatura hispana de los Estados Unidos* (2002), alone in the crop of recent anthologies, take up the challenge of constructing a vision of the Latino literary past in the single-group sense.[36] Co-edited by Agnes Lugo-Ortiz, José B. Fernandez, Erlinda Gonzales-Berry, Charles Tatum, and Alejandra Balestra under the general direction of Nicolas Kanellos, the narrow-margined pages of these substantial volumes have little spare room for the discussion questions, glossaries, and extended headnotes that characterize *Latino Boom* and the *Prentice-Hall Anthology*, resisting readymade classroom use. Both *Herencia* and *En otra voz* (which contains much of the same material, leaving out those works not originally composed in Spanish) adopt Kanellos's tripartite scheme of "three major manifestations of Hispanic culture in the United States," three modes of Latino literary production: Native, Exile, and Immigrant. "Native Hispanic" literature includes works penned by *californios, tejanos,* and *hispanos* of New Mexico and Arizona who wrote to maintain a communal memory even before the U.S. acquisition of their home places. But in *Herencia*, the category also extends into the late twentieth century to include most of what we think of as seminal Chicano works by Américo Paredes and Luis Valdez. The "literature of exile" predictably includes most Cuban American texts, from the nineteenth century forward, as well as the *México de afuera* writers of the 1920s whose intention was always to return to the *patria*. The "literature of immigration," characterized here as having a "double-gaze perspective: forever comparing the past and the present," happens to feature mostly writers of Caribbean origin—many of the Puerto Rican writers are put here—with a few exceptions from Mexico: an interesting choice given the dominance of Mexicans in contemporary immigration debates.[37]

Although Kanellos does not define them this way, the three modes describe different lived temporalities, different logics of time: "Native" writing insists on its distinctive communal memory as a counter-history to the dominant national one, and thus puts particular weight upon the past as the source of its civil-rights claims; "Exile" writing is oriented toward the unknown future moment of longed-for return; and "Immigrant" writing sees the present moment as a scene of transformation, working toward an eventual assimilation. While this three-way division invites intriguing, interestingly diachronic comparisons among Latino writers (e.g., an exile from Maximilian's Mexico together with one from Castro's Cuba), they do not always work so well as analytical categories. An exile may well imagine the future differently from a voluntary immigrant—but how many writers have access to knowledge of their place in this taxonomy *at the time they are writing*? Among today's transmigrants who shuttle between, say, Guanajuato and Watsonville, California, the sense of being in exile *now* is quite profound, regardless of whether some of those will *eventually* abandon their Mexican citizenship and remain in the United States—as many surely will.[38]

When these three major categories of Latino experience run out of steam, two others arise to fill the first and last places in the anthology's five major sections (the disproportion between these two and the three main categories is noticeable). A short first section deals with the "literature of exploration and colonization" by Spaniards; and an equally short final section is labeled "Sin frontera/beyond boundaries," including authors such as Guillermo Gómez-Peña whose work explicitly vexes national and identitarian boundaries, as well as those of genre and modality. Both of these are primarily spatial categories rather than *temporal* ones: "exploration and colonization" mark the writing as itinerant, having value primarily because of the place it describes; and "beyond boundaries" invokes, of course, the post-Anzaldúa notion of the borderlands and the transnational turn. But transnational literary studies itself has a history, and to limit discussions of "globalization" to the immediate present and the impending future is to participate, once again, in the foreshortening of the Latino past.

These critical observations are not meant to downplay the achievements of *Herencia* and *En otra voz*, which represent significant milestones in moving beyond national frames of literary analysis; they alone, among the anthologies I have mentioned, encourage more creative, illuminating intra-Latino comparisons outside the pan-ethnic umbrella model. They include texts that defy the more readily marketable models of "ethnic" subjectivity, and require readers to consider publication contexts and the shifting place of writers and readers in particular communities.[39] Moreover, *Herencia* clearly seeks to intervene in and disrupt U.S. national narratives of literary and cultural development. Speaking solely of the Chicano case but making a point germane for Latino literary history more broadly, José Aranda has argued that the ultimate goal of textual recovery should be to incite dialogue with such national traditions by disrupting their singular points of origin with multiple ones, and by encouraging diachronic comparisons: linking the Puritan "city on a hill" to the *Movimiento*'s imagined utopia of Aztlán, for instance.[40]

LIVING IN THE ETERNAL NOW

If the disruption of dominant temporalities in the United States constitutes an essential *part* of the work of this as-yet-unaccomplished

Latino history, it is clearly not the *whole* work. For, as Poblete reminds us, the appearance of transnationalism as a conceptual frame has not made nations, or nation-states, less important. Flores reiterates the dual nature of Latino identity even in its single-group usage, "the paradox of being 'nationals' in a thoroughly 'transnationalised' economic geography."[41] Latino studies, he concludes, must weave fluidly between national and transnational analyses, and this is no less true, I would argue, when discussing the past. What we need—as the tacked-on final category in *Herencia* indicates—is a way to develop the *temporal* dimension of the now primarily *spatial* notion of transnationality, to give it a durational identity that is more complex than casual references to NAFTA, for instance, will allow. That temporal dimension, as West-Durán writes, would necessitate constant reference to the entwined histories of the United States, the European colonial powers, and the other nations of Latin America:

> We must say that Latinos are an integral part of the US and its identity as a nation, and because of that, as well as the sometimes-tortured historical relationship between Latin America and the US, Latinos are also part of a global context that is local, national and transnational. We are here because the US is there, or in the words of Juan Gonzalez, we are "the harvest of empire." This means that analyzing Latino literature entails a larger understanding of greater forces that are at work.[42]

Put differently, "Latinos," as I have written elsewhere, were anticipated long before they were born. The Benjaminian overtone to that phrase is intentional.[43] Some of the most radical experiments in recent literary history have overtly modeled themselves on the loose structure of Benjamin's massive *Arcades Project*. In David Wellbury's *A New History of German Literature* (2004), contributors choose a single moment in time—not a traditionally deterministic event such as the outbreak of World War II, nor a vague marker such as a year of publication, but a rich moment such as a writer's first hearing of a life-changing piece of music—and then leap forward and backward in time to see how this fixed temporal–spatial coordinate radiates outward to a multitude of other texts. The idea of the "event" is flexible; the structure of time itself, horizontal and web-like rather than progressive and linear.[44] This approach highlights the constantly shifting definitions and valorizations of "the literary" over time and space. Unlike a traditional literary–historical survey, which carves up time into periods and establishes chronological causality, the *New History* largely leaves it to the reader or "user" to determine webs of influence and intertextuality; it encourages, rather than avoids, asynchrony and anachronism along the lines of Aranda's Chicano Puritans.[45]

With this in mind, we might think of Latino literary history as much more than a strategic field-provocation, a corrective to existing national and transnational volumes, curricula, or disciplinary habits. "The Latino past," in the single-group sense, represents not a specifically bounded set of facts but an *interpretive opportunity*. To seize upon that opportunity is to become critically aware of the pressure of prolepsis upon Latinos in the United States, and to counter the resulting denial of coevalness in past time. If the work of cultural criticism is to expose how certain language uses, metaphorical domains, and geographical imaginaries gain and lose power in particular contexts, then that work involves the interrogation of hidden temporal logics as well. The project of Latino literary history would thus involve cutting up the enormous body of knowledge about the space of the Americas in creative ways, revealing hidden continuities—or simply contiguities—among various kinds of Latino experience both within the United States and outside it. It would interweave the threads of that past experience with other cultural histories—U.S., Latin American, indigenous, African, European, Asian—recognizing the always-unequal and ever-shifting influence of each of these traditions upon any given set of writers and readers over time.

Jesse, in Véa's *Gods Go Begging*, leads his fellow soldiers in a mental exercise meant both to amuse and to distract them from the traumatic present: supposing. "*Supongamos, mis amigos*," he says, "Suppose the wind had been blowing just right back in the sixteenth and seventeenth centuries . . . that the Pilgrims had been blown south by a terrific gale and the *Mayflower* had run aground in the Yucatán peninsula."[46] But the manipulation of time, and the construction of counter-histories, becomes more than a game, or a narrative device, as the novel progresses. In its climax—a surreal chapter that may or may not be categorizable within the terms of *lo real maravilloso*—the living and dead characters from 1968 and 1998 actually touch and communicate with one another. Afterward (or is it?), Jesse explains the unbelievable event to his girlfriend:

> "Carolina, think about the stratifications of an open hillside, a place where earth has given way and time itself is left exposed, layer upon layer—silica, clay, diatoms, and ash. Down here at this level is the time of the swelling sea; here, the time of the desert when hot, rising air would have haunted our eyes; here is a jagged karst, a time when the

world shook an abrasion into its own skin; and here are the fossil dead, here you will find love and war in the same shamble of strewn bone. Here and there, where the world has shifted and cracked open, one era will touch another. And once upon the rarest time, human hands and eyes from the distant past can seek out and find . . . search for and contact . . . hands and eyes of the present time . . . our time." (282; ellipses in original)

As in Benjamin's mystical–Marxist *Theses*, a truly engaged response to history requires that one speak to, from, and as the "fossil dead." Informed by existing national and ethno-national time frames and spatial imaginaries, but not beholden to them, Latino literary history is charged with uncovering as-yet-invisible links among the chaotic layers of human experience. I eagerly await the coming of that unwritten volume so that I can love it, hate it, tear it apart, and plot its next regeneration.

Notes

1. Alfredo Véa, *Gods Go Begging* (New York: Plume, 1999); hereafter cited with the page number following the quoted text.
2. Julia Alvarez, *In the Time of the Butterflies* (Chapel Hill, N.C.: Algonquin Books, 1994); Victor Villaseñor, *Rain of Gold* (Arte Público Press, 1991). Both were originally small-press publications later reprinted in commercial editions.
3. The fact that Véa, a Mexican American born in a labor camp in rural Arizona and now an urban Californian, has expressed skepticism about the particularist claims of ethnic literature further complicates this question. See Véa's interview in The *Bloomsbury Review*, 20:1 (January/February 2000), where he states that U.S. Latino writers have "allowed ourselves to applaud the provincial in literature. That time is over. The artistic bar of literary fiction has been set for our time by Nabokov, Bellow, Faulkner, et al. We should study that bar—aim at it with every intention of leaping over."
4. Joan Flores, *From Bomba to Hip-Hop: Puerto Rican Culture and Latino Identity* (New York: Columbia University Press, 2000), 152.
5. Against Oboler's influential thesis about the divisive intentions of the U.S. government's first use of "Hispanic" as a term (not just a concept), Laura Lomas, in her forthcoming book *Translating Empire: José Martí, Migrant Latino Subjects and American Modernities*, rehearses the debates over whether José Martí's utopian conception of *Nuestra América* is really appropriate in the U.S. context and argues he did in fact develop a sophisticated concept of U.S. *latinidad*. For a useful review of the philosophy of temporality as it has structured historical writing, see Reinhard Koselleck, trans. Keith Tribe, *Futures Past* (Cambridge: MIT Press, 1990).

6. Suzanne Oboler, *Ethnic Labels, Latino Lives* (Minneapolis: University of Minnesota Press, 1995), 171.

7. Jorge J.E. Gracia, *Hispanic/Latino Identity: A Philosophical Perspective* (Oxford: Blackwell, 2000); emphasis mine.

8. Ibid., 50, 65.

9. Flores, *From Bomba to Hip-Hop*, 197. Flores distinguishes between "demographic," "analytic," and "imaginary" approaches to the question of Latino identity, challenging the first two as claiming a false quantitative objectivity. "Regardless of what anyone chooses to name it, the Latino or Hispanic community exists because for much of the history of the hemisphere, people have moved from Latin America to the United States, while portions of Latin America have been incorporated into what has become the United States" (192).

10. Gracia identifies himself as a philosopher, not an historian, and I have some quibbles with the examples he gives of what this shared history might be. Like many Latin American philosophers of racial mixing from Vasconcelos onward, he identifies the moment of Spanish–indigenous contact as the origin-point of the *mestizo latino*. This originary location renders secondary the introduction of Africans to the hemisphere: *mestizaje* trumps *mulatez* as the founding paradigm, and thus the notion of Afro-Latinos as a second-order population gets instantiated yet again.

11. In addition to Poblete's collection, see also *Transnational Latina/o Communities* (Rowman & Littlefield, 2002); Liliana R. Goldin, ed., *Identities on the Move: Transnational Processes in North America and the Caribbean Basin* (Austin: University of Texas Press, 2000). The journal *Latino Studies* has worked transnationalism into their mission statement, and the spring 2006 issue was devoted to transnational research. Rosaura Sánchez and Beatrice Pita's "Theses on the Latino Bloc: A Critical Perspective" (*Aztlán* 31:2, Fall 2006, 25–53) importantly redefines "Latino" not within the categories of identity formation, but as an ever-shifting, transnational bloc marked by multiple divisions as well as multiple possibilities of affiliation.

12. Earl Shorris organizes *Latinos* (New York: Norton 1992; rev. ed. 2001) both diachronically, by national-group history, and synchronically by "social problem" (!). Himilce Novas, *Everything You Need to Know about Latino History* (New York: Plume, 1998; rev. 2003), divides her chapters by ethno-national group. Lalo Alcaraz and Ilán Stavans, in *Latino USA: A Cartoon History* (New York: Basic Books, 2000), likewise begin with the Spanish-indigenous contact and cover all the relevant national-group experiences, though the different visual economy of the images allows, in my view, more commonality among groups. Juan Gonzalez's *Harvest of Empire: A History of Latinos in America* (New York: Viking Penguin, 2000), probably the best of these to date, has an initial section, "Roots," that works chronologically through the intertwined history of the Americas until the mid-twentieth century,

THE ONCE AND FUTURE LATINO ✦ 135

then a second section, "Branches," comprised of separate chapters on six ethno-national groups, and finally "Harvest," on contemporary issues. D.H. Figueredo, *The Complete Idiot's Guide(R) to Latino History and Culture* (New York: Alpha Books, 2002), which is full of factual inaccuracies and is derivative of both Shorris and González, has an introductory section, clearly aimed at non-Latinos, followed by a section on "origins" that gives a capsule history of Latin America as a whole (with one chapter devoted exclusively to Mexico), and then three sections on shared questions of culture and language. I am not including here Nicolas Kanellos's several versions of the *Hispanic American Almanac*, including the *Hispanic Chronology*, on the grounds that although Kanellos writes introductory narratives to them, these reference works are essentially meant to be read out of sequence by looking up a single entry rather than consumed in a linear way—though, as I will argue later, nonlinearity can be a good thing.

13. Paula Moya has challenged Gracia's vision of "historical unity" as too capacious in *Learning from Experience*. Although it is limited to the Chicana case, Moya's conception of "post-realist identity" is derived from a more general corrective movement within ethnic studies, and thus could be applied to the wider category of Latino. Moya defines "Chicana" as a local and personalized category of "political awareness: her recognition of her disadvantaged position in a hierarchically organized society arranged according to categories of class, race, gender, and sexuality; and her propensity to engage in political struggle aimed at subverting and changing those structures." Gracia's definition of historical unity is "too large and heterogeneous," writes Moya; "people's lived identities do not necessarily correspond to philosophical categories or intellectual traditions. Much more salient for a person is her historical sense (which is generally more localized than Gracia would allow . . .)." Paula Moya, *Learning from Experience* (Berkeley: University of California Press, 2002), 42.

14. Flores, *From Bomba to Hip-Hop*, 199.

15. John Christie and José González, *Latino Boom* (New York: Longman, 2000), 433.

16. From the mission statement: "*Latino Future* magazine is designed to help Hispanics on their path to greater business success and personal life style fulfillment. Our Mission: To unite and solidify our community by providing informative and enlightening articles that inspires [sic] and empowers our readers to maximize their resources and realize their dreams." http://www.latinofuture.com/about.html, accessed June 7, 2006.

17. Johannes Fabian, *Time and the Other: How Anthropology Makes its Object* (New York: Columbia University Press, 1983), 144. Italics in the original.

18. Samuel P. Huntington, *Who Are We? The Challenges to America's National Identity* (New York: Simon & Schuster, 2004), italics mine.

McClintock argues that Bush-era neologisms such as the "permanent war on terror" invite a state of "perpetual suspended panic": "the time of waiting is the time of imperial paranoia." This suspended temporal state invites "fantasies of engulfment and destruction by an enemy always about to arrive." Although her focus is on the war on terror, the same notion of "waiting for the barbarians to arrive" (she adapts the C.P. Cavafy poem) seem to me germane to the Latino immigration debate. See her "Paranoid Empire," in Russ Castronovo (ed.), *States of Emergency: Alternative Temporalities and US Studies* (UNC Press, forthcoming).

19. Samuel P. Huntington, "The Hispanic Challenge," *Foreign Policy* March/April 2004, 7. http://www.foreignpolicy.com/story/cms. php?story_id=2495, accessed June 7, 2006.

20. Blanca Silvestrini's essay on culture rights in *Latino Cultural Citizenship* cites as exemplary a Latina interviewee who resists the perceived demand to "lose" her personal history in order to claim public space in the United States: "you are requested to erase the past . . . it's like being asked to be born again in order to participate" (*Latino Cultural Citizenship*, eds. William Flores and Rina Benmayor [Boston: Beacon Press, 1997], 39). The speaker nicely repudiates not only the secular doctrine of assimilation, but the whole evangelical temporality from which Huntington writes.

21. In his first footnote, Hayes-Bautista writes that although "There are many Latino subpopulations," "About 77.1 percent of Latinos in California are of Mexican origin; therefore, the Mexican portion of the Latino experience predominates in this book" (xv). Even if it were impossible to give voice to that other 22.9 percent—a not inconsiderable number—at the very least, the tensions between some of these intra-Latino groups would seem to merit some of his attention.

22. For a summary of the different institutional histories of the Latin Caribbean vs. the Mexican border as sites of inquiry for Latino studies, see the revealing article by Pedro A. Cabán, "Moving from the Margins to Where? Three Decades of Latino/a Studies," *Latino Studies* 1 (2003), 5–25. This is not the place to pronounce on the merits or demerits of maintaining separate field divisions (Chicano studies in particular has tended to resist integration into Latino studies on the grounds that it does not share the historical stake that the Chicano Movement held in indigeneity). But it is surely uncontroversial to point out that the current West Coast/East Coast division tends to slight the experience of less politically powerful, but demographically very significant, national-origin groups in the United States, most notably Central American Americans and Dominican Americans. Additionally, the multiple affiliations of Afro-Latinos in the United States are perpetually slighted, as Silvio Torres-Sailliant has noted in multiple venues.

23. This kind of ideological burden is magnified when it comes to *literary* history because of the weight that the current moment places on literature (on the nonexperimental novel, the memoir, and on confessional poetry in particular) to move the reader toward a greater understanding of otherness through her or his empathetic identification with the author's voice. While literary scholars may wish to repudiate that affective work, many of the textual tools in circulation right now (many of which I will discuss later in this essay) are aimed at the general reader who believes precisely that. I don't have space to develop this question here, but on the problematic position of "ethnic" literature and readerly subjectivity, see Marcial Gonzalez, "A Marxist Critique of Borderlands Postmodernism," in *Left of the Color Line*, eds. Bill Mullen and James Smethurst (Chapel Hill: University of North Carolina Press, 2003), 279–297.

24. David Perkins, *Is Literary History Possible?* (Baltimore: Johns Hopkins University Press, 1992).

25. Emory Elliott, ed., *Columbia Literary History of the United States* (New York: Columbia University Press, 1988); Sacvan Bercovitch, ed., *Cambridge History of American Literature*, 8 v. (Cambridge and New York: Cambridge University Press, 1994–2005); Roberto González-Echevarría and Enrique Pupo-Walker, eds., *Cambridge History of Latin American Literature*, 3 v. (Cambridge and New York: Cambridge University Press, 1996); Mario J. Valdés and Djelal Kadir, eds., *Literary Cultures of Latin America*, 3 v. (Oxford and New York: Oxford University Press, 2004). It is worth remembering that both of these fields, in turn, became institutionally legitimated in large part because of a successful, seminal literary history. Pedro Henríquez Ureña's *Literary Currents in Spanish America* (1945; Spanish version 1949) decisively ruptured the declensionist narrative of peninsular-focused Spanish studies with its inventory of copious, understudied materials from the colonial *relación* to the *crónica modernista* that, when finally taken seriously as complex texts, reshaped the very parameters of "the literary." Likewise, although there had been earlier patriotic compilations of "American" works in the United States, Robert Spiller's *Literary History of the United States*, published in 1948, changed the landscape of British-dominated English studies by positing a distinctive theory of national literary evolution that was diverse, capacious, and not obviously indebted to chauvinistic political concerns.

26. Cyrus K. Patell, in Bercovitch, ed. *Cambridge History* v. 8, 671.

27. This does not exhaust the list of recent literary histories. Richard J. Gray's *A History of American Literature* (London: Blackwell, 2004), includes some colonial texts translated from Spanish as well as some material on the oral tradition of the southwest and a fifteen-page section near the end on Chicano/Latino writing. It is, in short, the *Heath Anthology* in narrative format.

28. In the third volume of *Literary Cultures of Latin America*, there is one essay on Chicano/Latino theater; one on Chicano writing in general; two on Puerto Rican writing in general; one on Puerto Rican theater; one on Cuban theater and another on Cuban American prose. Not only does this structure exclude Dominican, Central and South American literary production, it unevenly represents the output—both in terms of literary publications or performances and in terms of scholarship—from these constitutive groups. I do want to credit the editors of this work, Djelal Kadir and Mario Valdés, for their innovative design and their broad culturalist approach to literature as a shifting signifier that must be understood with reference to the social practices governing literacy, print communities, access to authorship, and reading in a particular place and moment. See "Beyond Literary History," Valdés' introduction to volume one. The *Cambridge History of Latin American Literature*, as I mentioned, has just two recognitions of Latino literature, both in volume two: one brief chapter on "Latin American [Hispanic Caribbean] Literature Written in the U.S." and another titled "Chicano Literature." This perfectly replicates the East/West coast divide within Latino studies.

29. For reasons having to do both with the market value of the multicultural exotic, literary productions by Latinos—as by other "ethnic" subjects—often make the leap from the "popular" to the "canonical" sphere very quickly; reference tools are frequently updated to account for "the new Cisneros." To the extent that marketing systems involve canny guesses, based on past demand, about where a new market force will emerge in the future, the question of Latino temporality also devolves ultimately on questions of the contemporary literary marketplace and its situation within what postmodern theorists have described as the space–time compression of life in the age of globalization and mass media. The Latino experience does not take place in some primordial outside of this culture; it is not simply, as Patell would have it, "emergent." Sánchez and Pita critique the corporatization of "Latin time" in their "Theses on the Latino Bloc." A romantic, retrograde association has surrounded visions of the Latino temporal experience at least since C.F. Lummis and D.H. Lawrence visited Mexico and the Mexican Southwest in the 1920s; the mythic "land of mañana" suggests not only a spatial "outside" to the "developed" world but a temporal outside to modernity. See Daniel Cooper Alarcón, *Aztec Palimpsest: Mexico in the Modern Imagination* (Tucson: University of Arizona Press, 1997).

30. Agnes Lugo-Ortiz, "La antología y el archivo: Reflexiones en torno a *Herencia, En otra voz*, y los límites del saber," in Kenya Dworkin y Méndez and Agnes Lugo-Ortiz (eds.), *Recovering the U.S. Hispanic Literary Heritage V* (Houston: Arte Público, 2006), 139–170.

31. Bryce Milligan, Mary Guerrero-Milligan, and Angela de Hoyos, eds., *Daughters Of The Fifth Sun* (New York: Putnam, 1995), 17. This

recognition was clearly influenced by the historical emphasis of Rebolledo and Rivera's *Infinite Divisions: An Anthology of Chicana Literature* (Tuscon: University of Arizona Press, 1993).

32. Ray Gonzalez, ed., *Currents from the Dancing River: Contemporary Latino Fiction, Nonfiction, and Prose* (New York: Harcourt Brace, 1994), xiv; emphasis mine.

33. Ray Gonzalez, *After Aztlán: Latino Poets of the Nineties* (Boston: David R. Godine, 1993).

34. The competing anthology by Victor Hernández Cruz, Leroy Quintana, and Virgil Suárez, eds., *Paper Dance: 55 Latino Poets* (New York: Persea, 2000). likewise focuses on the book's own future-oriented, utopian project of bringing all its aggregate Latino ethnicities together. There is no room in this essay to analyze every existing Latino/a literature anthology (including such bestsellers and Augenbraum & Stavans's *Growing Up Latino* [New York: Mariner Books, 1993], Carlson's *Cool Salsa* [New York: Fawcett, 1995], Poey and Suarez's *Iguana Dreams*, Castillo-Speed's *Latina* [New York: Touchstone, 1995], and Magill's *Masterpieces of Latino Literature* [New York: Harper Collins, 1994]), but the two dozen that I have analyzed all demonstrate the same problem of contemporaneity, with the exceptions I mention here. Typical is Eduardo R. del Rio's *Prentice Hall Anthology of Latino Literature* (2001), which, as the publisher's unhelpfully vague description states, does not even try to provide historical context but rather "emphasizes the similarities and differences between the culture and literature of the three primary groups [Mexican, Puerto Rican, Cuban] while also trying to emphasize the unique qualities and universal themes present in all of them." The regionally focused work by Rick Heide, ed., *Under the Fifth Sun: Latino Writing from California* (Berkeley: Heyday Books, 2002) does, however, provide a historical origin point in Spanish explorers, and makes an effort to include non-Chicano and non-U.S.-based writing about the place.

35. I have not made mention yet of Harold Augenbraum and Margarite Fernández Olmos's *The Latino Reader: An American Literary Tradition from 1542 to the Present* (New York: Houghton Mifflin, 1997). *The Latino Reader*, although it makes a gesture at the long sweep of Latino presence in what is now the United States by establishing Cabeza de Vaca as the first Latino author (an interesting, and controversial, decision), does not provide much framework for thinking about historical process, and its attention to the diverse groups of Latinos is virtually negligible.

36. *Herencia: The Anthology of Hispanic Literature of the United States* (Oxford and New York: Oxford University Press, 2001); *En otra voz: Antología de literatura hispana de los Estados Unidos* (Houston: Arte Público Press, 2002). Kanellos's introduction to *Herencia* acknowledges its ambition to be representative and grand-scale, if not

impossibly inclusive, in its title, "An overview of *the* Hispanic Literature of the United States": using the article "the" and the singular of the noun "literature" suggest that the study claims authoritative status. That "overview" begins by justifying the project proleptically, too, noting that "more and more Hispanic surnames have been appearing on the pages of book reviews and on college syllabi" (1). Moreover, the back-cover blurb, taken from a glowing review of the book by Julio Ortega, invokes the Latino future in a subtly urgent way: "*As a living memory*, this magnificent book opens its pages to the cross-cultural language of *our best future*" (emphasis mine).

37. Lugo-Ortiz, one of the coeditors of *Herencia*, illuminates the process by which this "tripartite" division was made ("La antología y el archivo," 147), and makes valuable points about the economic conditions such as royalties and marketing concerns that shaped the selection process (154–157).

38. Who gets to be considered an "exile" (e.g., Cubans with dry feet) and who an "immigrant" according to the baroque twists of current U.S. immigration policy is, of course, a politically charged issue within Latino communities. Another anthology, Recovery Project alumna Gabriela Baeza Ventura's admirable *U.S. Latino Literature Today* (New York: Longman, 2004), while focused on contemporary writing, also adopts the tripartite categories of "Native," "Exile/Immigration," and "Transcultural." The book's inexplicable inclusion of nineteenth-century Cuban writers such as José María Heredia and José Martí, without including other nineteenth-century Mexican writers, seems random.

39. Although it is not intended as a literary history, I want also to mention here Alan West-Durán and Maria Herrera-Sobek's two-volume reference work *Latino and Latina Writers* (New York: Scribner's, 2004), which offers no particular timeline, allowing the individual essayists to summarize work by author and simply using an alphabetical arrangement. The problem for them is one of canon formation—of selection—which lies beyond my scope here (the selection process, of course, would be another way to analyze the anthologies I have just mentioned). Works that establish and disseminate canons ("traditions"), however self-reflective or tentative, establish presumptive relationships between past, present, and future by constituting a community of readers across temporal and spatial coordinates. *Canonicity* may thus be seen as the process of being assigned historical meaning: the canon's beginning and end, as marked in each syllabus or anthology, constitute a theory of development, even if that theory, as in the anthologies, remains unarticulated. One of the tasks of literary history is, then, to be reflective about how the property or quality of canonicity changes over time: a recognition of those social factors that drive the identification of some text as exemplary, demonstrative, or

worthwhile. Manuel Martín-Rodríguez, in his *Life In Search of Readers* (Albuquerque: University of New Mexico Press, 2003), begins to establish this kind of methodology for the Chicano case.

40. José Aranda, *When We Arrive* (Albuquerque: University of New Mexico Press, 2004), xvi. Aranda critiques the Chicano Movement for proposing "a separate, singular, counternationalist literary tradition" (47), but he does not explore the potential of Latino writing more broadly for carrying on that challenge to the national *telos* of immigration/assimilation. His brilliant reading of the penultimate chapter of Tomás Rivera's *. . . y no se lo tragó la tierra* emphasizes the present-progressive temporal location of the protagonist's "arriving."

41. Flores, *From Bomba to Hip-Hop*, 214.

42. Alan West-Durán, "Canon a la cañona," *Latino Studies* 4 (2006): 140–146, 143.

43. "The past carries with it a secret index by which it is referred to redemption. Doesn't a breath of the air that pervaded earlier days caress us as well? . . . there is a secret agreement between past generations and the present one. Then our coming was expected on earth. Then, like every generation that preceded us, we have been endowed with a weak messianic power, a power on which the past has a claim. Such a claim cannot be settled cheaply." Walter Benjamin, "On the Concept of History," *Selected Writings* v. 4, ed. Howard Eiland and Michael W. Jennings (Harvard University Press, 2003), 390.

44. Wellbery writes, citing Erwin Panofsky, "every historical phenomenon 'represents the intersection of numerous frames of reference that confront each other as products of different spaces and times and whose interaction in each instance leads to a unique result.' Such interactions produce what Walter Benjamin called 'constellations,' configurations of historical facts that converge in a moment of sudden insight. Thus multiple paths radiate from each event to other events. Echoes, influences, and contrasts become perceptible. Sometimes these interconnections are chronologically proximate; sometimes they leap across centuries." David E. Wellbury, "Introduction," in *A New History of German Literature* (Cambridge: Harvard University Press, 2004), xxii.

45. Manuel Martín-Rodriguez, in "'A Net Made of Holes': Toward a Cultural History of Chicano Literature," *MLQ* 62:1 (2001), 1–18, proposes year-based explorations of this vast temporal–spatial terrain as a way to show both the "net" (the remaining record) and the "holes" (the losses and absences) in it. I find this an appealing model, and yet the years he chooses as examples—1598, 1848, 1998—have been rendered a little tired by their totemic invocation within the nascent field of Americas studies (e.g., Kaplan and Pease on 1898; Streeby on 1848). Now that those markers have performed their salutary function of bringing expansion and imperialism back into U.S. studies, we can surely extend our temporal imaginations beyond them. There are so many other suggestive starting points: substituting

1899, the year the United Fruit Company was incorporated, for the worn-out 1898 would highlight processes of economic neocolonialism in the hemisphere through the development of new methods of vertical integration. Or we could choose an originary event located *outside* the hegemonic power, for a change: to look at the trans-American 1928 starting from the publication of Mariátegui's *Siete ensayos de interpretación de la realidad peruana*, rather than from the election of Herbert Hoover, would foreshadow the movement toward indigenous autonomy rather than the Great Depression. The "progressive" nation would be lurching toward a terrible reversal, the "backward" one leaping ahead conceptually by a century, producing an entirely different *telos*, a new sense of relation, more like a collection of fragments with an end but not a *telos*, in the sense of the grand master narratives of Romantic historiography.

46. Véa, *Gods Go Begging*, 111–113.

CHAPTER 6

Hurricanes, Magic, Science, and Politics in Cristina García's *The Agüero Sisters*

William Luis

A Él

. . .

Vuelan, vuelan en sus alas
nubes y hojas a la par,
ya a los cielos las levante,
ya las sumerja en el mar.

¡Pobres nubes! ¡pobres hojas
que no saben dónde van! . . .
Pero siguen el camino
que les traza el huracán.

Gertrudis Gómez de Avellaneda

Ciclón

Ciclón de raza,
Recién llegado a Cuba de las islas Bahamas,
Se crió en Bermudas,
Estuvo en Puerto Rico.
Arrancó de raíz el palo mayor de Jamaica.
Iba a violar a Guadalupe.

> *Logró violar a Martinica.*
> *Edad: Dos días.*
>
> Nicolás Guillén

POLITICS I

I have asked myself what similarities may exist between 1898 and 1998, and how they relate to Latino U.S. literature and culture. Since we have begun a new century, I am tempted to associate the two dates with current debates surrounding the fin de siecle, or even with Frank Kermode's *The Sense of an Ending*—a need to imagine origins and endings in order to give meaning to our intermediary position and preoccupations.[1] But the ending as closure invokes its binary opposite, a beginning. In the case of 1898, its closing also connotes 1899, but more appropriately the advent of another century, or in Viconian terms, the start of a new cycle.[2]

The end of the nineteenth century brought profound changes to the United States, the Spanish Caribbean, and Spain. While U.S. historians may look to John L. O'Sullivan's ideas of Manifest Destiny, Capt. Alfred Thayer Mahan's proposition that the United States become a sea power, or to Dr. Albert W. Shaw's interpretation as the country's rightful outcome of events,[3] perhaps nature provided another explanation for the change. The Spanish-Cuban-American War of 1895–1898 spans a period of an unusually high number of hurricanes passing through the Caribbean. These natural forces, which contain their own endings and beginnings, create their own destructions, followed by man's desire to start anew, that is, to bring life back to a previous level of normality. In the period that encompasses the war, the Caribbean received seven hurricanes. One hurricane hit Cuba in October of 1895, two in September of 1896, one in October of 1897, and another one in October of 1898.[4]

HURRICANES I

Hurricanes are at the very core of a genealogy of Cuban and Caribbean cultures. In *El huracán*, Fernando Ortiz interprets eight Amerindian objects found in the eastern province of Cuba. He believes that the figures with heads and curved arms, one up and the other down, in a rotation or sigmoid motion, may have been symbols of the hurricane gods Guabancex, Maboya, or Jurakán. Hurricanes are one of the most devastating forces of nature. Strong winds, tidal waves, and furious rainstorms accompany them. While Ortiz recognizes that tornados have higher wind speed, they cover a smaller area and last for a shorter period of time. The hurricane envelops a wider region and lasts for many days. It is erratic in direction and appearance. Ortiz points out that in 1933 there were twenty-one hurricanes in the area of the Caribbean, while there were only two in each of the following years: 1911, 1914, 1917, 1929, and 1930.[5] I should add that 1933 signaled another change, one that brought the Machado dictatorship to an end.

Toward the end of the nineteenth century a similar kind of hurricane struck Cuba and the Caribbean, not natural but metaphorical, not from the South but from the North. On July 1, 1898, the early part of hurricane season, the most important land battle of the war was launched. Generals Kent and Wheeler attacked San Juan Hill, and two cavalry regiments, which included Teddy Roosevelt's famed Rough-Riders, captured the Hill, but not without suffering great loss of life.[6] During that day, six thousand U.S. soldiers attacked seven hundred Spaniards.[7]

On August 12, another man-made hurricane hit the islands in the form of a signed armistice. Spain relinquished to the United States rights over Cuba, and ceded Puerto Rico and the Ladrone group islands.[8] As an omen of what was to come, Puerto Rico received two punches. One was man-made and the other natural. On August 8, 1899, "San Ciriaco" reached the island with a tidal wave that destroyed most of the houses in Humacao. More than three thousand lives were lost throughout the island, and property damage exceeded $20 million dollars. The same storm made landfall in Florida and continued a path of destruction to Hatteras.[9] One year later, Puerto Rico was hit by a second blow, the Foraker Law, which made Puerto Rico a U.S. territory. At the start of the century, the Caribbean experienced six hurricanes. Of these one landed in Cuba, and another in Puerto Rico.

POLITICS II

The end of the century brought significant political changes. It signaled the end of Spain as a world power, and the emergence of the United States as an economic and military world force. With the success of the Guadalupe–Hidalgo Treaty of 1848, the United States expanded its borders west to the Pacific, and south to the Rio Grande. With the Spanish-Cuban-American War, the emerging giant seized territories outside of the mainland. In addition, U.S. journalism acquired a certain power that made it a de facto fourth branch of the U.S. government.

At the turn of the twentieth century, the United States played, for better or worse, a major role in the internal and external affairs of its prized possessions. Puerto Rico became a colony, and Cuba an economic, political, and military dependency, as the Platt Amendment to the Cuban Constitution of 1901 indicated. Whereas some Cubans welcomed the U.S. intervention, and indeed annexation had been part of the nineteenth-century discourse, others resented and even rejected the U.S. control over the island, frustrating decades of struggle for Cuban sovereignty.

The present recalls the past, with some important differences. At the end of the twentieth century the United States stands alone as the most powerful country in the world. Puerto Rico recently decided its political status, to remain a Free Associated State. Yellow journalism has continued and made inroads into former president Clinton's bedroom and the Oval Office. And 1998 experienced an above-normal hurricane season. The weather forecast center predicted ten tropical storms; of these six grew into hurricanes and two into intense hurricanes. In September hurricane Georges wreaked havoc over Puerto Rico, Hispaniola, and Cuba, before reaching the mainland.

Over the past one hundred years the United States has continued to play a decisive role in Cuban politics, even if each government is merely reacting to the other. Instead of taking political control of the island, as lawmakers intended to do prior to the outbreak of the Spanish-Cuban-American War, the influx of Cubans, Dominicans, and Puerto Ricans leaving their country of origin for the mainland is dictating the policies of many U.S. cities, where Hispanic and Latino cultures are thriving.[10] In fact, a certain active sector of the Cuban American community is setting U.S. policy toward Cuba. Mexican Americans continue to live in states that once belonged to Mexico; and migrants will ignore or defy a geopolitical border unrecognized by their forefathers and their culture.

Literature and Politics I

Let us review briefly what transpired in the field of literature during the same one hundred years. Toward the end of the nineteenth century, the United States provided haven for its Spanish Caribbean neighbors, as Cuban and Puerto Rican intellectuals and activists fighting the Spanish colonial government sought refuge on the mainland. Writers such as José María Heredia, José Martí, Félix Varela, Cirilo Villaverde, Gonzalo Pachín Marín, and Eugenio María de Hostos, among many others, fought for their country's freedom in the United

States, but also completed their most important works in cities like New York.

As we concluded the twentieth century and started the twenty-first, the descendants of Cuban, Puerto Rican, Dominican, and Chicano residents, immigrants, and exiles, Latinos born or raised and educated on the mainland, are at the forefront of a new literary movement that has opened up a new field in literature and criticism; it is both Hispanic and North American in character, and is helping to bring the two cultural groups and their literatures together. The United States has exerted a strong influence on anyone reaching its shores. For writers who were formed in their country of provenance, and have been considered pioneers of their countries' national literature, but later lived and wrote in Spanish in the Untied States, events unfolding on the mainland must be addressed when recontextualizing their works. I contend that critics should examine the time and place of writing as necessary elements for deciphering the text's complexity. In the present, Latino U.S. authors write in English about their characters' experiences both on the island and mainland. This body of work, which is bridging two languages and two cultures, is making serious gains in both U.S. and Latin American literatures.[11]

To understand the relationship between 1898 and 1998, and how the past and the present function in terms of each other, I have elected to study Cristina García's *The Agüero Sisters*, which in an uncanny way places itself at the center of some of the issues I have raised earlier. While the novel begins at the turn of the century, the beginning of a new cycle, when Cuba emerged as a so-called independent nation, the narration mentions the past of the Spanish-Cuban-American War, and refers to the three countries involved: the Spanish past of the sisters' grandfather, the past and present of Cuba's revolutionary government, and the current United States, where the two sisters live. As in *Dreaming in Cuban*, García situates the present political events within the context of the family's history. The present does not take place in a vacuum, but as a manifestation of previous events.[12]

Like Domingo Sarmiento's *Recuerdos de provincia* (Memory of the Province), in which the author associates his family with the founding of a modern Argentina,[13] García relates the Agüero family with the emergence of the Cuban nation. One will foretell the outcome of the other, for their destinies are inextricably intertwined. Reina and Constancia's grandfather, Reinaldo Agüero, traveled from Spain to Cuba at the conclusion of the Spanish-Cuban-American War, when Cuba began to develop as an independent nation. He represents the early migratory wave, different from the one known to García's parents, as Spaniards traveled in large numbers from their country of origin to Cuba, from the turn of the century well into the Machado dictatorship (1927–1933), many of whom were from the province of Galicia. As a reader in a cigar factory, Reinaldo represents the well-educated, skilled, and liberal sector of Cuban society. Fernando Ortiz's *Cuban Counterpoint: Tobacco and Sugar* but also Bernardo Vega's *Memoirs of Bernardo Vega* provide clear descriptions of how this crop is associated with a certain political ideology.[14] In Ortiz's book tobacco and cigar makers are opponents of sugar, central authority, the colony, and slavery. In Vega's memoirs the same workers fight oppression, and support Puerto Rican independence, socialism, and Vito Marcantonio, the Congressman from El Barrio in New York City.[15]

Ignacio Agüero was born October 4, 1904, two years into the birth of the country and the presidency of Estrada Palma, and the same year in which the national Congress was elected. Ignacio is an important barometer of Cuba's infant stage, as well as the years to come. There were impending signs of disaster for Ignacio and the country alike. The narration states:

> No sooner had she settled back on her matrimonial bed than Mamá spotted the shadow on the far wall. Straight ahead, standing guard between the open shutters of the bedroom window was a siguapa stygian owl. My mother did not know its official name then only that it was a bird of ill omen, earless and black and unmistakable. It was doubly bad luck to see one during the day, since they were known to fly about late at night, stealing people's souls and striking them deaf [. . .]
>
> The owl alarmed Soledad, who grabbed an etched glass lamp and threw it at the owl, and it precipitated her labor. Soledad delivered a nine-pound baby boy. The owl watched the birthing of Ignacio, and remained still, waiting for the placenta to emerge, snatching it with its beak up from the floor, and flying out the window.
>
> Later, my mother learned that the bird had flown low over the President's parade with her placenta, scattering the crowd and raining birthing blood. Even President Palma, trembling with fear, crossed himself twice before jumping headlong into a flowering angel's-trumpet bush, his crisp linen suit spattered with Mamá's blood. (29)[16]

The Congressional elections proved to be a farce. Both the Republicans and the National Liberals attempted to win by *el copo*, which prevented the minority from any representation. By the time Ignacio had celebrated his first birthday, the aging and incompetent Estrada Palma, with the help of some 150,000 fraudulent votes, was reelected without opposition to the presidency on December 1, 1905.[17]

MAGIC I

There is a relationship between Ignacio's birth and the nation's destiny. In some ways his life represents the country's outcome or future. Ignacio was born on October 4, the day of Saint Francis of Assisi, who in Cuban Santería is known as Orula or Orúnmila. If Ignacio's birth is associated with tragedy, Orula's life begins in a similar manner. Orula, the son of Yemmu and Obatalá, at birth was taken away by his father and buried up to his waist next to a Ceiba tree. After his older son, Ogún, betrayed him by committing incest with his mother, Obatalá had vowed to kill all of his sons. Elegüá witnessed the burial, and told his mother Yemmu. She begged Elegüá to feed her son, who was also protected by the Iroko tree. Yemmu had another son, a charming black boy by the name of Changó, whom Obatalá liked and did not harm. Obatalá's daughter, Dadá, who after age four brought Changó to his father, raised him. From conversations with her, Changó learned to hate Ogún. He found out that Orula was still alive, and with permission from his father, Changó saved him; he grabbed Orula by the shoulders and unearthed him. Not knowing how he would make a living, Changó, owner of oracles, took a branch from the tree, made an oracle board, and gave it and the gift of divination to Orula, to help others. Orula's first words were of praise: "Maferefún Changó, maferefún Elegua, maferefún Obatalá, maferefún Olofi." From that moment, Orula became the god of divination.[18] With his actions, Ignacio will foretell the future of his country.

In Spanish, the bird of ill omen is called "un pájaro de mal *agüero*." Whether Ignacio is the origin of the bad omen that besets his family, the country, and the president, there is little doubt that from its infancy, the country will be struck with the same outcome that clouded the family of *The Sisters of Ill Omen*, as a retranslation of the novel's title suggests.

HURRICANES II

The Agüero Sisters is at the crossroads of Cuban history, culture, religion, and literature. Just as the Agüero family is plagued by tragedy, the Platt Amendment, the Machado dictatorship, and the most recent stage of the Cuban revolution handicapped the Cuban nation. Both family and island-nation will experience similar tragedies.

At the close of the chapter that contains the mentioned quotations about Ignacio's birth, Ignacio makes a startling revelation: "Years later,

I learned that Mamá had had a child out of wedlock long before I was born, a little girl named Olivia, who'd drowned when the Guamá River overflowed one rainy September: "I remember my mother was always saddest in September, and to this day it seems to me the bleakest of months" (33). September is the darkest month, because it refers to hurricane season, which claimed Olivia's life. In another chapter Ignacio clarifies that Olivia was born in 1890, and died four years later "when the Guamá River overflowed its banks" (154).

In *Hurricanes, Their Nature and History*, Ivan Tannehill tells us that from September 18 to 30, 1894, a strong hurricane passed through the Caribbean, affecting Haiti, Cuba, and Florida. The wind produced considerable damage in Cuba, and the rivers overflowed.[19] However, Olivia's death also may have occurred one year after, on September 30, 1895, when another hurricane reached the island, producing floods in the provinces of Havana and Pinar del Río, where the Guamá River is located, causing great loss of life. That Soledad had Olivia many years before Ignacio was born places this part of the family history at the start of the Spanish-Cuban-American War, and refers to the death of Olivia, foretelling the outcome of the Cuban uprising, and the Cuban nation. The name Olivia may also allude to another ending; that of the present Cuban government, whose revolutionary soldiers gained distinction with their *olive* colored uniforms. In addition, Olivia's illegitimacy refers to the past and future, to its treatment in literature in Cirilo Villaverde's *Cecilia Valdés*, Cuba's national novel, and in García's narration of Ignacio's wife Blanca's extramarital affair, which resulted in Reina's birth. García's description inverts Villaverde's novel. If the Cuban master writer described the white Cándido Gamboa, who has extramarital relations with Cecilia's mulatto mother, the Latina writer narrates the relationship between Blanca and an unknown black or dark-skin mulatto. The white male exploitation of a *mulata* in the nineteenth century is avenged by a black's relationship with a light-skinned woman in the twentieth. However, there is another interpretation that we cannot overlook, one based on the women's movement in the Untied States, between the liberated "white" woman who defies the pressure of her culture and society and chooses a mulatto for her lover.

POLITICS III

As in *Dreaming in Cuban, The Agüero Sisters* unfolds in the present. The political tension between the U.S. and Cuban governments

continues to divide the Cuban family. Reina, whom we first meet atop
a telephone pole repairing high-voltage cables outside El Cobre, the
city of Cuba'a patron saint, symbolizes life in the revolution. Her
older sister Constancia, who has become an astute businesswoman
selling cosmetics and who achieves the American Dream, represents
life in the United States. One is dedicated to the cause of her society,
and the other lives a superficial life of topical creams and powders and
material goods. And if García's first novel described events on the
island up to the takeover of the Peruvian Embassy in May 1980, leading to the mass exodus of Cuban refugees through the port of Mariel,
the second one narrates the most recent stage in Cuba's ever-changing
culture and economy. The present action takes place ten years after, in
1990, when Castro announced the Special Period. This was the period
in which the Berlin Wall fell, and the Soviet Union ceased to be a
world power. In the present, Russia struggles to keep the country
together while moving precariously to a market economy.

If the Cuban past was bad, the present is even worse. Whereas the
Soviet Union subsidized Cuba's sugar industry, Russia requires pay-
ment in hard currency. The depressed sugar prices have forced the
Castro government to look elsewhere for another source of revenue.
Similar to the Batista dictatorship, Castro found a quick remedy for
Cuban problems in tourism, one of the country's natural resources.
This shift in the economy implied that all other sectors would be
sacrificed; those who work in tourism have become part of a new privileged class. Workers with access to tourist dollars are the *nouveaux
rich*; other workers have no alternative but to share the scarce resources
the government has made available to them. The realignment of
Cuban society has placed tourism and the dollar at the center of the
country's economy. Well-qualified professionals abandoned their jobs
to seek new ones, of lower prestige and less education, that pay in dollars and goods enjoyed by tourists, otherwise not found in state-run
stores. It is not difficult to see that with this societal shift, Cuba will
soon experience a management crisis, similar to the one that became
evident at the outset of the revolution, when middle and upper class
professionals abandoned the island.

During the present time of the narration, Reina's daughter, Dulce
Fuerte, in order to make ends meet, has turned to a new wave of prostitution. She and other women are not the typical professional prostitutes; rather they are students, professionals, housewives, mothers, or
daughters who need to survive. Dulce, whose father was one of the
leaders of the revolution, has turned her back on the government,

which came to power for the sake of her generation. She begins her section with the following commentary:

> Sex is the only thing they can't ration in Havana. It's the next-best currency after dollars, and much more democratic, if you ask me. The biggest problem is competition. Then policemen. Almost everyone I know my age, male or female, turns a trick once in a while . . .
>
> Despite what my mother suspects, I'm not a professional. I only buy what I *need*. I only buy what I *need*. Right now, I'm out here earning pocket money until my visa comes through for Spain. (51–52)

Dulce is only deluding herself, because she is always in need. Even when she leaves the country, she does not change her frame of mind. Dulce, one of two characters privileged with the first-person narration, represents the present-day Cuba as she prostitutes herself in order to go on with her life. Reina, for different reasons, feels liberated but cannot live without a man.

In spite of the political events that separate and define Reina and Constancia's lives, both women are tied to the past. The past exists in the present and the present in the past. The past is defined as the past of the family, and the sisters' attempt to come to terms with their parents' relationship. As I have mentioned, Blanca disappeared and returned to Ignacio with an illegitimate pregnancy. Years later, Ignacio shoots his wife and also commits suicide. These events, without a doubt, have led to each of the sisters' trauma. But all the children live with their parents' past. Ignacio is tied to the life of a Spanish father who traveled to Cuba and married Soledad, a woman ten years his senior and who had an illegitimate daughter, Olivia, who died. Constancia's son, Silvestre, also lives with his past. And just as his grandfather, Ignacio, killed his grandmother for betraying him, Silvestre does the same with his father.

All the children have been denied a parent. Soledad suffers a heart attack while Ignacio works in the Zapata Swamp; Blanca's mother was trampled by a stampede of pigs; Ignacio shoots Reina and Constancia's mother and later commits suicide; Reina never gets to know her biological father; Dulce's father drowns; Silvestre murders his father; and Heberto, Constancia's husband and Isabel's father, is killed as he and other exiles invade the island. If we continue to read the past as a manifestation of the present, the following question arises: Will the children of the revolution turn their backs on the same government that has provided for them?

SCIENCE I

Just as the novel refers to the past of the children, it also conveys another past. This one is not related to the past of the family, but to a natural time, prior to the island's development. The novel returns us to an earlier and more primitive time, to Cuba's Garden of Eden, as evident in Blanca and Ignacio's trips to document rare and extinct specimens that once roamed the Cuban countryside.

> As naturalists, Ignacio and Blanca Agüero had traversed Cuba with a breadth and depth few others achieved over considerably smaller territories. They knew intimately every cleft of the island's limestone mountains, every swell of its plains and pine forests, every twist of its rivers and underground caves. Together they had spent years cataloguing the splendor of Cuba's flora and fauna, and had decried with each passing season the decline and extinction of once populous species.
>
> The Agüeros often imagined what Cuba must have been like before the arrival of the Spaniards, whose dogs, cats, and rats multiplied prodigiously and ultimately wreaked havoc on the island's indigenous creatures. Long ago Cuba had been a naturalist's dream. Why, then, had so much been sacrificed to successive waves of settlers and spreading monotony of sugarcane fields? (4)

Although the narration opens on September 8, 1948, during the Carlos Prío administration, which like so many others was plagued with corruption, the description of Cuba's flora and fauna provide a different referent. The narration recalls Christopher Columbus, who in his *Diary* documented Cuba's natural beauty. But it also suggests Cirilo Villaverde's description of Vuelta Abajo in his *Excursión a Vuelta Abajo* in the province of Pinar del Río, a region also familiar to Ignacio, and in his *Cecilia Valdés*, which describes the countryside from a New York perspective, where the author completed his novel. García's depiction of the Zapata swamps evokes Colón, Villaverde, and Gómez de Avellaneda's descriptions of the lush vegetation of Cuba's countryside.[20] For García writing becomes a way of recovering a memorable, but lost past.

The natural past refers to Cuba's Garden of Eden, but also to Thomas Barbour's *A Naturalist in Cuba* (1945). In a lucid essay entitled "*En búsqueda del paraíso perdido: La historia natural como imaginación diaspórica en Cristina García*," Adriana Méndez Rodena shows that the carácter Dr. Samuel Forest is based on Barbour's life and works.[21] In fact and in fiction Barbour, a Biology professor at

Harvard, founder of the Botanical Gardens of the city of Cienfuegos, fostered collaboration between the United States and Cuba. In García's novel, Dr. Forest becomes Ignacio's mentor, and the professor's concern for Cuban ecology, as well as his examination and collection of species, are also reflected in the student's actions. Méndez further shows that if Barbour depends on his Cuban colleague Carlos de la Torre for his observations, and views the Cuban landscape through his eyes, the relationship is inverted as Forest instructs Ignacio, and repeats it between Ignacio and his student wife Blanca. Equally important, García reproduces Barbour's trips to Matanzas in search of bats, to one of Cuba's many caves to look for a rare shrimp species, and to seek out the world's smallest frog.

As an ornithologist, Ignacio travels throughout the countryside, but concentrates on the Zapata region, full of thick vegetation, isolated and untouched by modern society, where he finds rare "crab hawks, spotted rails, purple gallinules, even a peculiar local crocodile, unknown anywhere else in the world" (4). The Zapata Swamp, which opens and closes the narration, transports the reader to a paradisiacal past, but also embraces the infernal present. This was the same region in which the counterrevolutionary forces landed in April 1961, and initiated a failed uprising against Castro's newly formed government. It was not the rare birds that the Rebel and Militia armies caught, but the invading forces seeking shelter in the marshes. Moreover, the Zapata Swamp alludes to the Florida Everglades, a natural region also used by man for his means. In the present 1990, Heberto trains with other Cuban exiles for another failed invasion, thus once more closing this option as a solution to Cuba's problems. Cuba's problems are internal and they must be solved from within.

Although the novel's title speaks to the lives of two women divided by politics, the first-person narration is not used with either one of them; rather, it is employed with Ignacio and Dulce, who belong to different genders and generations. In *Dreaming in Cuban*, García only uses the first-person narrative voice with the children, thus giving them a voice that allows them to relate their experiences from their own perspective. In *The Agüero Sisters* the author denies Constancia's children, Silvestre and Isabel, a voice, but privileges Ignacio's story by allowing him to speak. This is of particular interest since the "Prologue," which situates the wife's murder on September 8, 1948, ends with the following lines: "Ignacio Agüero waited until nightfall, watched and waited until a lone red-tailed hawk soared above them in the sky. Then he carried his wife seventeen miles to the nearest village and began to tell his lies" (5). The ending of the novel repeats the same information, but from Ignacio's point of view. In some respects the novel is a search for the truth, which is provided by Ignacio's own words and perspective.

SCIENCE II

Ignacio's narration provides insights into the past. In the present, the past is recollected and read through Ignacio and Blanca's ornithological specimens, but also through pictures, a passport, and other assorted items that belong to the parents and are passed down to Reina. Constancia, who does not have access to these items, has little memory of her family and Cuba's past, preferring to live in the present and future. The novel, I believe, addresses how one represents the past in the present and how the present represents the past. The issue of representation is aptly addressed in Eugenio Donato's "The Museum's Furnace: Notes Toward a Contextual Reading of *Bouvard and Pécuchet*," where he studies Flaubert's characters and their understanding of the Library and Museum as representation.[22] He observes that the library is made up of pieces of works, without an origin, and does not make possible any mimetic or representational veracity of fiction, which would delude the reader into accepting its complete state. The library does not allow the possibility of obtaining a certain order, totality, or true representation.

Bouvard and Pécuchet abandon books as mediation and turn to science. The museum, which privileges archeology, geology, and history, also makes metaphysical assumptions about origin, representation, and symbolization. For example, the original archaeological artifacts are used to explain the meaning of a larger history. Like the Library, the Museum is expected to represent human history through selected artifacts. In so doing, it suppresses the heterogeneity of the object, and homogenizes the differences that exist among the artifacts. According to Donato, the fiction of the museum only works if we believe that a metonymic displacement can produce an understanding of totality and, therefore, of the world. For without that fiction, the Museum is reduced to "bric-a-brac." Donato explains:

> Flaubert's critique seems radical enough to question, by means of the Museum, the possibility of reaching any truth, essence, or origin through a representational mode. If the Museum as concept has at its origin the same metaphysical ambition that the Library has in other contexts, namely, to give an adequate ordered rational representation of reality, nevertheless its project is doomed from the start because

representation within the concept of the museum is intrinsically impossible. The museum can only display objects metonymically at least twice removed from that which they are originally supposed to represent or signify. The objects displayed as a series are of necessity only part of the totality to which they originally belonged. Spatially and temporally detached from their origin and function, they signify only by arbitrary and derived associations.[23]

In his critique of Foucault's *Les Mots et les choses*, Donato shows that a reliance on archeological metaphors does not solve the problem of linguistic representation. Botanical and zoological taxonomies did not originate in some space between words and nature in the Classical period, but in the eighteenth century, as part of the epistemology that would later be associated with archeology.[24]

SCIENCE III

Let us return to *The Agüero Sisters*. Ignacio is the author of *Cuba's Dying Birds*, the *Owls of Oriente*, and another book on the mating habits of tropical bats, and in 1933 was promoted to full professor of general science and biology. Just as the Museum collects artifacts and represents them metonymically, and, in accordance with Forest's instructions, Ignacio appears to do the same with the endangered species. Certainly, Cuba's flora and fauna have been altered and any semblance of the past can only be captured metonymically. After all, at the outset of the narration Blanca and Ignacio were in the Zapata Swamp "hunting ruddy ducks for a new museum collection in Boston" (3). Therefore, Ignacio and Blanca lived with the fiction that they were gaining access to a veridical representation of the Cuban past, which they attempted to reconstruct and reproduce through books and specimens. In fact, Ignacio had a sizable collection, which Reina will donate mostly to the Natural History Museum of Gibara, and the best of the lot to the Carlos de la Torre Collection in Holguín.

This archeological reading of the novel allows for another understanding of why Ignacio may have killed his wife, who left him for another man. It is possible to conclude that Ignacio murdered his wife out of revenge. She betrayed him, and returned pregnant with the soon-to-be born Reina. Though convincing, there is another interpretation that suggests that the shooting was an accident. The narration clarifies this reading of the novel: "*On cloudless days like this*, the light in the Zapata was so fierce that even the most experienced travelers were deceived, made to consider all manners of ruinous delusions.

The swamp was known to exert a hypnotic effect on ambition, that all-welcoming peril" (emphasis in the original; 4). Thus, when Blanca spotted the bee hummingbird, no bigger than a wasp, Ignacio lost sight of the background where his wife stood.

There is still another explanation of Blanca's death, one that responds to Ignacio's professional interests. His desire to capture rare birds is a way of preserving them before they become extinct and lose what makes them special. Like the birds, Blanca is an exceptional individual. The narration describes her as being unusually beautiful; and her actions, including her betrayal, made her even more attractive to Ignacio. According to this interpretation, when Ignacio raised his gun to shoot the bee hummingbird, he moved the shotgun and focused on a more rare and soon-to-be extinct creature, his wife. The narration makes allusions to her as an extinct bird. For example, in the chapter "The World's Smallest Frog," which describes Ignacio and Blanca's meeting, Ignacio is struck by her delicate beauty and compares her to a bird: "Blanca was slight, as delicately boned as certain birds, and she had a cascade of blue-black hair that fell past her shoulders" (183). In the chapter "Owls of Orient," which explains Blanca's return to Ignacio, and highlights her transformation, Ignacio states "Blanquita was dying like the rarest of birds" (266). And when Blanca throws Ignacio a party, the scene is described as a forewarning of what would take place later in the Zapata Swamp:

On the night of the party, Blanca transformed herself into a dazzling bird. She wore a filmy pink bodice, a long swirling skirt, and a diadem of artificial jewels. Reinita was outfitted in a dragonfly costume that Blanca had sewn together from crepe de chine scarves. And I, rather too sensibly, dressed up as if for one of my expeditions, complete with rubber boots, a flashlight, and my fine-mesh net. (267)

If we were to superimpose this event on what follows in the swamp, Ignacio's shift from the bee hummingbird to Blanca is a way of metaphorically preserving and understanding his wife, and saving his stepdaughter.

The last chapter of the novel confirms my interpretation, that Blanca was an exceptional individual, indeed the rarest of birds. And like his birds, Ignacio also wanted to preserve her. The novel ends with a letter Ignacio writes, in which he describes the death of his wife. He recapitulates: "I do not recall taking aim, only the fierce recklessness of my desire, the press of the twelve-gauge shotgun against my shoulder, the invitation from the bird itself. I moved my sight from

the hummingbird to Blanca, as if pulled by a necessity of nature"
(299). The closing words of the novel suggest that this was a habitual
act when Ignacio saw a rare bird. The grammatical construction establishes an equivalency between the hummingbird and Blanca. They
both have equal value. And as with his cataloguing of rare birds,
Ignacio needed to preserve his wife, before she and her surroundings
continued to change. Not having the cameras and recording devices
used by young naturalists during Ignacio's days: "One simply had to
kill a creature to fully understand it" (150).

If Ignacio is trying to understand and perhaps recover the Cuban
past metonymically, Reina attempts to do the same thing, but twice
removed. She has inherited her stepfather's collection of specimens,
books, and other artifacts, which she believes provide insight into an
uncertain past. Reina surrounds herself with them, and makes an effort
to reconstruct what her life was or would have been with her mother
and stepfather. However, she does not know her exact origin; she met
her biological father once, but knows nothing about him or her parent's relation. Her real past has been denied to her. The metonymic
relationship Reina has with her stepfather's artifacts becomes even
more distant when she decides to abandon the island, leaving all the
artifacts behind. Her only access to the past is what she remembers
about them.

Reina, armed with her memories in the United States, confronts
Constancia about their parents' past, which the older Agüero prefers
to forget, believing her father's story that their mother had committed suicide. After she learns of Heberto's failed attempt to overthrow
the Castro government, Constancia makes a trip to Cuba to recover
his body and her father's letters, artifacts left of the past. Like a trea-
sure hunter or an archaeologist, Constancia looks for and finds the
box her uncle had buried. She digs and retrieves the artifacts, and
gains some insight into the past. She reads her father's letter and
understands that he unintentionally shot his wife. Although this is a
startling revelation, which confirms what Reina had told her, neither
she nor Reina or the reader knows why Ignacio murdered Blanca.
Access to this information has been lost and the reason for her death
will never be resolved.

Science IV

Bouvard and Pécuchet, Donato tells us, failed in their pursuits because
they were epistemologically flawed. Although Flaubert's characters
are exposed to fire and heat, they are incapable of understanding the

laws of thermodynamics, which ushered a new concept of time and history, subverting that of the Museum and archeology. According to the second principle of thermodynamics, energy moves from a differentiated state to an undifferentiated one. From the perspective of thermodynamics, the metaphors of history abolish all differences. García seems to be aware of this. After their parents' deaths, and the sister's departure from Cuba, the Agüero sisters have only a few artifacts that provide any insight into the past. Reina's case is even more dramatic. Her mother has died and she will never know the past of her biological father. And as we have seen with the final letter, it only reveals what happened, and not the reason behind the action. Without any context for the artifacts, the family past will fade and memory will become undifferentiated.

HURRICANES AND MAGIC I

There is a relationship between the Museum's furnace in *Bouvard and Pécuchet*, and the hurricanes in García's novel. Although my reference to the hurricanes at the outset of this study may have been seen as gratuitous, it is at the core of the novel. Let us remember that the novel starts with Blanca's murder, on September 8, 1948, during hurricane season. In that same year, the Caribbean saw ten tropical storms, and of these six attained hurricane strength. The eighth and ninth storms crossed over western Cuba in excess of 100 mph. The latter one caused damages of over six million dollars, with eleven dead, and three hundred injured.[25] I should also point out that Ignacio's father, Reinaldo, dies in the month of September; and Ignacio is born in October. And if we were to follow the present time of the narration, as outlined by the chapter months, the "Prologue" is dated September 8, 1948, the novel starts with "Acts of God: El Cobre, December 1990," and the last month mentioned is September, hurricane season.

If we were to read the novel with this time frame in place, the novel either ends in September, the last month mentioned, or in the final section, "Coda: A Root in the Dark," when Constancia travels to Cuba, perhaps in September or in the beginning of October. The novel favors September but also October. September is the ninth month of the year; nine is the same number of times García allows Ignacio to speak, the number of pounds Ignacio weighs, and the number of days Constancia has to burn the fifteen candles she offers to Ochún. The novel opens and closes with the actions that unfolded in the ninth month of September. Furthermore, Constancia is in Cuba during Silvestre's birthday, September 8, which also commemorates the day of Ochún, La Virgen de la Caridad del Cobre, Cuba's patron saint, the date that also opens the novel.

However, if we privilege Ignacio's discourse, then October, Ignacio's birth month, also becomes important. Let us remember that Ignacio is born on October 4, the day of Orula, the god of divination. October may also be the month he wrote his letter, which appears at the end of the narration. Therefore, September represents the month in which myths are created, and October is the act of writing. September, which begins and ends the novel, opens and closes a cycle; October starts another one. From the perspective of Santería, September and October, the only two month with corresponding days and years in the novel, are related: one refers to Oshún, and the other to Orula, who were also husband and wife. If we were to insist on an Afro-Cuban reading of the novel, Oshún and Changó, who in the Catholic religion is Saint Bárbara, fall in love with each other, and their union produces the birth of the sacred twins, the Ibeyis.[26]

Reina's lineage and subsequent change or transformation is evident from the start of the novel. In the first chapter, "Acts of God," Reina's spiritual mother and father are already present during her change or transformation. At the outset we meet Reina working on high-voltage cables outside of El Cobre, the town that carries the name of La Virgen de la Caridad del Cobre to whom she pays homage. When Reina kneels before Our Lady of Mercy and says: "Bless me, *Virgen*, for I have sinned," (12) and offers her a wrench from her tool belt, she is not only praying to cure her insomnia but is also asking her spiritual mother for help. At the conclusion of that chapter, Reina performs her last assignment in El Cobre, to fix the electric water pump. It's raining and something goes amiss, and Reina finds herself riding the pump downhill, which stops before a mahogany tree. The accident almost kills Reina. "The impact rattles Reina's spine, breaks her nose and both thumbs, and loosens a back molar. A tangle of her hair is pulled out by the roots" (17).

The next chapter in which Reina appears, "Conditions of Survival," reveals more information about the accident and pertains to her father. When Reina wakes, she notices that her skin smelled like sweet smoke, and that lightning had saved her life: "Many thousands of bolts strike the earth daily, searing their fatal messages. Yet Reina cannot accept a rational explanation. What she knows is this: that she was singled out to die but, instead, has survived" (37). The story that follows, that Oyá, Changó's first wife, stole lighting from her husband, can be interpreted as a way of using Reina to get even with Changó. But in this story, lighting is used not to harm Reina but, like the mahogany tree with healing powers, to save her. In the story, Blanca abandons Ignacio for her mulatto lover, and later returns with her daughter Reina. The mulatto lover is Changó and Reina represents the Ibeyi twins. As the daughter of Changó and Oshún, Reina is the Ibeyis. Reina can be viewed as a twin of herself. She has two incarnations: one before the lighting that almost claimed her life and one after the skins of others were grafted onto her own; one in Cuba and the other in the United States. Reina's power is not only a manifestation of women who grew up in the revolution, but as an Ibeyi she is endowed with magical powers.[27]

Ortiz's study of hurricanes is also useful here. He tells us that other representations of hurricanes come from the Quiché pantheon, which imagined it as an anthropomorphic god with one leg. The one extremity may have represented the marine waterspout, a tornado over water. The hurricane also has a Yoruba designation, and can be associated with Osaín, god of the tempest, with one eye, one ear, one arm, one testicle, and one leg. In Santería, he is coupled with Eleguá, the god of the roads, represented as a spirit with only one leg. According to Ortiz, he inhabits the crossroads and plays with the winds.[28] But he is also associated with St. Francis. The knotted roped used by the Franciscan friars to secure their habits have been interpreted as a way of knotting (*amarrar*) people or spirits, just as one would knot the stomach of a pregnant woman so that she would not abort. Castilian sailors believed that bad weather resulted from St. Francis undoing the three knots from the spiraled rope that hung from his habit, thus releasing a tempest against sinners. The tradition of St. Francis of Hurricane passed on to the Congolese of Cuba, whom they called Tata Pancho Kimbúngila, made up of the words Father, Francisco, and whirlpool. As mentioned earlier, in Afro-Cuban syncretism St. Francis is Orula, the god of divination. When a babalao, an Afro-Cuban priest, finds himself in danger, he ties around his waist his ókpele, that is, a devise "to speak to St. Francis," which is the equivalent to the knots on the rope holding this holy saint's robe.[29] Since Ignacio was born the day of St. Francis, he also represents the hurricane, the force that destroys Blanca, and affects the course of Cuban history. Other sources point to Oyá as the destructive force. As a Catholic representation is Our Lady of Candelaria, St. Teresa of Avila, and Our Lady of Montserrat. Oyá is also the strong wind, the waterspout, who precedes Changó with the tempest as her skirt. Equally important, Oyá is the guardian of death and of the cemetery and her number is nine, thus suggesting Oshún, but let us not forget that this numeral also refers to Ignacio; it represents the month in which he kills Blanca.[30]

Hurricanes, Magic, and Science I

September and October are also in the middle of hurricane season; and they are the two months with the most hurricane activity. Like heat and the furnace in Donato's study of *Bouvard and Pécuchet*, the hurricane produces similar results. It destroys everything in its path, moving it from a differentiated to an undifferentiated state. Although Constancia takes the piece of bone for her sister, with time it too will lose meaning.

For the author and other Cubans or Latinos, whether immigrants or exiles, who have left their country of origin, or were born and raised in the United States, they travel to the adopted country with few belongings. Life back home can only be recovered metonymically. Like Reina and the specimens on the island, or Constancia and her father's letters, for the exile Cuban culture can only exist in fragments, without a context, and without representation, as a fiction, allowing for the creation of narratives. In the United States, Constancia has reduced José Martí's poem "Flor del destierro" to a brand of perfume with a citrus scent. Martí did in fact write a collection of poems, not "Flor del destierro" but *Flores del destierro*, published posthumously in 1933, which corresponds to the stage of *Versos libres* (1913), where he emphasized content over form. Like Constancia, for the author Martí's works have taken on a different meaning.

There is yet another movement toward un-differentiation that is also supported by the novel. If we were to apply the theory of thermodynamics to history and culture, it would lead to the abolishment of difference. Donato states:

> In contrast to Newtonian history, based upon points of presence, thermodynamics will substitute a notion of history based upon the metaphors of decay, decadence, corruption; in a word, a notion of history based upon any metaphor that can be read as abolishing difference.[31]

The science of thermodynamics but also the natural forces of hurricanes, tend to support an undifferentiating representational notion of history.

Conclusion I

The increasing numbers of Latinos, but also Hispanics, in the United States will force them to recreate their customs on the mainland, but this action inevitably distances them from their parents' culture, which also has been mitigated by time. Here I make a distinction between

Hispanics and Latinos, terms that gain significance, not in Spanish, but within a U.S. context. Hispanics are those born, raised, and educated in a Spanish-speaking country, and Latinos are those born, raised, or educated in the United States. Hispanics are closer to their language and country of origin, and Latinos attempt to negotiate the culture and language of their parents and those of the United States. U.S. culture and society will impact the traditions of Hispanics and Latinos. However, Hispanic and Latino cultures will also affect U.S. traditions. Each will develop and influence the other.

On the mainland, Cuban culture will become as real as or more real than the one back on the island, which continues to evolve according to the current political and economic circumstances. Let us remember that the magic of Santería is as important for Constancia on the mainland as it is for Ignacio on the island. And as we have seen, Santería is also a necessary backdrop for García when writing *The Agüero Sisters*. During this current stage of un-differentiation, U.S. and Hispanic histories and cultures will interact and affect each other. They will come together and produce a synthesis, which García's novel and Latino literature represent.

NOTES

I dedicate this chapter to Roberto Negrón.

1. Frank Kermode, *The Sense of an Ending: Studies in the Theory of Fiction* (New York: Oxford University Press, 1975).
2. See *The New Science of Giambattista Vico*, trans. Thomas Goddard Bergin and Max Harold Fisch (Ithaca, NY: Cornell University Press, 1984).
3. See, e.g., Samuel Flagg Bemis, *A Diplomatic History of the United States* (New York: Henry Holt and Company, 1936), 443.
4. Ivan Ray Tannehill, *Hurricanes, Their Nature and History* (1938, rpt.) (Princeton: Princeton University Press, 1956), 261–262. See also P. Simón Sarasola, S.J., *Los huracanes en Las Antillas* (Madrid: Imprenta Clásica Española, 1928), 244–245.
5. Fernando Ortiz, *El huracán: su mitología y sus símbolos* (México: Fondo de Cultura Económica, 1947), 50.
6. According to Hugh Thomas, the United States suffered 223 deaths, 1,243 wounded, and 79 missing in action. By comparison, the Spaniards counted 102 deaths and 552 wounded. See *Cuba: The Pursuit of Freedom* (New York: Harper & Row, 1971), 393.
7. Ibid., 394.
8. Bemis, *Diplomatic History*, 463–464. See also Thomas, *Cuba*, 406.
9. *Tannehill*, 261.
10. For an explanation of Hispanic and Latinos, see William Luis, *Dance Between Two Cultures: Latino Caribbean Literature Written in the*

United States (Nashville: Vanderbilt University Press, 1997), and chapter eight, "Post Meditation on Latino Race and Identity," in particular.

11. See, e.g., Luis, *Dance Between Two Cultures*; hereafter, "Dance."
12. Ibid., 214–234.
13. Domingo Sarmiento, *Recuerdos de Provincia* in *Obras XLIX* (1850 rpt. Buenos Aires: Imprenta y Litografía Mariano Moreno, 1896).
14. See Fernando Ortiz, *Cuban Counterpoint: Tobacco and Sugar*, trans. Harriet de Onís (New York: Knopf, 1947); and Bernardo Vega, *Memoirs of Bernardo Vega: A Contribution to the History of the Puerto Rican Community in New York*, ed. César Andreu Iglesias, trans. Juan Flores (New York: Monthly Review Press, 1984).
15. See my study of this figure and Bernardo Vega in *Dance Between Two Cultures*, 99–120.
16. Cristina García, *The Agüero Sisters* (New York: Alfred A. Knopf, 1997). All references to this novel will appear parenthetically in the text.
17. Thomas, *Cuba*, 473–474.
18. Jorge Castellanos and Isabel Castellanos, *Cultura afrocubana 3: Las religiones y las lenguas* (Miami: Ediciones Universal, 1992), 38–39.
19. Tannehill, *Hurricanes*, 225–226.
20. *Cecilia Valdés* (Havana: Letras Cubanas, 2001); *Excursión a Vuelta Abajo* (Havana: Editorial Letras Cubanas, 1981); and *Sab* (Madrid: Cátedra, 1997).
21. "En búsqueda del paraíso del paraiso perdido: La historia natural como imaginación diaspórica en Cristina García," *MLN* 116.2 (2001): 392–418.
22. Donato, "The Museum's Furnace: Notes toward a Contextual Reading of Bouvard and Pécuchet," in Josué Harrari (ed.), *Textual Strategies: Perspectives in Post-Structuralist Criticism* (Ithaca, NY: Cornell University Press, 1979), 213–238.
23. Ibid., 223–224.
24. Ibid., 226.
25. Tannehill, *Hurricanes*, 288–289.
26. Castellanos and Castellanos, *Cultura afrocubana*, 51.
27. Mercedes Cros Sandoval, *La religión afrocubana* (Madrid: Playor, S.A., 1975), 259.
28. Ortiz, *El huracán*, 436.
29. Ibid., 78–80.
30. Castellanos and Castellanos, *Cultura afrocubana*, 45–47.
31. Donato, "The Museum's Furnace," 236.

CHAPTER 7

Latin Americans and Latinos: Terms of Engagement

Román de la Campa

The 1990s witnessed increased attention in Latino studies from many different disciplines and ethnic groups, including larger number of specialists in Latin America. A certain eagerness to engage the topic became evident, as the Latin American studies center of gravity began to shift from area studies toward border and U.S. Latino issues. To fully grasp this turn in American academia, however, one must take a closer look at the Cold War paradigm of disciplinary order established during the 1960s, an epoch of massive government initiatives such as the Alliance for Progress that created the first set of large-scale opportunities for Latin American scholars to visit and ultimately reside in the United States as students and faculty, a sort of academic migratory pull fostered by granting agencies and foundations such as the Social Science Research Council, the American Council of Learned Societies, Ford, Rockefeller, and Tinker. In literary studies, this moment coincided with the new Latin American novel, the "boom" that brought worldwide prestige to Latin American letters for the first time, as well as the creation of new professional organizations such as the Latin American Studies Association, largely devoted to social science research at that moment.

Roughly speaking, this period generated an increasing demand for Latin American topics that could only be met with a broadening of the field's scope, and the inclusion of large numbers of visiting scholars and graduate students. Many of them came from the middle and upper classes of Latin America, though they often understood their own presence in the United States in the context of the geopolitical unevenness and inequality that marked the history of U.S.–Latin-American relations. These students and scholars could thus be understood, by and large, as privileged visitors who often harbored subaltern feelings. That complex and interesting contradictory position, however, did not necessarily imply an affinity to the human and social reality of Latinos, which remained distant if not foreign to them. When Latin Americans met Latinos on U.S. campuses during this period, the two barely recognized each other, as widely different national, racial, and linguistic ideologies stood in the way of their mutual intelligibility. This can be easily tested with even a cursory look at the initial Latin Americanist reception of Latino topics within academic disciplines and institutions. By the end of the Cold War, however, the divide between these two populations began to narrow somewhat, as Latin American studies moved from a primary embodiment of the "Latin other" in Anglo-America, to a position of shared, contested, or perhaps conflated spaces with Latinos and Latinas.

It could thus be reasonably argued that Latin American and Latino academic interests—or perhaps even destinies—inched closer to each other since the late 1980s. Moreover, this proximity continues to gain significance, if not impetus, as one gathers from Néstor García Canclini's latest book, *Latinoamericanos Buscando Lugar en este Siglo* (2003), which envisions Latinos as key players in Latin America's future.[1] This is not to deny the need for pertinent distinctions and boundaries on both sides of this growing nexus, but one can't fail but notice the search for shared grounds between the two fields, as evidenced in recent anthologies such as *Borderless Borders* (1998), *Mambo Montage* (2001), *Latinos: Remaking America, Critical Latin American and Latino Studies* (2003), *and Latino Cultural Citizenship* (2004).[2] In any event, it seems clear that the waning of the Cold War and its corresponding academic paradigm brought about a stage of unexpected encounters between Latino and Latin American peoples and topics, at times promising to chart new territory. Where it leads remains an open and difficult question equally prone to enticing new work as to readymade disciplinary answers.

It is widely known that the nation has always been an arresting point for American Latinos, a conflictive site claiming multiple territories, historical, mythical, or literary. An obsession with the nation left behind—by oneself or by one's forebears—surfaces time and again, even in writers and thinkers who otherwise feel their future only makes sense in the United States as traditionally understood. How else does one explain Richard Rodriguez's obsession with his father's Mexico in *Days of Obligation* (1992), which he thought he had left behind in *Hunger of*

Memory (1989) or, for that matter, how does one account for his current celebration of a mestizo America in *Brown* (2002), given his earlier loathing of racial and ethnic politics?[3] A different but perhaps analogous example of conflictive entanglements could be found in the sentimental logic spelled out in *Heaven's Door* (1999), by the Harvard economist George Borjas, who movingly recalls his arrival in the United States as a Cuban refugee in the early 1960s, even as his book calls for migratory policies that would basically ban future Latino refugees like him.[4]

In this transnational sphere, filled with differing claims, dreams, and ideas, Latino and Latin American motifs continuously imbue each other. Latina writers such as Julia Alvarez and Cristina Garcia, for example, probe the forgotten secrets of Caribbean history through voices residing in English and in the United States; and the work of Ana Castillo and Sandra Cisneros shows that retracing Mexican history in the United States always resides beyond national boundaries. Indeed, the voice of women figures prominently in the new cartography of the Americas. It therefore seems pertinent to ask how, when, and why the spheres of Latinos, Latin Americans, and Caribbean peoples converge and what significant patterns emerge or dissolve in such a rapidly widening nexus. In that context, certain books from the 1990s draw our attention, for they provide a survey of contradictory accommodations on matters of language, nation, culture, and gender that generally traverse the space of Latin Americans and Latinos. One such book would be Ilan Stavans's *The Hispanic Condition* (1995).[5] Stavans, a Mexican writer with strong Jewish cultural roots who first came to the United States as a theology student, now offers an outright embrace of Latino issues and themes, as he claims to understand them. In that pursuit, his book provides a telling index of the Latin American arrival in Latino studies; indeed, some might say Stavans has undertaken the task with a vengeance, as his continuous production on Latino topics since 1995 has now amassed dozens of titles.

The Hispanic Condition remains quite representative of the main tenets in Stavans's writing on Latinos, as evidenced in recent iterations such as *Spanglish* (2003). At its core one finds a Latino/a with a postmodern bent, a mixing of popular culture with literary history as conduit for a new, lighter style of academic work aimed at an undergraduate audience. Its main points could be summarized as a script for a triumphant new Latino subject organized around the following contours:

1. The American way now includes a sense of beat and style with deep roots in Latin America but Latin America itself can be left behind due to its endemic political and economic flaws.

2. Chicanos and Nuyoricans established themselves in the United States at an earlier, more difficult time, as evident in their culture and their literature of redress; that situation has now changed to one of celebration, with the arrival of so many other groups and the wider fusion of Latin American and Hispanic culture within the American fabric.

3. Spanish is here to stay, but only as a secondary language that doesn't represent a threat to the United States; all Latinos in time become English-dominant, but their real language may be Spanglish, since their Spanish leaves a trace that turns into an inter-lingual condition.

4. Spanish speakers who want to cultivate their mother tongue are to be commended, but Spanglish is fun, creative, and inevitable; it should be embraced and celebrated, much the way hip-hop commercials do.

These are obviously deeply contentious positions begging for further scrutiny, but one should first reckon with the deeply conflicted Latin American derivation of this author's Latino identity. Ilan Stavans describes his relationship to his native Mexico in equivocal, if not distant, terms. In a published letter to his son he speaks of having lived there in:

A self-imposed Jewish ghetto, an autistic island where gentiles existed and Hebraic symbols prevailed. Money and comfort, books, theater, and art. What made me Mexican? It's hard to know: language and the air I breathed perhaps . . . Surrounded by the Other, I, together with my family and friends, inhabited a self-sufficient island, with imaginary Borders build in an agreement between us and the outside world, completely uninvolved with things Mexican.[6]

One is led to conclude that Mexico never provided a sense of homeland for Stavans, and that his Jewish ethnicity may have found itself more isolated in a less-tolerant, Catholic nation such as Mexico than it is in the United States. Yet the new homeland he now fully embraces is not simply American, or even Jewish American, but American Latino, a construct built around language and literature that allows him to incorporate both his Yiddish and Latin American background within the privileged locus of English and the United States.

Stavans's Latino thus appears to closely follow a self-styled Yiddish experience layered with negative residues from his Mexican past, a life of culture in the Diaspora completely decoupled any idea of a return to a promised land; to this he adds a little Latin beat and a Spanglish tinge, all of it particularly available in the United States. One would have to assume, however, that such a model raises a number of important issues, particularly in the unexamined claims it makes for culture and language. First, it conjures a middle-class sense of belonging that takes for granted higher education and its corresponding high levels of consumption. One should also notice that the important weight of Anglo-American culture—including professional command of English—in such a life remains unacknowledged, except as an empty screen of economic opportunity. Second, Stavans's script turns Latin American culture into a set of readily translatable styles without any link to concrete communities and social experiences, except for post-modern media celebration or the light academic writing it inspires. One is thus left with a Latino model defined by a floating new American ethnicity that has been superimposed on a very conflictive, if not embittered, disposition toward Mexico, and Latin America by implication. In this construct, Latin America comprises a set of nations without a future, even if its culture and literature seems worth cherishing from afar, in English, Spanish, or even better, in Spanglish.

Stavans's notion of language also deserves attention, particularly in his more recent book *Spanglish*, where he attempts to translate the Spanish classic *Don Quijote de la Mancha* into an inter-lingual register he claims to command, one which, by implication, places a special focus on a reality shared by many if not most Latinos. But he fails to make crucial distinctions between those for whom Spanglish consti-tutes a form of play and those for whom it affords an important, if not primary, means of communication. Indeed, for someone in firm command of both Spanish and English whose real-life experiences with Spanglish generally occur in the classroom of an elite undergradu-ate college (Stavans teaches at Amherst), mixing these languages as a grammatical exercise amounts to a ludic enhancement of mainstream credentials, perhaps a way of empathizing with a few minority stu-dents on campus.[7] But when spoken as a primary means of communi-cation, *Spanglish* responds to more serious entanglements, particularly if it also comes with a shakier hold on Spanish, English, or both. The unmitigated celebration of difference thus runs the risk of failing to account for both the benefits and difficulties of inter-lingual compe-tence within a world of serious consequences, particularly those per-taining to socioeconomic conditions. All of this is left summarily unattended by *The Hispanic Condition*.[8]

The much-debated topic of national or cultural identity, often entwined in theoretical debates, demands a much closer look at the lives of American Latinos who now find themselves surrounded by waves of Latin American immigrants from different points of origin, in some cases searching for a new identity, as the case of Stavans indi-cates. Both groups must confront the advent of a globalized economy that feeds the constant lure of migration northward, as well as the network of Latin American economies dependant on hard-currency remittances from U.S. Latinos. But the history preceding this moment of proximity between Latinos and Latin Americans should not be neglected, given the initial disconnect between these two groups during the earlier phases of the Cold War, as well as the negative representation of Latinos in American media, in which *West Side Story* stands out as looming testimony from the 1960s. Many Latin Americans residing in the United States may have always understood such Latino casting as a stereotype, but perhaps they also suspected it would not be applicable to them as long as they aligned themselves with different national, class, and racial bearings, an assumption challenged as their stay in this country grew longer and as the American Latino label crossed their paths of cultural, ethnic, and linguistic differences.

This emerging but unexplored nexus among Latinos and Latin Americans constitutes the primary concern of Suzanne Oboler's *Ethnic Labels, Latino Lives* (1995), a book that simultaneously engages cultural studies, ethnic theory, and language policy issues, while also deploying data and ethnographic research.[9] *Ethnic Labels* also tells the story of a Latin American scholar who comes to the United States and discovers the growing Latino ethnic paradigm, to which the author responds with both personal alarm and intellectual intrigue. The book begins by probing how ethnicity is constructed in the United States, fully aware that this exercise, if it is to make sense to Latin Americans, must provide a contrast with the way race and ethnicity function in Latin America itself. That crucial realization brings the author to a much wider spatiotemporal terrain, because the imprint left by race on a culture always harks back in time, in this case for both continents. Oboler furnishes not policy recommendations or corrective measures but rather an uncompromising spotlight on the intractable issues underlying American Latino identity, drawn from her review of applied as well as theoretical research, together with interviews of twenty-two Latinos and Latin Americans—men and women—from nine different countries of origin and professional experience in both the United States and Latin America.

Taken together, these elements yield an intricate methodology that weaves in and out of key themes repeatedly, as if to show that only with multiple passes can one unveil the ways in which race, nation, and ethnicity unfold across the plane of different times and national domains. For the sake of discussion, I will organize her arguments around three interrelated sets: race and nation, the ethnicity paradigm, and the inter-American problematic. Latino ethnicity, argues Oboler, arises from the persistent conflation of race and nation, a way of thinking seldom examined cautiously, in spite of its long history in the United States. In this case, the author finds that Latin American or Hispanic nationalities are grafted onto the American black–white racial divide, leaving behind a unique, homogeneous conflation called Hispanics or Latinos that retains traces of the nations left behind. Latino ethnicity thus contains three elements that must be studied separately, even though they function as one:

1. A fusion of multiple national origins onto a homogeneous American ethnic category.
2. Racial undertones remain within that American concept of ethnicity, historically established as part of the manifest destiny of the United States and its hegemonic relationships south of the border.
3. Traces of Latin American modes of racialization also persist in Latino ethnicity due to historical and continuous patterns of Latin American back and forth migration.

In that light, both the American ethnic paradigm and the Latin American race/class modality must be taken into account. The former disguises inherent inadequacies as it applies to Latinos, a category enveloped in an underlying racial and geopolitical structure, and the latter masks its own mode of discrimination seldom analyzed by immigrants.

Indeed, after considering a growing body of scholarship on the matter, Oboler concludes that ethnic theory, by and large, defaults when it comes to mapping nonwhite populations. This might lead one to think that a subdivision of Latinos into white and nonwhite remains possible whereby the former assimilate as an ethnic group, and the latter converge as a racialized minority. Yet, as Oboler explains, at times with a sense of personal dismay, there may be no way for white Latin Americans in the United States to escape the trace of racial undertone established during the nineteenth century, for it was built into the structure of foreign relations between the United States and Latin America prior to its deployment toward Latino minority populations in the 1960s. Thus, when Latin Americans arrive here, they are given an ethnic label thoroughly racialized at two separate but interlinked moments, first during the nineteenth-century expansionist wars with the South and later through minority group formation in the twentieth.

Oboler methodically delves into these intractable problems of Latino ethnic formation, observing why for many Latinos, white and nonwhite, it leads to a feeling of ambivalence, if not an insistence on clinging to national designators. But she also examines the gaps within Latin American identity formation, particularly the commanding role of social class within its elaborate hierarchy of racial distinctions, which only accentuates the conflation experienced by Latin Americans on their arrival in the United States, as many find it difficult to discern between two competing sets of racial/ethnic structures. She cites the important example of the Mexican philosopher José Vasconcelos and his "cosmic race" notion, which seems to vindicate a form of *mestizaje* when viewed from the U.S. Latino racial divide, but which actually privileges the Latin American understanding of whitening. This often ignored problematic comes into full view through the interviews conducted by Oboler, which show how her subjects came to realize, after arrival in the United States, the extent to which their Latin American identity was a category they had never fully understood, thereby compounding their sense of ambivalence, if not loss, with one of discovery as well upon arrival at a new, albeit conflicted American ontology.

The author set out to probe the inner lining of the Latino label, particularly as it confronts the thoughts and feelings of Latin Americans who regard themselves as white, move to the United States, and are then confronted with an ethnic label that implies something other. Along the way, she (as well as her subjects) discovered implicit contradictions within Latin American racial categories, an outcome the author may have not quite foreseen. Through her sustained critique of racial and national conflation, Oboler ultimately reveals that for those who must choose among ethnic labels they do not quite approve or understand, the debate over what designator to use, *Latino* or *Hispanic*, most likely leads to a dead end. Moreover, she add that it can't be solved by latching on to the Latin American identity, either, given that adherence to national bearings will not detain the homogenizing process to which both Latinos and Latin Americans must submit in the United States, in many ways beyond their control. But it seems pertinent to suggest that this otherwise complex reflection on Latino ethnic labeling, and the racialization it implies, might have also considered the ways in which ethnicity has given earlier groups of Latinos a sense of being in the United States that was unavailable to them in their native lands. Oboler is not inclined to consider this angle of an otherwise thorough critique of the racial gaps and masks that history has left behind both sides of the North/South divide.

My brief journey through the Latin American reflection on Latinos during the 1990s will conclude with a look at the Latino reflection on this growing array of imbrications published in the new century: *Harvest of Empire* (2000) by Juan Gonzalez, *Latinos, Inc.* (2001) by Arlene Dávila, and *Living in Spanglish* (2002) by Ed Morales. These texts signal yet another turning point, for they bring the growing voice of New York Puerto Ricans to the intricacies of transnational Latino understanding.[10] As such, these books denote a new stage in which historical Latino scholars come into the field with fresh templates, eager to engage it as a broad intellectual project, not just as an extension of their given cultural group. Indeed, these authors display a distinct awareness of the large and consequential Mexican American presence among Latinos, often neglected by East Coast academia. Together with new Mexican American scholarship found in books such as *Latino Metropolis* (2000), by Victor Valle and Rodolfo Torres, and *Barrio-Logos: Space and Place in Urban Chicano Literature and Culture* (2000), by Raul Romero Villa, one can point to novel paths in Latino research in various academic disciplines such as history, media and popular culture, as well as literary studies.[11]

As grand narratives go, *Harvest of Empire* seems predictable. Gonzalez depicts the uneven relationship between the United States and Latin America as the matrix from which Latino identity originates, a history of American imperial ambition that he sees as currently embodied by global market pressures. This explains his choice of "roots," "branches," and "harvest" for chapter headings, arboreal metaphors that underline his emphasis on external causality, or imperialism, which at times borders on dependency theory, a 1970s-style approach to U.S. imperial history, in this case inspired by Eduardo Galeano's *Open Veins of Latin America* (Siglo XXI, 1973), a modality often privileged unguardedly by Latin American postcolonial theorists as well. Then again, *Harvest of Empire* has much to tell contemporary readers, for it could not have a more timely central concern: the interrogation of American values and priorities at this moment of globalized economies and unyielding migration, precisely the issues that concern Samuel Huntington, though leading to radically different conclusions and recommendations.

Gonzalez wants to take us past the point of ethnicity and internal solutions to Latinos, to focus instead on the hemispheric contexts and geopolitical ramifications that pertain to the topic. He is tired of what he calls "safari" approaches to Latino studies, by which he means authors unwilling to consider the inevitability of a new, yet common destiny for American Latinos, Latin America, and Americans at large.[12] A product of the global imaginary, *Harvest of Empire* opens the twenty-first century with a comprehensive Latino version of American history, both North and South, conveyed by a New York Puerto Rican, brought to the United States at the age of one, a former member of the Young Lords party, raised in *el barrio*, now an accomplished journalist who has honed his craft as writer and historian and has spent eight years on this book, amassing information, conducting hundreds of interviews, and shaping arguments through various intellectual models from both sides of the border. At heart, the book reveals a deep appreciation for American democracy and the fairness of its common people, as well as a suspicion toward an elite class historically known for its imperial ambition. The telltale moment of global capital, according to the author, has arrived; it will either shake or ratify the inherent split in the American character if an inclusive, historically sensitive agenda comes into play. The contrast with Huntington's *Who Are We?*[13] could not be more precise.

Gonzalez puts his faith on the side of fairness, and his hope for a future America is predicated on the following set of premises:

1. Latinos will compose a quarter of the nation's population by mid-century, and maybe half by the end, thus the need for Latinos to imagine the nation from the standpoint of partners, or as part of the majority, seems paramount. Latinos, like most other Americans, either don't know the history of Manifest Destiny, or they cannot break through the filters masking it.

2. Globalization deemphasizes national constructs, at times disenfranchising common folk, economically and culturally; for nations to survive, they must reconstitute themselves through new collective narratives; one likely scenario for the United States would be for it to reconstruct itself along inter-American lines, instead of Euro-American ones.

3. Such a scenario would benefit if the history of the Americas, and of changing U.S.-Latin American policy, were unveiled.

The contrast between Gonzalez and Stavans comes now into full view. The former, a historical Latino, wants to involve Latin America in a New American imaginary, the latter, a former Latin American, now a self-styled new Latino, aims to abandon all southern territories. Yet, one could also question the accuracy or predictability of many or all of Gonzalez's premises. For example, his diagnosis of American expansionist traditions fails to consider that the elite structure of Latin American ruling classes has played a key role in colonization. Indeed, he appears to conceive those nations as stable entities beyond the need for radical refashioning. Were he to engage the global imagination in that direction as well, his neo-Bolivarian dream would likely require a closer inspection of the internal causes of inequality that pertain to Latin America.

Nonetheless, *Harvest of Empire* convokes a set of issues and arguments that cannot be ignored in future thinking in the Americas, and most particularly in the United States, given this nation's centrality as both hemispheric power and headquarters for global markets and designs. Mapping America on this new canvas demands a new economy of imaginaries, that is, the capacity to envision oneself beyond the realm of sacred texts—whether historical, legal, or theological—in response to new media representations that continuously reshape the world. Gonzalez asks his readers if this radical simultaneity in space and time should not also change the stories we tell about the past. As such, his work ultimately challenges its own naiveté toward Latin America history as well.

No sphere of inquiry comes closer to the essence of globalization than the study of marketing. This is particularly so in the case of Latinos, for the growing trope of marketing offers a direct window onto the fanciful link between products and the self-image that must somehow confront the duplicities and conflicts attendant to this tangled label. In *Latinos, Inc.*, Arlene Dávila takes on this topic with a unique study of television advertising and with a wealth of information drawn from extensive ethnographic research on the industry, specifically examining the media creation of a pan-Latino identity. She discovers a process that, from the perspective of ethnic theorists, is rich in contrasts, for Latino media consistently rely on a homogeneous image of hispanicity that features Spanish language, whiteness, traditional family values, and spirituality, a set of characteristics in many ways closer to a Latin American or even Spanish stereotype than to the reality of historical Latinos she understands.

Davila's critique of the media construct of Latinos includes the following main points:

1. Media representations tend to make Latinos more invisible to mainstream America even as they create the illusion of greater visibility that comes with more advertising.
2. Such packaging promotes the idea of an exotic, foreign population of non-speakers of English and an identity ill-disposed to change, while the rest of the population is portrayed as dynamic and open to constantly changing stimuli.

3. This fixed, nostalgic image disregards long-established patterns of community survival by Latinos (particularly historical communities) in the United States, groups that in time became more independent of the cultural and linguistic models prevalent in the countries of origin. The emphasis on Spanish as the deepest foundation of pan-Latino values seems regressive to a U.S. Latino culture whose distinctive presence, indeed its difference, ought not to depend on the use of Spanish, and much less on the use of "proper" Spanish, or the racial types imposed by such imaging.

The pretense of one big, happy, Spanish-speaking family as the core of Latino identity finds a concentrated critique in Dávila's book. More specifically, she brings special attention to Spanish-language use as perhaps the most regressive practice, for she holds that "language is to Hispanics as race is to African Americans, that which over and above other indexes of difference marks them as outsiders within the dominant norms of the white and monolingual U.S. national community."[14]

It could be said, however, that this important critique fails to consider other aspects, for it has been shown that Spanish-language television in the United States presents challenges to mainstream media, which, as we know, conjures the image of one, big, happy, English-speaking American family, always able to absorb difference, whether in the news of the world or in the array of hyphenated cultures within the nation.[15] Indeed, English today constitutes what may be called the lingua franca of globalization. Thus, the question would be to what degree a Latino, English-speaking media could exist that is sufficiently independent of Anglo-American culture, or even whether a differently conceived Latino media could actually replace the one now nurtured by Latin American linguistic and racial preferences.

Dávila's highly suggestive critique also leads to other crucial questions and complications. One could ask, for example, if Latino television, even when tied to the medium of Spanish language, presents an unexpected threat to Latin America's cultural elite, given its role in setting national values. It could be argued that while pan-ethnic Latino images in the United States come about in Spanish, actual media programming—Sábado Gigante, Laura, and Cristina, for example— offer a popular culture manifestation that arguably departs from metropolitan values in Latin America. Undoubtedly, more research on the Latin American reception of such images could be instructive. Beyond that, Dávila's emphasis on the exclusive problem of language poses another crucial question. To the extent that advertising dollars respond to data in the purest sense—the pursuit of profit—the marketing of

Latinos in Spanish points toward the growing power of that "other" language in the United States, itself an important contradiction in a broader spectrum. She is right to point to the racial stereotypes implicit in Spanish-language casting of Latinos, but we know that advertisers only bet on a sure thing. Hence advertising in Spanish seems to bank, among other things, on a Latino audience willing to absorb many otherwise contradictory messages. It also seems to belie predictions of decreasing use of Spanish based on surveys of the English-dominant offspring of immigrants. Needless to say, Dávila has opened a line of research that requires much more debate; it also underlines the importance of an English-speaking, nonwhite definition of Latino culture, before it is totally masked by the dictates of high-stakes transnational television.

One could argue, nonetheless, that Hispanic and Latino culture must now be understood in terms of a plurality that comprises an extraordinary array of languages, including a role for Spanish difficult to ascertain and evaluate, as Dávila's and Stavans's contrastive positions on the matter indicate. Spanish now comes close to a second national language for Latinos and perhaps even Americans at large. On strict utilitarian grounds, Spanish as a second language has gained value as a means to gain employment in most urban centers in the United States and parts of Canada. It also seems clear that this incipient national bilingualism contributes to a global sense of Spanish in which Spain and Latin America have found an unexpected reentry of sorts, one that is not strictly defined by a sense of national empowerment but rather by the opportunities of investment in cultural and linguistic dissemination, a sort of transnational Spanish marketing, with its main theater of consumption in the Americas—including, importantly, the United States.[16]

Globalization does not entail an end of the nation, as many have augured, but rather a dispersal of its deepest moorings, hence the new language–culture equation enacted by media industries whose main products include manufacturing desire through television and computer technologies. This turn points to an intricate melding of citizenship and consumption, a new logic for molding the symbolic capital necessary to enter the middle class. It remains unclear, however, how discourses centered on language use, literature, immigration, and ethnicity—perhaps the core themes of Latino studies—will respond to this challenge. The space once known as "the street" now breaks into the fold with a new force and legitimacy; it is no longer just an intruder that overturns the high–low cultural divide. In that context, the place of the researcher, or intermediary, becomes irremediably more public and ultimately more anxious, because capitalism itself demands it. By way of example, and as conclusion to this essay, I will turn to the book *Living in Spanglish* by Ed Morales.

Morales brings us directly to the world of lived experience, where high and low cultures commingle, a world in which he has participated as journalist, as cultural theorist, and at times as a performance artist, for over fifteen years. His topics include music, dance, literature, art, and boxing. His narrative has historical aspirations, but it combines expository prose with moments of poetic rhapsody, such as his definition of Spanglish as that "catchy catapult for the imaginary proliferation of everything."[17] Though his story begins with the nineteenth century, it is largely focused on the twentieth, especially the era of movies, television, mass culture, mambo, big-band music, and later salsa, rap, and hip-hop.

Morales traces Latino contributions to that great—perhaps defining—century of American culture, with an eye trained to discern deep-seated connections that are often overlooked. He outlines, for example, how much the American cowboy culture depended on Mexican *vaquero* motifs and how the 1950s offered a prelude to the current Latino cultural boom that was delayed through the 1960s due to rock and roll and the civil rights struggles. His focus on the 1960s features a new reading of the West Coast Chicano influence on Latino music, particularly through its association with rock and alternative forms, a richness he finds necessary for mapping Latino cosmopolitanism. These musical connections are an awakening for him, as they will be for anyone accustomed to thinking that Latino hip-hop owes everything to East Coast Caribbean influence.

Spanglish, for Morales, doesn't simply pertain to a mixing of languages, cultures, or races, although all of these references form part of the American Latino cultural history. As he sees it, simply calling Latinos a brown race fails to complicate the white–black binary, a blurring he considers necessary and possible now, given the cultural presence of American Latinos and changes within global capitalism. "Spanglish," he asserts, doesn't refer exclusively to language hybridity because even if American society now surrounds us with slogans such as "Yo quiero Taco Bell" and "Hasta la vista, baby," these are "merely the iconographic residues of a society in transition, like rock and roll, Andy Warhol, or phone sex." For Morales, Spanglish is an ontological condition, "a perpetual state of flux," in which Latinos have special competence, as national subjects accustomed to doubt and as racial subjects who refuse the black–white American divide, "while at the same time having the capacity to be both." Alas, Spanglish amounts to an ultramodern state of being particularly inflected by musical form, the "endless pursuit of resolving contradictions in politics and art, a state of perpetual transition."

Like most contemporary authors of Latino books, Morales wants to save America, not on behalf of Anglos, Latinos, or Latin Americans, but by revising "the entire idea of being American" with a new aesthetic that fuses North and South, with Latinos in the role of cultural intermediaries and translators that they have performed for over a century. He sees that process as an infusion of Latino elements into an American pop culture that has been bogged down by its own market-driven formulas. Moreover he understands these elements to constitute a return to a more organic sense of culture, one that mitigates the damage done to human affect by the crass elements of global marketing. He thus invokes a utopian notion in which Latinos represent the solution to America's future, rather than the obstacle seen by Huntington. As he sees it, Latinos provide an antidote of cultural conservatism to an Anglo-American culture that has become too materialistic; yet Latino culture, he argues, also points toward the future, particularly through music, which absorbs the flows of marketing creatively, without contradiction. Morales seems totally convinced that Latinos can replenish and renew what it means to be American, thereby positing a direct opposition to Huntington, even if it arguably comes close to an analogous exaggeration.

I hasten to add, however, that of the books discussed in this essay, Morales addresses the question of race most directly. He argues it should be neither avoided nor essentialized; neither neutralized through ethnic labeling, nor turned into a mystique possessed by, or imposed on, a given phenotype. Instead, he insists on a cultural understanding of race as the most promising approach to the Latino experience, not because he ignores the racialist implications of *creole* and *mestizo* constructs, or Huntington's nostalgia for the Anglo-Saxon creed, but rather because he sees that the white–black racialist ideology has entered a cul-de-sac in global capitalism. He realizes that the two most resistant anchors of the American identity have been race and language, elements that consistently define the path to ethnic assimilation, but he also understands that new markets leave nothing untouched or unchanged, including a cultural identity based on racial and linguistic substrata. In that sense his Spanglish is quite distinct from the aseptic linguistic play of Stavans.

The American Latino conceived by Morales does not celebrate arrival to the United States as an end in itself, nor does it glorify identity as a proud and stable brown synthesis, but rather as a careful calibration of the politics of culture in the shadows of capital, a logic that imposes continuous transformations on all national bearings. His concept of Latinos/as is thus largely imbued by a deep understanding of contemporary music, the necessary counterpoint of a nimble subjectivity whose history reveals pragmatic as well as creative accommodation between otherwise intractable political and cultural entanglements. The future conjured by that utopia, one gathers, will hopefully lead to an enriching meeting of cultures in which racial differences and monoligual rule will play a much less prominent role. How that leaves the terrain shared by Latinos and Latin Americans remains to be seen, but it is safe to assume that there are no safe assumptions on this question other than the need to tread it with as much rigor and sensitivity as one can summon.

Notes

Research for this essay was conducted with a grant from the Tomas Rivera Policy Institute.

1. Nestor García Canclini, *Latinoamericanos Buscando Lugar en este Siglo* (Buenos Aires: Paidos, 2003).
2. Frank Bonilla, Edwin Meléndez, Rebecca Morales, and María de los Angeles Torres, eds., *Borderless Borders* (Philadelphia: Temple University Press, 1998); Agustín Laó-Montes and Arlene Dávila, eds., *Mambo Montage* (New York: Columbia University Press, 2001); Juan Poblete, ed., *Latinos: Remaking America, Critical Latin American and Latino Studies* (Minneapolis: Minnesota UP, 2003); William V. Flores and Rina Benmayor, eds., *Latino Cultural Citizenship* (Boston: Beacon Press, 2004).
3. Richard Rodriguez, *Days of Obligation* (New York: Viking, 1992); *Hunger of Memory* (New York: Bantam, 1989); *Brown* (New York: Viking, 2002).
4. Borjas defines an index of skills in which only educated and skilled immigrants would be allowed in the future. George J. Borjas, *Heaven's Door* (Princeton: Princeton UP, 1999), preface.
5. Illan Stavans, *The Hispanic Condition* (New York: HarperCollins, 1995), 195; hereafter cited as "HC." Also see his *Ilan Spanglish* (New York: HarperCollins, 2003). Hereinafter cited as "S."
6. *HC*, 202.
7. Stavans has established himself as a writer in both English and Spanish. Moreover, he teaches at prestigious Amherst College, an undergraduate institution in Massachusetts.
8. Language is one of those topics that can be approached from many different fields, albeit with varying levels of specificity. It therefore seems important to consult the work of linguists. A fresh perspective can be found in Giorgio Perissinoto, "Linguistic Constraints, Programmatic

Fi, and Political Correctness: The Case of Spanish in the United States," in *Critical Latin American and Latino Studies* (Minneapolis: Minnesota UP, 2003), 171–190.

9. Suzanne Oboler, *Ethnic Labels, Latino Lives* (Minneapolis: Minnesota UP, 1995). Vasconcelos quote.

10. Victor Valle and Rodolfo Torres, *Latino Metropolis* (Minneapolis: U. of Minnesota P, 2000); Raul Romero Villa, *Barrio-Logos: Space and Place in Urban Chicano Literature and Culture* (Austin: University of Texas Press, 2000).

11. See also the far reaching bi-coastal approach of Lisa Sánchez González's *Boricua Literature* (New York: NYU Press, 2001).

12. Ibid., xvii.

13. Huntington, *Who Are We?* (New York: Simon and Schuster 2004).

14. Arlene Dávila, *Latinos, Inc.* (Los Angeles: University of California Press, 2001), 187.

15. América Rodríguez, *Making Latino News: Race, Language, Class* (Sage, 1999). (New Delhi: Sage Publications, 1999).

16. Néstor García Canclini (op. cit) details how Spain has strategically invested in these key areas, while Latin American governments have failed to do so. *Latinoamericanos Buscando Lugar en este Siglo*, 20–48.

17. Ed Morales, *Living in Spanglish* (New York: St. Martin's Press 2002).

CHAPTER 8

"Inheriting" Exile: Cuban-American Writers in the Diaspora

Andrea O'Reilly Herrera

The notebook was jammed with yellowed newspaper clippings, an assortment of black-and-white photographs and thin translucent flowers someone had pressed between the pages that now crumbled at Lilly's touch. Knowing that Margarita never bothered with the contents of the drawers of her escritoire, Lilly had claimed the photographs and the green Morocco notebook—along with the leather compact—as her own, sensing that it connected her to a past her mother had . . . denied her—an image of the past, she thought, that had begun to inhabit her deepest dreams.

Re-examining the photographs one by one, Lilly tried to imagine the world beyond their serrated borders. She could not help but feel as though she were standing outside a closed door set within a stone wall she could not climb alone . . . Overturning the photos like a deck of tarot cards, Lilly searched in vain for some clue, some hidden message. Given that her mother had taken a vow of silence about her past, she herself would be forced to fill in the blanks and the voids with her own imagination.

Lilly perched herself on the edge of the bed, trying to make sense of the mosaic of dreams that spliced together the photographs in the green notebook with inexplicable fragments of her unconscious life . . . Rising with restless agitation, she opened the drawer of the nightstand in search of the tooled leather compact she had discovered alongside the notebook. With great effort she undid the S-shaped hook that fastened it shut, for the clasp had rusted into place. One side was lined with creased blue velvet and a mirror was on the other. At first she saw only her own reflection, but as she tilted the mirror from side to side, a pair of eyes that were not her own suddenly gazed out at her—then the bridge of a nose and the curve of a mouth came into view. Lilly drew the glass toward her to get a closer view, but the face vanished like a ghost. Startled at the sight of the unblinking green eyes that gazed at her in the mirror, she dropped the compact on the floor—nearly breaking it in two—and then she began laughing at herself when she realized that they had been her own eyes staring back at her from the surface of the glass. For an instant, she hadn't recognized her own image.

Standing at the window in order to get a better look at the woman in the glass, she held the open compact up to the light, moving it back and forth until the ghostly image in the mirror came clearly into view. A stern-looking woman in a wide-brimmed hat stared out at her. She was sitting stiffly in a tall wicker peacock chair that was placed between tall potted plants. One of her arms encircled the waist of a little girl with long corkscrew curls—in the other she cradled an infant. Lilly guessed by the obvious age of the daguerreotype that she was probably her great-grandmother.

Cocking the compact sidewise, Lilly saw her own reflection once again. This time only one of her eyes and the corner of her mouth were visible. As she turned it length-wise, both of her eyes came into view outlined by dark tiaras of eyelashes and thick brows shaped into arches that joined together like the wings of a bird at the bridge of her nose. Lilly began to move the mirror around in small circles, watching all the while as her arched brows, pale green eyes, fleshy pink lips, cheekbones, pearl earrings, and wave of black hair flashed across the surface of the glass. Then gradually she began to move the glass around faster . . . and faster . . . until her features blurred and blended into indistinct shapes. Growing tired of the game, she held the mirror at arm's length until the living puzzle was pieced back together again.

—from *The Pearl of the Antilles* by
Andrea O'Reilly Herrera

Public dissent in Cuba—over ideological differences or as a result of disintegrating economic and social conditions—has been witnessed on a large scale by the exodus that followed in the wake of the 1959 revolution. Since that time, more than one-tenth of Cuba's present-day population has migrated to the United States alone.[1] Although the exodus is ongoing, historians have tended to divide the Cuban Diaspora into several distinct periods. The initial wave occurred between January 1, 1959, and October 22, 1962, when all air traffic between Cuba and the United States ceased as a result of the Missile

Crisis. As historian María Cristina García notes, this first wave brought approximately 248,070 Cubans to the United States including some 14,000 children who were sent off the island unescorted as part of an initiative called Operation Peter Pan.[2] Despite the cessation of air traffic in 1962, some 56,000 Cubans migrated to the United States via third countries such as Mexico, Venezuela, and Spain from October 1962 to September 1965. As García points out, the postrevolutionary migration out of Cuba followed a logical socioeconomic progression. Cubans of the elite classes were the first to leave, followed by members of the professional middle class. By the end of 1960, close to 40,000 Cubans arrived in the United States and their numbers increased by one-thousand–fifteen-hundred per week. Wishing to export even more dissenters, on September 28, 1965, Fidel Castro announced that Cubans with relatives in the United States who wished to leave would be permitted to do so. In a "memorandum of understanding" between the two countries, the United States agreed to send chartered planes to Varadero twice each day. The "freedom flights" continued until April, 1966, when the Castro government suspended emigration to the United States. By this date, 3,048 flights had carried 297,318 refugees to the United States.

By 1974, the Cuban Refugee Program had resettled 299,326 of the 461,373 Cubans; in April, 1980, following the storming of the Peruvian Embassy, the Castro government allowed Cubans to emigrate out of the port of Mariel. The Mariel boatlift brought 124,776 Cubans to the United States from April to October of 1980. The most recent wave of post-Castro Cuban migration was the *balsero* or rafter crisis, which occurred during the last two weeks of August 1994; the U.S. Coast Guard rescued an average of 1,500 balseros each day.[3]

Though I consciously wish to avoid the notion that the Cuban case is exceptional, the post-1959 scattering is distinct from other diasporic experiences in regard to a series of combined factors such as its volume and longevity; the idea that the majority of exiles left the island—either voluntarily or forcibly—under varying degrees of duress and, therefore, cannot or will not return; and the fact that the largest sector of the exile population resides in South Florida in close geographical proximity to the homeland. It is this particular historical and political context out of which Cuban-American diasporic writing emerges. And thus, whereas the key contemporary historical developments that serve as the foundation for Chicana/o, Puerto Rican, and Dominican-American literature are rooted, in the case of the former, in the civil rights struggle, and in the latter two groups in a colonial and/or neo-colonial context, ideological divisions and post-1959 migration, as Claudia Sadowski-Smith points out, continue to assume a central role in the identity formation of multiple generations of U.S. Cubans and, in turn, in Cuban-American literary production.[4]

The Cuban diasporic population is now witnessing the birth of a fourth generation of what I refer to as Cub*ands* outside the Island;[5] it is the ongoing nature of this scattering, with specific reference to its cultural expressions, that I wish to focus upon particularly in this essay. This single aspect of the Diaspora calls for a more nuanced theoretical approach to exploring the complex relationships among diasporic Cubans and their offspring; examining the manner in which the various generations have adapted to and transformed their receiving cultures and preserved their ethnic identity; and analyzing the various multigenerational manifestations of Cuban cultural expression outside the island.

THE POLITICS OF EXCLUSION

Due in part to a politics of exclusion that is determined according to a sociopolitical hierarchy is based upon historical longevity and degree of economic, social, and institutional oppression, Cuban-American literature written in or translated into English still tends to be largely overlooked in current mainstream Latina/o literary criticism in the United States and consequently abroad, and understudied in Ethnic Studies and English departments. Unbeknownst to many, a pattern of Cuban migration, especially to the United States, was established over centuries; a more significant and diverse migration occurred, however, after the 1860s as a result of the Cuban independence movement.[6] Although Cubans possess a long history of exile in the United States, which includes members of the various communities established primarily in New York, Tampa, and Ybor City during the decades preceding the war for independence from Spain,[7] the relatively new presence in the United States of significant numbers of Cuban refugees and/or exiles[8] following the 1959 revolution, coupled with the preferential treatment they received (and in some cases continue to receive) upon their arrival as a result of the Cold War,[9] and their comparative economic success disqualifies Cuban exiles and Cuban diasporic literature in the view of some scholars from serious or extensive consideration. Nevertheless, gradually increasing attention has been given to Cuban-American writers by non-Cuban academics as witnessed by this volume as well as others.[10]

Generally speaking, first-generation Cuban-American writers are loosely divided into two broad categories: Cuban-American ethnic writers, a group that generally consists of the 1.5 or one-and-a-half generation (those who arrived in the United States as adolescents and are situated between their Cuban-born parents and their American-born children);[11] and American Raised Cubans or ARCs (those who were born on the island, but left during infancy or early childhood).[12] For the most part their claim to cultural and ethnic authenticity and authority within the Diaspora is territorial and based upon birthright.

In contrast to other U.S. Latina/o literatures, which according to Sadowski-Smith tend to emphasize colonialism and neo-colonial domination or economic immigration, the central tropes in contemporary first-generation Cuban-American writing are displacement and exile.[13] Writers such as Cristina Garcia (*Dreaming in Cuban*, 1992, *The Agüero Sisters*, 1997), Yvonne Lamazares (*The Sugar Island*, 2001), Margarita Engle (*Singing to Cuba*, 1993 and *Skywriting*, 1995), and J. Joaquín Fraxedas (*The Lonely Crossing of Juan Cabrera*, 1993) depict specific phases of contemporary life in postrevolutionary Cuba, and Pablo Medina's more recent fiction explores the possibility[14] of a return to a post-Castro Cuba (*The Return of Felix Nogara*, 2000) as well as the prospect of dying in exile with the unfulfilled hope of returning to the island (*The Cigar Roller*, 2005). Nevertheless, as Cuban-American literary critics Eliana Rivero and Isabel Alvarez Borland, among others, point out, the exigencies of transitioning from refugee or exile status to that of a U.S. ethnic or racial minority centrally informs the work of many contemporary first-generation Cuban-American writers. Broadly and variously treating the interconnected themes of assimilation, cultural continuity, and identity formation, authors such as Hilda Perera, Roberto Fernández, Virgil Súarez, Achy Obejas, and Elías Miguel Muñoz (as well as Garcia, Lamazares, Engle, and Fraxedas), examine the manner in which Cuban exiles coexist among themselves and define themselves both within and against dominant culture.[15]

When compared to one-and-a-half generation authors, those of us who number among the second- and even third-generation of Cuban Americans have widely divergent relations to the island. Though we represent a distinctly new wave in U.S. Cuban diasporic writing, our critical and creative work takes up many of the same fundamental themes as our predecessors. Representing vastly different perspectives and experiences, which are inflected by our own particular social locations (informed by categories such as race, class, religious and/or sexual orientation, geographical location, age, and gender), our work collectively expresses a second-hand sense of displacement,[16] and is centrally concerned with the themes of hybridism and transnational identity as well as cultural transmission, continuity, and transformation.

More fundamentally, it speaks to a phenomenon that Marianne Hirsch refers to as *post-memory*—the historical traumatic effects that persist in haunting us through generations, like phantom limbs, at both the unconscious and conscious levels.[17]

Though we cannot pretend to lay claim to any direct experience of exile itself, many second- and third-generation Cuban Americans (myself included) are acutely conscious of their unstable positioning in the larger diasporic community.[18] Despite our recognition that we are impressed in varying degrees with American mores and attitudes, our social consciousness and cultural identities are nevertheless primarily rooted in our shared Cuban heritage. In other words, we share what Carolina Hospital calls a consciousness of exile (*una consciencia de exilio*).

Although our received memory of Cuba has been conveyed erratically or unevenly among us, one of the factors that distinguish second- and third-generation Cuban Americans from one another is the manner in which we explain the Caribbean component of our identities. In her essay "Los hijos del exilio Cubano y su literatura" (The Children of the Cuban Exile and Their Literature), Hospital accounts for this Cuban sensibility as an acquired phenomenon—a strict product of socialization and acculturation, which results from the external influence of kinship networks or our extended communal associations. As Hospital puts it:

> Some people ask how it is possible that . . . individuals who are either raised or born outside of Cuba can have a consciousness of exile. The answer resides in their participation in an exile community that has strong ties with the Cuban situation . . . The works of these writers effect a search for forms, images and themes that permit them to grow in this new experience of being between two cultures. (113)[19]

Unlike Hospital, others articulate a more essentialist formulation of cultural identity and received memory by insisting that they have genetically "inherited" (as opposed to having been acculturated to model) a Cuban way of being in the world. According to this latter group, *cubanía* or Cubanness[20] depends upon the ability to apprehend an accepted body of knowledge that can only be accessed through intuition or a surviving consciousness. This approach is somewhat akin to the notion of cell memory—a concept that argues the body holds or spiritually records memories and experiences. According to many who adhere to this theory, an inherited memory of Cuban culture, exile, and displacement persists and is passed down through generations of diasporic Cubans; in the same vein, the long-term effects of traumatic rupture from family members, friends, and *patria* or nation have been ingrained not just in the history but in the character or nature of the Cuban people. For others, Cuba is a romantic, almost mythopoetic "idea" or space, a "lost paradise" simultaneously tied to and un-tethered from historical events or, for that matter, an actual physical place. In other words, *cubanía* is a state of mind; and Cuba is (to borrow Althusser's notion) a "'[s]pace without places, time without duration.'"[21]

Clearly we account for our Cuban "inheritance" in different ways, yet our relationship to our collective past and our cultural heritage as well as our future—our post-memory to borrow and recast Hirsch's term—is indelibly informed by this second-hand experience of loss and displacement as well as the attendant realities of transnationalism and globalization, and the consequent ambivalences and ambiguities of modernity. Many of those who inhabit this shifting, intermediary space, therefore, insist that they experience by association a profound and perpetual sense of cultural un-belonging, despite the fact that they were born or bred outside the island. They perceive themselves to be strangers in their own land searching for a cultural "home." The emphasis then is not so much on locating home, but on the fluid process of voyaging between identities and worlds; in other words, the journey is home. In this sense, we are also post-national.

Despite a pressing and growing presence, our critical and literary contributions to the ever-expanding canon of Cuban diasporic writing have gone largely unexplored. As a result, we belong to what I collec-tively refer to as the *lost generation*—lost because we virtually do not exist in the dominant intellectual and political discourses emanating from both the island and the Diaspora, let alone in discussions of con-temporary U.S. Latina/o writing.[22] Rather than analyzing the work of specific authors, the remaining portion of this essay is dedicated to formulating a more versatile critical approach to Cuban diasporic writ-ing, which operates both inside and outside the realm of history and geography; admits multigenerational cultural transmissions that reflect a kind of nouveau post-nationalist diasporic consciousness; and allows for the discrepant histories and discursive practices that collectively constitute this traveling nation that is Cuba.[23] In the process, my intention is not to create a false illusion of equivalences or obscure the multiple and various experiences that distinguish Cub*and* authors living outside the island. On the contrary, my proposed reformulation of Cuban diasporic identity, both in general and in regard to its liter-ary production, strives to maintain historical and cultural specificity and emphasize generational links that extend into the future at the same time that it de-emphasizes geographical points of origin or geopolitical boundaries.[24]

THE HIERARCHY OF AUTHENTICITY

Although members of the first generation such as Cristina Garcia have been taken to task on occasion for what some regard as their unclear political views or stereotypical and exaggerated portraits of Cubans and Cuban culture,[25] the focus on issues of identity formation in the writing of second-generation Cuban-American authors is frequently treated as inauthentic or characterized, as Claudia Sadowski-Smith puts it, as perpetuating preconceived notions and clichés about Cuba and/or U.S. Cuban culture.[26] The response to the work of Pulitzer Prize-winning author Oscar Hijuelos provides perhaps the best example as he has been snubbed consistently or denigrated by a host of literary critics, many of whom are prominent in Cuban-American critical circles.

Despite the fact that Hijuelos has attracted serious and extensive critical attention abroad as a Cuban-American writer, a number of U.S.-based scholars regard him as an American author who simply happens to have been born into a displaced Cuban family and who, therefore, exploits and capitalizes upon his ethnic roots or heritage. As Sadowski-Smith points out, critics such as Juan Bruce-Novoa suggest that in *The Mambo Kings Play Songs of Love*, Hijuelos taps into U.S. mainstream expectations drawn largely from sources such as the media and popular culture in order to put forth some picture of what is purportedly authentic Cuban culture.[27] Taking up a similar tack, Enrique Fernández claims that "Hijuelos's book smelled wrong, of other shores, certainly not Cuba's . . . Hijuelos's [characters act] like some generic 'ethnic' family seen through gringo eyes."[28] Gustavo Pérez Firmat, on the other hand, equates authenticity with language. In his view, *The Mambo Kings* "does not pledge allegiance to its Cuban roots, for it is very much a novel written away from Spanish and toward English." "In one sense," Pérez Firmat argues, "Spanish is everywhere in the text: in the place and character names, in the characters' hispanicized diction, and in the constant references to Cuban music. In another sense, however, Spanish is nowhere, for Hijuelos has rendered in English all of the characters' thoughts and words."[29]

In its search for unity and its rigid codification and formalization of what constitutes *real* or *genuine* Cuban cultural production, these particular exclusionary forms of critical practice ground themselves in what amounts to an essentialist, territorially and linguistically based concept of national and cultural identity. In the process they erect an authoritative hierarchy of authenticity that purportedly determines who *qualifies* as a true Cuban or Cuban diasporic writer and who does not. Although the impulse to exclude may ultimately signal the anxiety of displacement that occurs in response to what Homi Bhabha refers to as the irredeemably plural modern diasporic condition, this particular form of critical discourse is nevertheless tangentially linked to a specific and parallel strain of exilic self-fashioning, which clings to the notion of some unchanging point of origin, and insists on fixity and heterogeneity as a means of self-preservation and survival.[30]

Although any claim to an authentic Cuban cultural identity is in some measure essentialist and politicized, both within the larger ideological context of the warring post-1959 discourses emanating from the island and sectors of the diasporic population and in regard to U.S. identity politics, all such claims impose (as Stuart Hall phrases it) an *imaginary coherence* on the experience of dispersal and fragmentation that is diaspora as well as any correspondent notion of cultural or ethnic identity. Ultimately, all such approaches obscure the particularities and structural differences or social determinations that differentiate and distinguish the various sectors of a diasporic population that is spread across the globe.[31]

In order to speak to these distinctions and particularities, I am compelled to adopt in an eclectic fashion an idiom developed by scholars of postmodernism, postcolonialism, cultural studies, and transsexual studies. The divergent theoretical paradigms from which this language has sprung address fundamentally the notion that all social and cultural identities are simultaneously fluid and on a continuum, and they acknowledge the ambivalent and *chiasmatic* intersections of time and place that constitute the problematic "modern" experience of the nation.[32]

Not unlike postcolonial identities, diasporic identities have their own particularity in that they imply multiple and constantly shifting transnational subject positions. In the case of diasporic Cubans, these shifting positions can be best understood in the larger dual contexts of Cuban and Caribbean history, which are inherently informed by rupture, scattering or dispersal, displacement, and, ultimately, cultural transformation or re-inscription. By its very nature, any concept of diaspora, as Stuart Hall, James Clifford, and Homi Bhabha most notably have commented, "exceed[s] a binary structure of representation" and "denotes hybridity and heterogeneity."[33] The attendant notions of postcolonialism, transnationalism, and globalization inadvertently put into relief the conceptual limits and shortcomings of all nationalistic discursive paradigms and practices that conceive of the nation as a fixed entity. In an attempt to "displace the historicism that has dominated the nation as a cultural force," and expose the "profound limitations of a consensual and collusive enunciation of cultural community," Bhabha emphasizes the temporal, situational, linear, and ultimately allegorical nature of nationalist discourse. As "an apparatus of symbolic power," Bhabha observes, the "ambivalence of the 'nation' as a narrative strategy . . . produces a continual slippage of categories . . . What is displayed in this displacement is the nation as the liminality of cultural modernity." And thus, any given representation of the nation and the nation-space is at best the product of a temporal process. Nevertheless, the shadow of the nation inevitably falls fully upon the condition of exile.[34] A diasporic perspective thus demands that we take account of the profound limitations of any monolithic idea of community, nationhood, or national culture, and the adjacent manner in which this ossified and superannuated notion shapes and informs the exilic condition even as it is experienced through multiple generations.

Rather than locating national or cultural identity solely in linear historical events, a restrictive notion of geographical territory or locale, or a fixed or nativist idea of identity, postcolonial scholars such as Bhabha theorize from the "boundaries" of ideology and discourse, the borderlands of culture. In this manner they take into account the evolving and protean nature of diasporic identities and cultural productions as well as the crucial role that the collective memory and "the reconstructive imagination" *play*[35] (or stand to *play*) in perpetuating and reinscribing cultural identity not only in diaspora, but, in the case of Cuba, in a futurist, post-Castro future.[36] In spite of the fact that they invoke or *play* against the concept of nation, transnational diasporic identities as defined by Bhabha "replace" their claim to a "purity of origins with a poetics of relocation and reinscription," for they are located (at the same time that they are dis-located) in a "contingent 'in between' space," which is on a continuum with the past yet constantly interrupts the present and ultimately intimates the future.[37] In other words, as Bhabha argues, diasporic cultural identifications or differential identities are formulated in "an interstitial future that emerges in-between the claims of the past and the needs of the present."[38] They are dis-located in a present that is always negotiating between the past and the future. This "in-between" space thus becomes what Bhabha refers to as the perpetually contingent borderline condition in which cultural translation and production occurs. "The borderline work of culture," Bhabha writes,

> demands an encounter with "newness" that is not part of the continuum of the past and present. It creates a sense of the new as an insurgent act of cultural translation. Such art does not merely recall the past as social cause or aesthetic precedent; it renews the past, refiguring it as a contingent "in-between" space, that innovates and interrupts the performance of the present. The "past-present" becomes part of the necessity, not the nostalgia of, living.[39]

Diasporic identities and cultural expressions thus operate at the juncture point of an array of seemingly antithetical subject positions, social locations, and perspectives, and thereby play simultaneously on difference and similarity. In this sense, they put into relief the complexities that reside not only among themselves, but within all cultural identities and productions.[40]

When accessed from this in between space, diasporic transnational identities and cultural expressions depend on something in addition to, but not wholly apart from, actual historical events or physical spaces. Although multigenerational diasporic cultural consciousness in all of its various forms and manifestations hinges upon memory's relationship to history and geography, the distortions, transformations, and reliance on a recollected past that occur in the process of ReMembering outside of Cuba simultaneously unbind it from temporal categories, historical events, and physical space.[41] In this sense, diasporic identity as well as its cultural expressions reside in "mid-air" so to speak,[42] in the tenuous balance and the "conversion" that occurs at the axes of history, memory and imagination—a concept somewhat akin to Jan Assman's notion of mnemohistory.

Acknowledging the constant interplay between memory and history in the construction and perpetuation of cultural identity, Assman defines mnemohistory as:

> Reception theory applied to history. But "reception" is not to be understood . . . in the narrow sense of transmitting and receiving. The past is not simply "received" by the present. The present is "haunted" by the past and the past is modeled, invented, reinvented and reconstructed by the present.[43]

According to this approach history is "a collection of the most notable facts in the memory group." It "starts" only when tradition is threatened or "ends" and "the social memory is fading or breaking up." Collective memory is distinguished from a formal or more conventional approach to history in that it is "a current of continuous thought whose continuity is not at all artificial, for it retains from the past only what still lives or is capable of living in the consciousness of the group keeping memory alive."[44] Memory, on the other hand, is not simply "the storage of past 'facts,' but the ongoing work of re-constructive imagination. The past, therefore, cannot be stored but always has to be 'processed' or mediated." "If 'We Are What We Remember,'" Assmann observes,

> the truth of memory lies in the identity that it shapes. This truth is sub-ject to time [and erosion] so that it changes with every new identity and every new present. It lies in the story, not as it happened but as it lives on and unfolds in the collective memory.[45]

Cuban diasporic memory in all of its manifestations and transmis-sions is an amalgam of multiple and sometimes contradictory accounts regarding the lived, the recollected, and the "inherited" past. Although it may strike a precarious balance on the precipice of relativism, the concept of mnemohistory challenges, at the same time that it enter-tains, all versions of the past including those that are deemed official or authorized as well as those that are regarded as illegitimate, inau-thentic, or unauthorized. Mnemohistory "surveys the story-lines of tradition, the webs of intertextuality, the diachronic continuities and discontinuities of reading the past. [It] is not the opposite of history, but rather one of its branches or sub-disciplines."[46]

Adapting Assman's concept in order to apply it to Cuban diasporic identity in general and Cuban diasporic cultural expression in particu-lar puts into high relief the manner in which the multivalent past,[47] as well as the ongoing effects of historical trauma, is variously and some-times vicariously reconstituted in the diasporic psyche and consequently channeled across generations through a process of socialization and sto-rytelling. The idea of Cuba as transnation is thus constructed in terms of continuity (to borrow Benedict Anderson's notion and reiterate Bhabha's), movement, and dispersion, as opposed to mere physicality or some notion of linear temporality. Diasporic communities, or even sectors of these communities, and their cultural productions "are [therefore] not to be distinguished by their falsity or genuineness," but rather by the "style" and (I would add) the conditions and pur-poses or ends in and to which they are constructed.[48] The significance of a given memory or idea of the past and the transnation thus resides not so much in its "factuality" or "actuality," but in the role it plays in the collective memory, which, Anderson argues, "extends as far as the memory of the group composing it."[49]

ReMembering the Past

Most assuredly, mnemohistory as a concept and a critical practice has its problematic dimensions, among them the potential dangers of inscribing or preserving the self from a position that is not so much concerned with the "truth of memory," but rather with the manner in which the past is remembered. Overlaid with the patina of fiction, it becomes doubly troublesome. At the same time, one is always inadvertently and inevitably implicated in the very structures of discourse that are being challenged or reinscribed, for the desire to stake a claim within or against any hierarchical or hegemonic system risks its own kind of essentializing and, as Stuart Hall reminds us, necessarily "implicates the position from which we speak."[50] Assman's concept possesses nonetheless strategic and positive implications for a radically different approach to transnational diasporic identity and cultural production, especially in regard to the manner in which cultural memory is inherited or channeled through the generations. Rather than authenticating or ranking any given memory's or interpretation's place or role within the collective, and thereby determining which narratives (both fictional and nonfictional) ought to be validated or suppressed or which are more or less authentic, it provides a critical model that emphasizes continuity at the same time that it assumes that all identities—be they individual, communal, or national— are constructed in a state of backwash and flux amid changing sociopolitical and historical circumstances. In consequence, each account or interpretation of the past, each individual memory or memory group has its own intrinsic value, yet none can be read in a vacuum, for they always constitute a part of a larger dynamic—a larger, albeit unfinished or incomplete, whole that ultimately gives to the future beyond.

Although some may feel that such an approach presents a pluralist anarchy of seemingly discontinuous realities or alternative histories of the excluded, Assman's theory of mnemohistory allows for a radical and open-ended expansion of the concept of diasporic community, which acknowledges what Edward Said referred to as a contrapuntal modernity.[51] What his system fails to take fully into account is the manner in which the act of translation and transformation that occurs in all diasporic cultural expressions mandates an encounter with newness that juxtaposes and renders contemporaneous the ever-changing historical present with both the past and the future. To put this a bit differently, Assman's theory does not adequately consider the manner in which the diasporic present is "haunted" by the future just as it is haunted by the past.

Set within the larger context of a "Communist future" that has already become a post-utopian thing of the past (as Mikhail N. Epstein suggests in an analysis of contemporary Russia),[52] the Cuban diasporic present—in its Janus-like stance—posits its own kind of liminality and temporality[53] as it reaches backward with Proustian-like nostalgia to times past, and forward into the uncertain future or the realm of the "beyond" in an effort to ensure its continuity or survival in the face of historical obliteration. The narrative of diaspora thus strives to secure some semblance of stability and continuity at the same time that it is compelled to acknowledge transition and cultural or social transformation. In this sense, it partakes simultaneously in the past, present, and future.

In light of its contemporaneous nature, the diasporic experience and its culture expressions must, therefore, be understood in relation to both the past and to the beyond, for they exist in some dis-located fashion in a kind of third space on the borderlines of the "present." For Bhabha, the beyond;

> signifies spatial distance, marks progress, promises the future; but our intimations of exceeding the barrier or boundary—the very act of going beyond—are unknowable, unrepresentable, without a return to the "present" which, in the process of repetition, becomes disjunct and displaced [and, one might add, is always linked to the past]. The imaginary of spatial distance—to live somehow beyond the borders of our times—throws into relief the temporal, social differences that interrupt our collusive sense of cultural contemporaneity.[54]

"Being in the 'beyond,'" he continues:

> is to inhabit an intervening space . . . But to dwell "in the beyond" . . . is to be part of a revisionary time, a return to the present to redescribe our cultural contemporaneity; to reinscribe our human, historic commonality; to touch the future on the hither side.[55]

The boundaries and borderlines that apparently separate present, past, and future or the beyond are thus something other than "'that at which something stops,'" as Bhabha observes (drawing his inspiration from the work of Martin Heidegger); rather, they are "'that from which something begins its presencing.'"[56]

If one accepts Bhabha's notion, the dis-located space of the beyond accessed by diasporic artists and writers intervenes in a present that exists both inside and outside an historical continuum. The condition for cultural translation, transformation, and invention occurs in this extra-territorial and a-temporal third space. This space, in turn, is post-nationalist in that it extends beyond what Bhabha refers to as the paradigmatic colonial and postcolonial condition of being un-homed, for home is simultaneously here and elsewhere.[57] It is this un-homely space of intervention that renders asymmetrical the past, present, and future, the center, boundary, and frontier, at the same time that it disrupts and displaces the binary divisions of the here/*aquí* and there/*allí*, the real and the false, the authentic or undiluted and the illegitimate or adulterated. This creative asymmetry and disruption allows for the possibility of presencing to which Bhabha and Heidegger allude, for all of these temporal categories and geo-political spheres are "mirrored" by an in-between spatiality and temporality that articulates fully the experience of fragmentation, liminality, inter-subjectivity, and the alternately antagonistic and propitious displacement that characterizes diasporic identity and its multiple expressions. As Bhabha puts it, this interstitial passage between fixed identifications, this encounter with newness that relies on indeterminacy, "opens up the possibility of a cultural hybridity that entertains difference without an assumed or imposed hierarchy."[58]

Although it is not its entire subject, the excerpt from my novel *The Pearl of the Antilles*[59] (which serves as the epigraph to this essay) speaks directly to the encounter with newness that occurs when the present confronts both the past and the future. On one level, this passage suggests the deep-rooted connection that those of us born into the diasporic community have—at both the conscious and unconscious levels—to the generations that have gone before us. Reflecting upon the fragmentation that can occur as a result of voyaging between cultures and geographical locales, it examines the *lost generation's* relationship to a physical place many claim to know in "a certain kind of way" (to borrow Antonio Benítez-Rojo's phrase)[60] despite the fact that we, for the most part, have little to no first-hand experience regarding life on the island and, on the other hand, reside in a culture dominated by a peculiar set of institutionalized race politics that more often than not fail to acknowledge in any complicated way, let alone accommodate, identities that are hybrid, multiethnic, and multiracial.

The fragmentation of the original (the nameless great-grandmother) and the replica (Lilly) is partly a result of the cultural and historical transmission and translation that has occurred in spite of the fact that Margarita—Lilly's Cuban mother—has consciously concealed or buried her past. Lilly nevertheless attempts to unearth her suppressed heritage and past, signified by the ghostly image of her great-grandmother as well as by her mother's and grandmother's green Morocco dream diary, which is written in Spanish—a language she literally cannot comprehend. Her discovery of the tooled leather compact emphasizes the conditionality and contingencies of her position. This particular moment in the novel also alludes to the inversions that occur as the unrepeatable past is repeated; in this sense the historical present is haunted by the past and signified through mimetic "repetition" or uncanny "mirroring." Lilly, like her great-grandmother, is thus caught in the ghostly time of repetition, the time of cultural displacement and disjunctive temporality. Because Lilly represents the future as much as she represents the past, her encounter with newness cannot be contained as this fragmentation suggests in the "mimesis of original and copy." Unable to translate or fully apprehend the inherited past, Lilly occupies, albeit unconsciously, the space of the "untranslatable."

For Lilly, Cuba remains untranslatable in its totality for it exists in her imagination between photographic frames. As a result of her effort to access and decode the unspoken and un-representable past, Lilly nevertheless acknowledges the manner in which this past intervenes in both the present and the future. Her attempt to interpret and translate her suppressed cultural heritage not only signals the complex positionality that is inherent to the heirs of the diasporic condition, but in her desire to be a writer, it suggests the artist's responsibility to acknowledge the unspoken and un-representable—the past that "haunts" both the historical present as well as the "beyond." Lilly's unconscious reckoning with her "inheritance," which manifests itself at another juncture in the novel in her dream of "returning" to the island with her mother, resides in the realm of the hither side. In her displacement of memory, she lives beyond the borders of time and experience.[61]

Conclusion

Loss and survival, "migration," "cleavage," and "in-betweenity" are inextricably interwoven into the story of Cuba and its various migrations dating back to the time of the first Spanish colonial intervention. This nomadic, migratory dimension of the island's history not only shares in the social and cultural imaginary of the Caribbean as a whole but, as Juan Flores suggests, in a larger Latino imaginary.[62] Clearly, the tendency or impulse to insist upon the sovereignty of geographical and cultural boundaries and thus guard them against the changeable future bespeaks the unresolved anxieties that underscore the diasporic condition. Nevertheless this shifting of critical focus and performative discourse heralds the ultimate survival of a culture that has been in transition perpetually, for the presencing that begins at the diasporic borders and boundaries prefigures the future possibility of suturing the wounds that currently divide so many Cub*ands* residing on and off the island.

It would be erroneous and misleading to reduce Cuban diasporic identity to a single notion or factor such as its a-temporality or instability (as Antonio Benítez-Rojo cautions in his discussion of the Caribbean). What I am calling for on the contrary is an alternative poetics of indeterminacy that allows for the creative possibility that resides in a-temporality and instability. Only then can we begin to forge a new vocabulary with which to speak of diasporic transnational identity and cultural expression—an idiom that establishes simultaneously a conception of the present in a continuous state of flux and interruption and acknowledges the critical existence of the poly-rhythmic elements to which Benítez-Rojo repeatedly refers in *The Repeating Island*—elements that somehow together constitute an ensemble. "Within this chaos of difference and repetitions, of combinations and permutations" in the Caribbean, Benítez-Rojo writes, "there are regular dynamics that co-exist."[63] Cuban diasporic space is simply a variation upon variations of the poly-rhythmic, for as I have suggested consistently throughout my critical and creative work, it connotes difference and repetition, transformation and continuity.

Approaching Cuban identity in general and all forms of Cuban cultural expression in particular from the vantage point of diaspora, and privileging instability over fixity not only speaks directly to rupture and traumatic displacement, but it also allows for a more complex continuation of Cuban culture both inside and outside the island. This open-ended spatiality and postponement of a fixed meaning acknowledges the shifting nature of Cuban cultural identity—with its long history of relocation and intermingling, its seams of continuity, and its recognition that *difference resides alongside continuity*. To borrow Bhabha's words once again, "[w]hen historical visibility has faded, when the present tense of testimony loses its power to arrest, then the displacements of memory and the indirections of art offer us the image of our psychic survival."[64] It is this displacement of memory, I would argue, that has not only allowed Cuban culture in all of its manifestations to persist over the centuries, but it is in some sense the key to its future survival.[65]

NOTES

1. For more information on this subject, see María Cristina García's essay "The Cuban Population of the United States: An Introduction," in Andrea O'Reilly Herrera (ed.), *Cuba: Idea of a Nation Displaced* (SUNY Press, 2007), and her critical work *Havana USA, Cuban Exiles and Cuban Americans in South Florida, 1959–1994* (Berkeley, CA: Berkeley University Press, 1996).

2. Operation Peter Pan was an initiative sponsored in large part by Father Bryan Walsh under the auspices of the Catholic Welfare Bureau beginning in December of 1960 and ending in October of 1962. For more information on this subject, see Yvonne Conde's critical work *Operation Pedro Pan: The Untold Exodus of 14,000 Cuban Children* (New York: Routledge, 1999); and Victor Triay's *Fleeing Cuba: Operation Pedro Pan and the Cuban Children's Program* (Gainesville, FL: University of Florida Press, 1998), as well as http://www.pedropan.org.

3. All facts and figures are drawn from García's "The Cuban Population of the United States: An Introduction," which appears in *Cuba: Idea of a Nation Displaced*.

4. See Claudia Sadowski-Smith's essay "'A Homeland Without a Home': Diaspora and Exile in Cuban-American Writing" in *Cuba: Idea of a Nation Displaced*.

5. Cub*ands* is an elastic and all-inclusive term I developed in order to simultaneously take account of the layered or sedimented presences that constitute Cuban cultural and national identity (such as Spain, Africa, Ireland, France, the United States, and the former Soviet Union, etc.) as well as allow room for the hybrid identities that are continuously transforming in an ever-changing diasporic context, which is at once global and transnational. See my introduction to *ReMembering Cuba: Legacy of a Diaspora* (Austin, TX: University of Texas Press, 2001), xxvii–xxx.

6. Following the conclusion of the Ten Years War, a cohort of separatists, as well as thousands who sought work outside Cuba as a result of the economic depression that occurred in the aftermath of the war, abandoned the island. Exiled separatists established themselves in various parts of the United States, Latin America, and Europe. The most prominent figure in this struggle was the renowned poet, journalist, and philosopher José Martí, who led the *Cuban Junta*, a separatist society in New York.

7. Exiled independence fighters who had participated in revolutionary activities from the 1860s and fought in Martí's army, and their descendents established two major exile settlements in the United States in the 1880s: Ybor City and West Tampa. Both of these communities became key centers for the independence movement. Cigar manufacturing formed the basis of these immigrant communities. For more on this

subject, see Susan Greenbaum and Linda Callejas's essay "'We All Lived Here Together': The Hidden Topic of Race in Tampa" in *Cuba: Idea of a Nation Displaced*.

8. At the outset of the revolution, Cuban immigrants were classified as political refugees. As it gradually became apparent that their stay in the United States could be permanent, their legal status shifted to exile.

9. According to María Cristina García, "[a] number of federally-funded vocational training programs targeted the working class. One program in particular entitled 'Aprenda y Superese,' or 'Training for Independence,' helped unskilled Cuban women become self-supporting. Women received intensive English-language instruction, as well as training in any of a number of skills: hand-sewing, sewing-machine work, office machine operation, clerical work, nursing, domestic service, and even silk-screen art work. Women were later resettled to cities where jobs were available for them. Aprenda y Supérese was so successful that it became a model for the amended 'Aid to Families with Dependent Children' (AFDC) program in 1968." See *U.S. Cuban Refugee Program, Training for Independence: A New Approach to the Problems of Dependency* (Washington, DC: Social and Rehabilitation Service, 1968). For more information, see *Havana USA* and "The Cuban Population of the United States: An Introduction" (in *Cuba:* Idea *of a Nation Displaced).*

10. See, e.g., Alvina Quintana's edited volume *Reading U.S. Latina Writers: Remapping American Literature* (NY: Palgrave Macmillan Press, 2003).

11. See Isabel Alvarez Borland's essay "Displacements and Autobiography in Cuban-American Fiction." *World Literature Today* 68:1 (1994): 43–48, and her discussion of first-generation Cuban-American writers in *Cuban-American Literature of Exile, From Person to Persona* (Charlottesville, VA: University of Virginia Press, 1998), 7.

12. See my discussion in the introduction of my edited collection *ReMembering Cuba*, xvii–xxxiii.

13. Sadowski-Smith, "'A Homeland Without a Home.'"

14. See Eliana Rivero, "From Immigrants to Ethnics: Cuban Women Writers in the U.S.," in Asunción Horno-Delgado, Eliana Ortega, Nina M. Scott, and Nancy Saporta Sternbach (eds.), *Breaking Boundaries: Latina Writing and Critical Readings* (Amherst, MA: University of Massachusetts Press, 1989), and Alvarez Borland's *Cuban-American Literature of Exile.*

15. See Alvarez Borland, *Cuban-American Literature of Exile*, 11. See also my essay "Women and the Revolution in Cristina Garcia's *Dreaming in Cuban." Modern Language Notes* 27:3, 4 (fall/winter 1997): 69–90.

16. See my testimonial expression "Una cubanita pasada por agua" in *ReMembering Cuba*, 317–20.

17. Marianne Hirsch, *Family Frames: Photography, Narrative, Post-Memory* (Cambridge, MA: Harvard University Press, 1997), 22.

18. For more on this subject, see my essay "'The Consciousness of Exile': Memory and the Vicarious Imagination in Cuban-American Literature and Art" in the *Journal of West Indian Literature* 8:1 (October 1988): 82–98.

19. Carolina Hospital, *Explicación de Textos Literarios* 16:2 (1987): 103–114.

20. *Cubanía* is a term developed by Cuban anthropologist Fernando Ortiz to signify the a-temporal, essential characteristics that bind all Cubans together.

21. This quotation is drawn from Homi K. Bhabha's critical work *The Location of Culture* (New York: Routledge, 1994), 204.

22. In my essay "The Politics of Mis-Remembering: History, Imagination and the Recovery of the 'Lost Generation,'" which appears in my edited volume *Cuba: Idea of a Nation Displaced*, I attempt to theorize a critical space for this *arcing* sector of the diasporic population, whom I dub as the *lost* generation, an intentionally ironic re-inscription of Hemingway's phrase, which refers to those of us born and raised outside the island. The term *arcing* refers to the fact that we now traverse several generations. Portions of this essay have been extracted from "The Politics of Mis-Remembering."

23. "Cultural Identity and Diaspora," in Jonathan Rutherford (ed.), *Identity: Community, Culture, Difference* (London: Lawrence and Wishart, 1990), 234.

24. Although I have long sought to redefine Cuban diasporic identity in this manner, I was inspired by and have consequently refined my argument after recently being introduced to Daniel and Jonathan Boyarin's essay "Diaspora: Generational Ground of Jewish Identity" in *Critical Inquiry* 19.4 (1993): 693–725. In this essay the authors propose to "articulate a notion of Jewish identity that recuperates its genealogical moment—family, history, memory, and practice—while problematiz[ing] claims to autochthony and indigenousness as the material base of Jewish identity."

25. Within the mainstream, Garcia's *Dreaming in Cuban* (New York: Knopf, 1992) garnered overwhelming critical acclaim and achieved popular success, however, the response from sectors of the Cuban exile community has been less positive. Among other things, her critics contend that despite the fact that *Dreaming in Cuban* addresses and represents a host of antithetical political issues and positions regarding the revolution, Garcia fails clearly to position herself politically. Moreover, a small coterie of critics—regarding Garcia's work as being in conflict with the conservative arm of the Miami exile community—have questioned her authenticity and criticized her for not having been raised in a Latino community. As one critic observed,

Garcia "failed to experience [the] deep sense of loss or nostalgia common to many Cuban-American children" (see, e.g., Joseph Viera's review in *Poets and Writers*). Others have accused her (like Hijuelos) of presenting a cliché-ed portrait of Cubans and Cuban Americans and have pointed out her frequently erroneous and stereotypical portrayal of Santería and its practitioners.

26. For an in-depth discussion on this subject, see Sadowski-Smith, "'A Homeland Without a Home.'"

27. Juan Bruce-Novoa, "Hijuelos' Mambo Kings: Reading from Divergent Traditions." *Confluencia* 10.2 (1995): 11–22.

28. Fernández is quoted in Lori Ween's "Translational Backformations: Authenticity and Language in Cuban American Literature." *Comparative Literature Studies* 40.2 (2003): 131.

29. Gustavo Pérez Firmat, "Rum, Rump, and Rumba: Cuban Contexts for The Mambo Kings Play Songs of Love." *Dispositio* 26.41 (1991): 61–69. Debates about the authenticity of Cuban-American literature are often linked to questions of language. For an extended discussion of this issue, see Ween's "Translational Backformations" for example.

30. See Bhabha's *The Location of Culture*, 213, as well as my critical essay "The Politics of Mis-Remembering."

31. See "Cultural Identity and Diaspora," 224.

32. In his effort to develop a traveling theory of nationhood and cultural identity, Bhabha observes, "the space of the modern nation is never simply horizontal. Their metaphoric movement requires a kind of 'doubleness' in writing; a temporality of representation that moves between cultural formations and social processes without a centered causal logic . . . The secular language of interpretation needs to go beyond the horizontal critical gaze if we are to give 'the non-sequential energy of lived historical memory and subjectivity' its appropriate narrative authority. We need another time of writing that will be able to inscribe the ambivalent and chiasmatic intersections of time and place that constitute the problematic 'modern' experience of the Western nation." *The Location of Culture*, 203.

33. "Cultural Identity and Diaspora," 228; "Diasporas," 244–77 in Rutherford, *Identity*.

34. Bhabha, *The Location of Culture*, 140, 200–04.

35. In this passage I am consciously riffing on Stuart Hall's concept of *play*. In "Cultural Identity and Diaspora," Hall discusses the "play of 'difference' within identity" and observes, "I use the word 'play' because the double meaning of the metaphor is important. It suggests, on the one hand, the instability, the permanent unsettlement, the lack of any final resolution. On the other hand, it reminds us that the place where this 'doubleness' is most powerfully to be heard is 'playing' [for example] within the varieties of Caribbean musics . . . At different places, times, in relation to different questions, the boundaries are resisted" (228).

36. I am borrowing historian Jan Assman's terminology here. See *Moses the Egyptian: The Memory of Egypt in Western Monotheism* (Cambridge, MA: Harvard University Press, 1999), 14.

37. For more on this subject, see Bhabha's *The Location of Culture*, 225, 7.

38. Ibid., 313.

39. Ibid., 10.

40. "Cultural Identity and Diaspora," 228–29.

41. In my edited collection of testimonial expressions *ReMembering Cuba*, the usage of capital letters suggests the multiple ways in which a ruptured and scattered nation, and consequently Cuban identity, can be reassembled. In other words, it speaks to the fluid and protean nature of diasporic identity construction and the possibility of unity in the face of fragmentation and division. Although I am clearly referencing this text, the usage of this term shifts throughout the course of the essay thereby signaling a realignment with other kinds of discursive "rethinkings" such as Toni Morrison's concept of "rememory," which she introduces in her novel *Beloved* (New York: Plume, 1987).

42. In the preface to his novel *Tres Tristes Tigres* (Barcelona: Seix Barral, 1975), Guillermo Cabrera Infante characterized Cuban discursive practices as a language "in flight." See also Damián Fernández and Madeline Cámara Betancourt's discussion of "the Cuban thirst for ingravity" in their co-authored introductory essay "Interpretations of National Identity," in *Cuba, the Elusive Nation*, (Gainesville, FL: University Press of Florida, 2000) 12.

43. Assman, *Moses the Egyptian*, 14.

44. Ibid., 9–10.

45. Ibid., 14.

46. Ibid., 9.

47. The fact that no two people—on or off the island and even within generations—recall the same Cuba testifies to the notion that the "idea" of the past is malleable and infinitely diverse; that memory is ultimately selective and subjective; and the idea of nation is an evolving concept subject to constant change.

48. *Imagined Communities* (London & New York: Verso, 1991) 114, 6.

49. Assman, *Moses the Egyptian*, 9.

50. "Cultural Identity and Diaspora," 223. Although I have been tempted to embrace the notion that the *lost generation*, in its presence and absence, is "creatively" unstable, my overriding hope is to depart from more traditional ways of constructing cultural and national identity.

51. See Bhabha's discussion in *The Location of Culture*, 8.

52. See the reference to Epstein in Aleš, Erjavec, ed., *Postmodernism and the Postsocialist Condition* (Berkeley: University of California Press, 2003), 20.

53. See Jana Evans Braziel and Anita Mannur's discussion of this topic in the introduction to their edited volume *Theorizing Diaspora* (Malden, MA: Blackwell, 2003, 2005).

54. Bhabha, *The Location of Culture*, 6.
55. Ibid., 10.
56. Bhabha is quoting from "Building, Dwelling, Thinking," by Martin Heidegger. See *The Location of Culture*, 1 and 7.
57. Bhabha, *The Location of Culture*, 13.
58. Ibid., 5.
59. Andrea O'Reilly Herrera, *The Pearl of the Antilles* (Tempe, AZ: Bilingual/Review Press, 2001).
60. See Antonio Benítez-Rojo, *The Repeating Island* (Durham, NC: Duke University Press, 1992).
61. I am consciously borrowing Bhabha's terminology here and drawing primarily from concepts he develops in his critical work *The Location of Culture*.
62. See "The Latino Imaginery," in Linda Martín Alcoff and Eduardo Mendieta (eds.), *Identities: Race, Class, Gender, and Nationality* (Oxford: Blackwell, 2003), 100.
63. Benítez-Rojo, *The Repeating Island*, 27–28, 81.
64. Bhabha, *The Location of Culture*, 26.
65. Paul Gilroy uses this phrase throughout *The Black Atlantic: Modernity and Double Consciousness* (Cambridge, MA: Harvard University Press, 1993). I am adapting Stuart Hall's claim that "Difference . . . persists— in and alongside continuity," "Cultural Identity and Diaspora," 228.

PART IV

Ideology and Labor

CHAPTER 9

"So Your Social is Real?" Vernacular Theorists and Economic Transformation

Mary Pat Brady

The struggle among politicians in the United States to leverage their fortunes to both the backlash against immigration and the mass movement to clarify and improve working conditions for immigrant laborers points to a singular question of articulation: the difficulty with which popular accounts have failed to offer a vernacular theory of the ongoing economic transformation (beyond broad categorical turns such as "outsourcing," and, well, "globalization") that immigration and its backlashes signal. A vernacular analysis of economic structural shifts is of course crucial politically since the lives of the most vulnerable people in the United States are, to some extent, at stake. Put differently, how does a broad cross-section of people come to understand a forty-year-long process in which the U.S. economy has become much more dependent on the production, not of things, but of services (e.g., computing and real estate) and of servicing capital (finance, insurance)? How do people begin to assimilate the transformation of the manufacturing economy into a service economy in both the formal sense of service to capital and in the informal sense of the growth of low-wage, service-oriented jobs (e.g., gardeners, housecleaners, nannies, short-order cooks) accompanying the disappearance of manufacturing jobs? To articulate this radical process merely as a question of supply and demand, remittances and anxiety, is to avoid accounting for the broader structural shift—to miss the emergence of a neo-feudal serving class of highly skilled, but poorly paid workers. That is to say, the formal service economy has been accompanied by a growing, largely informal economy made up of servants. The service sector's professional and managerial class, valorized and well-remunerated, demands attention from servants; its consumption patterns favor service-intensive restaurants, labor-intensive specialty and gourmet foods, elite child and doggie day care, house and apartment cleaners, personal shoppers, and so forth. Servants accompany service.[1]

While the immigration that has accompanied the development of this service economy has been the subject of a right-wing media frenzy, much of the actual labor immigrants perform flies under the radar of official economic reports. Their labor goes unreported and few official mechanisms have been developed beyond hysteria and paranoia to account for their economic contributions. The Federal Reserve, charged with recording every aspect of the U.S. economy, does not even try to collect data on this informal economy despite the evidence of its significance. This refusal to collect data belies the emergence of this multiscalar service economy composed of various formal and informal subsystems that have been a crucial aspect of global restructuring. Yet unfortunately when globalization analysts note the informal service economy, it is frequently in relation to broader changes in immigration, where immigration becomes a confirming sign of globalization. Globalization discourse has largely concerned itself with the workings of the elite, with the cultural impacts of global change on "global cities" rather than with what we might call *el otro lado*, the other side of the service economy. Attention to this far side reveals that conversations about global restructuring are taking place in multiple registers even though many political economists remain unaware of them.

Yet even if regulatory systems refuse to offer a transparent account of the impact of the informal economy, a range of writers and visual artists are developing a vernacular theory of both global change and U.S. economic shifts that deserve serious attention. Certainly, an impressive number of Latino/a artists, writers, and scholars have been deeply engaged in a critique of these processes of global restructuring, have been sensitive to refashioned subjectivities and dilemmas, and have configured an array of artistic, imaginative responses by refusing to mystify the valuation dynamic that works to produce a structure of exclusion by over-valorizing some forms of labor and under-valorizing others. In recent years a cluster of novels, sociological texts, anthropological, legal, and ethnographic work along with short stories, visual art, novels, films, poems, rock operas, and memoirs have focused on servants.[2] Much of this cultural work analyzes global change, assesses the results of U.S. structural adjustment programs, and tests a variety of responses and survival strategies while also exploring new forms of narrative and subjectivity. This material often starts with the social contradictions and constraints of a discursive order that depends on the simulation of fixed categories and on the repression of conflicts undergirding civic memory. Alma López, Esmeralda Santiago, and Denise Chávez operating from perhaps quite different understandings of these shifts, offer an analysis of global change and its affective figurations that demand attention.

Highlighting the density of the service economy and the mechanisms both institutional and mythic that serve it, Alma López's well-known digital print, "California Fashion Slaves" (1997), provides a useful starting point for my discussion.[3] Here a typical Los Angeles cityscape occupies nearly two-thirds of the print's area: the relatively few tall buildings stand in contrast to the surrounding urban sprawl; the sky is a picturesque blue; the clouds over the distant mountains billow protectively over the surface below. Woven through the landscape and unsettling it, however, is a sepia-toned photograph of women garment workers. The sepia photo does not obscure LA; the buildings and city seep through the bodies and clothing of the women, implying that the figures haunt the city, or more precisely, that their laboring bodies are intertwined with the more visible and recognizable symbols of a global city, even though their bodies are not what the purveyors of official memory wish to enshrine.[4]

Yet memory is crucial to "California Fashion Slaves." In homage to the groundbreaking series of paintings of the Virign de Guadalupe by Yolanda López another photo in López's print, one apparently taken more recently, shows a woman sewing.[5] Her fabric, however, is not the ordinary cloth of a sweatshop but the starred mantilla adorning *la virgen*. That mantilla blends into the landscape of the lower section occupied by an old map marked "*E.U. con Mexico.*" On that map, along the presumed border, a figure runs from the border patrol, heading, apparently, toward the image of la virgen whose seraph has been stamped over with "1848." An arrow with the words "Manifest Destiny" points at the image, and disrupts the lyrical quality of the print. Why might that arrow point at la virgen instead of at the workers or even the running figure? On the one hand it invokes the dearly held belief that Cortez invaded Mexico precisely so that la virgen would appear to Juan Diego. In this sense "Manifest Destiny" is turned slightly, a reworking of the Anglo-protestant concept that fueled U.S. expansion. Yet the graphic quality, the forcefulness of the arrow, and the stark color render this interpretation ironic and leave open to question, whose destiny has been so manifested? The workers? The border patrol? The global city built by the laboring poor?[6] Is this the ongoing destiny the print highlights?

The astute, acerbic vision projected by Alma López contrasts with a very different, if densely ambivalent, narrative of service. Published in 1996, Esmeralda Santiago's *América's Dream* recounts the experiences of América Gonzalez, a maid employed at a tourist hotel on the island of Vieques, Puerto Rico.[7] América is plagued by a jealous and violent lover, Correa, and troubled by a frustrated, angry daughter and an alcoholic mother. After her daughter runs away and Correa's violence becomes intolerable, América escapes by taking a job with a wealthy family she had worked for while they vacationed at the tourist hotel. This new job requires her to leave the island and travel to a New York suburb to work as a live-in nanny and housekeeper. After only a few months, Correa tracks her down, terrorizes her with alternately pleading and threatening phone calls until he comes to the mainland, breaks into the house, and assaults her. In staving off his brutal attack, América accidentally kills Correa.

Both bildungsroman and allegory, *América's Dream* tracks América's education, her transformation from Correa's frightened object to a woman aware of a discourse of rights to which she may claim access; it similarly tracks her growth as a parent caught in a cycle of violence. That her education is mediated by a gendered brutality and exploitation ratchet the bildungsroman genre into another set of relations. Doubling as an allegory, the novel offers an allegorical account of Puerto Rican struggles; América becomes a figure for Vieques, bombed and collared by the U.S. Navy as part of its defense system. In this sense Correa's name, which translates as leather strap or leash, further signals the allegorical desire of the novel. The novel suggests the difficulty that Vieques, and by extension Puerto Rico, would have in finding liberation from its batterer, from gaining access to a discourse of rights that establishes privileges and access through a system dependent on exclusionary mechanisms. In *América's Dream* the two modalities of allegory and bildungsroman structure each other as a means both to offer a critique of what Anibel Quijano calls the "coloniality of power" and to suggest, albeit elliptically, that these very generic forms may also participate in processes of domination.

The opening passage establishes many of its themes:

> It's her life, and she's in the middle of it. On her knees, scrubbing behind a toilet at the only hotel on the island. She hums a bolero, a love

song filled with longing. She's always humming, sometimes a ballad, sometimes a lilting cha-cha-chá. Often, she sings out loud. Most of the time she's not even aware of the pleasing music that comes from her and is surprised when tourists tell her how charming it is that she sings as she works. (1)

The narrator's dispassionate introduction establishes an odd tone or stance toward its subject, implying that this figure is immersed in her world without much opportunity for reflection and even suggesting a kind of passive attitude of acquiescence. Figured first not physically or even in terms of a name, but as an object, laboring, she appears. Her task signals her status. This status and task contrast with the figure's response—she sings and hums romantic lyrics. Deploying the mechanisms of romance and leisure the narrative establishes a contrast with her labor even as it invokes the network of musical articulations that help to construct an image of latinidad. By signaling her status as slightly unaware, the novel also suggests her need for a broadened consciousness, which the narrative will plot out for her. But the narrator signals its own ambiguity by making boundaries unclear. In this particular case it is difficult to tell just what América finds surprising—that her music is "charming," that she has been singing, or that tourists have bothered to speak to her and acknowledge her presence cleaning toilets.

The opening passage continues:

The tiles are unevenly laid behind the toilet, and she catches a nail on the corner of one and tears it to the quick. "Ay!" Still on her knees, she moves to the sink and runs cold water over her middle finger. The bright pink crescent of her nail hangs by the cuticle. She bites it off, drawing salty blood.

"¡América!"

The scream bounces against the concrete walls of La Casa del Francés. (1)

Even before her name appears, before she speaks, she bleeds. The scream of her name accompanies the blood flowing into the sink. Her labor is cut short by the wound and the wound prefigures her hailing. In this manner the opening passage warns of the battering and loss to follow, wherein América seems almost not to exist without physical violence, without her body being battered and threatened. Conversely, she comes into being as a named figure, not when she is called charming—in that moment she still retains object status, but when she is bleeding. The scream itself is a public event, as if her being called reverberates throughout the hotel she spends her days scrubbing. This hailing also initiates the allegorical form of the novel; the opening scene recalls another memory of another America sought (and discovered) bleeding.

Like the title of López's print, the title of the novel also creates an ironic distance from narratives of consumption, indeed from the processes of producing citizens by producing consumers, or rather conflating the status of citizen with that of consumer. This story counters the commodified version of an "American dream" used to lure laborers to the states.[8] If the introductory scene suggests América's eccentricity as a subject, it also calls attention to the seemingly naturalized narrative identifying women with nation and land and to the novel's troubled deployment of that narrative.

Santiago further underscores this allegorical critique in the account of América's first romance with Correa. The chapter, which briefly recounts their first meeting, begins with the short sentence, "It's all uphill from Esperanza to Destino" (16). That even the island's place names signal the allegorical mode may be heavy-handed, (Esperanza [hope] is the village where the laboring poor live, Destino [destiny] the locale of wealthy, anglo residents from the mainland), but it also reinforces the novel's critique of the conflation of women with land and colony and its own ambiguous deployment of that very conflation to criticize U.S. policy. Such a critique appears when the narrator turns to the familiar terms of courtship used in colloquial Spanish: "Correa had come to the barriada with the contractors improving the roads, stringing electric wires from tall poles, digging up ditches to lay pipes for running water and sewers . . . La conquista, the seduction, didn't take long" (25). Correa arrives with development, during the period when the United States invested heavily in Puerto Rico, showcasing it as an alternative to socialism during the dicey early moments of the Cold War.[9] The romance of development, its seeming promise is quickly overturned.[10] Vieques remained poor and undeveloped, continually shuddering from the U.S Navy's rounds of live ammunition and targeted bombing. Like the conquerors of the American hemisphere, Correa maintains a tight hold on his possession: "In the fifteen years Correa has been in her life, no other men have dared enter it, for fear he will kill her" (25).

The novel suggests the impossibility of distinguishing between Correa's battering of América and the U.S. treatment of its colonial holdings, exemplified by the repeated bombing of Vieques. Yet América often appears unaware of the problematics of her situation, resigned to the violence ("she's in the middle of it"), unaware that

she might defy Correa, and largely untroubled by the political or
environmental consequences of the Vieques occupation ("This is history, and América doesn't think about it," 16). So the narrator's attitude toward an allegorized América does begin to take a strange tone.
It is as if, the novel suggests, Puerto Rico has acquiesced too easily to
conquest, has failed, unlike Cuba, to resist U.S. demands. It might be
argued that the novel's attitude ultimately mirrors the United States'
own bullying stance toward Puerto Rico. What is worrisome is that an
allegorical figuring of Puerto Rico (and given América's name, of
Latin America as well as the Caribbean) as a battered, naïve, domestic
servant participates far too easily in an already well-burnished discourse
of coloniality that figures the colonized country as weak, passive, and
in need of colonial rule. In this sense, the novel's ambivalence, or perhaps the narrator's lack of clarity, highlights the ambivalent politics of
an allegorical mode for discussing gendered violence as colonial violence. This allegorical account is mired in the long history of U.S. por-
trayals of the Spanish empire as a shrewish female beast in need of
Uncle Sam's taming practices.

Oddly enough, the novel as allegory becomes more complex when
the plot molts into bildungsroman after América travels to the mainland to become a live-in nanny. *América's Dream* shifts its focus to a
critical portrayal of white professionals and suburban structures. The
story of América's psychological development picks up speed as she
learns to navigate English, the bourgeois family structure, the sub-
urbs, and trips into New York City to stay with her extended family.
The narrative focus also shifts to the dynamics of what one critic calls
"the regime of labor intimacy."[11] Or as América puts it, "All these
Americanitos are learning about life from us" (228).

Here the novel offers an analysis of domestic labor that, along
with Barbara Neely's mystery series featuring Blanche White, antici-
pates the house servant's return to popular culture. The past five
years has evidenced a remarkable focus on women servants from
bestsellers, such as *The Nanny Diaries* and Barbara Ehrenreich's
Nickel and Dimed, to Jenifer López's film, *Maid in Manhattan*;
Broadway has offered *Carolyn or Change*, LA's Taper Forum
commissioned a stage version of *Nickel and Dimed*, Benjamin
Cheever has published *The Good Nanny* to mixed reviews, and Dino
Ignacio and Rex Navarette teemed up to make the internet-released
short cartoon about the servant who cleans the Superfriend's super-
hero Hall of Justice, *Maritess versus the Superfriends*. Most of these
texts offer critical portraits of the hierarchical labor regime structuring
the service economy.[12]

Unlike many of these efforts however, *América's Dream* more clearly participates in the critique of the shifts in social reproduction accompanying global restructuring by staging a number of scenes that suggest how global change and structural adjustment programs have served to benefit white middle- and upper-class women to the detriment of laboring, poor women of color. Such programs have forced the migration into the United States of millions of women who subsequently agree to work below minimum wage as housekeepers and nannies.[13] As such they relieve middle- and upper-class white women from these responsibilities and enable them to work outside the home in better paying and higher status jobs, while preserving the romanticized notion of family. The economy thus captures two labor pools at once and, with the increase in spending capacity of dual-income households, channels new capital through the system.[14]

América's Dream amply illustrates this dynamic. The Leveretts, América's employers, reflect the imagined nuclear family. Charlie Leverett works in Manhattan, is rarely home, does none of the work of child care or housekeeping. Karen Leverett too works outside of the home, but also manages América, instructs her, arranges her schedule, and in a short time begins to increase her duties at every turn without corresponding pay increases. When América protests, Karen dismisses her concerns and dismisses the labor she performs as exaggerated and inefficient. Not surprisingly, given the failure of feminist efforts to renarrate reproductive labor in the broader social imagination, Karen's dismissal echoes the ongoing dismissals of homeworkers' contributions to the economy.

If América begins to develop a critique of her labor conditions on her own, her interactions with other workers solidify and extend that critique. Such interactions are crucial aspects of job negotiations and socialization because, as Pierette Hondagneu-Sotelo reminds us, "Suburban homes are increasingly replacing inner-city factories as the places of economic incorporation for new immigrants."[15] Yet for domestic workers, working "interna"—that is, living in an employer's home or as they might say, "se encierra"—having enclosed oneself, is the least desirable option because it tends to be the most exploited and poorly paid of positions. Domestic workers share knowledge about jobs, living conditions, and wages as well as legal systems governing labor and housing. For those working *interna*, such conversations can provide crucial insights for navigating the U.S. informal labor system and formal juridical machinery. The novel emphasizes this point when, in an extended conversation with other domestic workers, América "discovers" the rights her citizenship status makes available:

> "Why would you work interna if you're Americana?" Adela asks one day while they're watching the children at the playground.
>
> "But I'm not Americana," América protests, "I'm Viequense, Puerto Rican I mean. It's just that Puerto Ricans have citizenship."
>
> Adela doesn't understand the distinction and until Adela started asking her questions about her legal status, America hadn't given it much thought.
>
> "So your social is real?" Adela asks. (218)

What follows is the revelation that many of the women employed in domestic work do not have formal immigration papers. The agitated question, "So your social is real?" refers of course to América's status as a U.S. citizen and her authentic social security number and implicitly to the methods by which workers without papers fabricate their citizenship status in order to gain employment. While it may be that América's citizenship is so invested in a colonialized hierarchy draining her status of much of its immediate meaning or consequence, the women she meets urge her to learn what citizenship may provide. With a real social, they tell her, she can get a better job. The lack that drives the other *empleadas'* phantasmagoric "social"—a social without any of the guarantees of security—is precisely the lack of State commitment to their care and well-being, even while it demands their labor.[16] These *empleadas* thoroughly understand the simulated status of the real, its crucial dependence on fantasy and bureaucracy. The distinctions the women face—América's so-called real and their simulated socials— illustrate the uneven legacy of U.S. colonial involvement in both the Caribbean and Central America.

And yet one may well ask just how "real" América's social may be. Beyond the material implications of her social security number, her status as Viequense, as Puerto Rican, remains remarkably complex. Puerto Rico, as a number of legal cases dating from 1850 to the more recent arguments over the prison camp in the Guantanamo Bay Naval Base in Cuba, has repeatedly been described by the courts as "foreign in a domestic sense." This declaration means that to a certain extent, the law as practiced in the United States differs in practice in Puerto Rico.[17]

That is to say América's social is not quite as real as a simple assertion of citizenship status might imply. Put differently, the legal status of Puerto Rico and her uncertainty about the social to which she may subscribe point to a central insight of the novel—that spatial relations mediate, at times even determine, the relationships between individuals and the State. For example, with the 1901 Insular Cases, the U.S. Supreme Court declared that Congress did not have to extend Constitutional protection over territories such as Puerto Rico. U.S. citizens residing in Puerto Rico may lay claim to fewer constitutional rights than those residing in the United States.[18] América would have understood, as a Viequense, that she had, for example, no constitutionally guaranteed right to a trial by jury. What would have told her then, that upon shifting ground, she might lay claim to new rights? Her suggestion of the slim meaning of citizenship reflects the extent to which citizenship is spatially mediated.

The question, "So your social is real?" also suggests the unreality and invisibility of the servant's economy in the broader U.S. imaginary. For the mainline imaginary, these servants' socials are certainly not real. One has only to watch popular films such as Paul Mazursky's *Down and Out in Beverly Hills* or James L Brook's *Spanglish* to get a sense of the popular imaginary's limited capacity to understand a so-called servant's interiority. As the novel will go on to suggest, América's social is no more real to her employers than it is to the directors of Hollywood films.

The two generic modes, allegory and bildungsroman, come together in the novel's final pages. As América steadily gains self-confidence and awareness and becomes more assertive—in some sense laying claim to the bourgeois individualism her citizenship status would seem to grant—Correa discovers where she has been living and comes to the States. In a convenient plot twist Karen and Charlie Leverett leave for the weekend, forcing América to care for their children for a vague promise of overtime pay. Correa subsequently breaks into the house and attacks América with a knife, slashing her face and throat; she kicks him; he hits his head on a granite coffee table and dies suddenly.

During her recovery in the hospital, América becomes the subject of media speculation with a headline announcing "Housekeeper Kills Intruder" (322). A subsequent headline, appearing after América's daylong interrogation by police, reads "Intruder was Maid's Lover" (323). Initiating her own close reading, and reminiscent of the discussion of terminology with the other empleadas, América dryly "wondered why she was a housekeeper the first time and a maid the second" (323).

This scene suggests the ways in which the service economy participates in a range of discourses and relies on a classificatory system consonant with the earliest structures of colonialism and the emergence of property law. In the first headline, the underlying emphasis is on the significance of property. What the headline implies of course is that the housekeeper had fended off a threat to her employer's property. América's status as housekeeper signals the centrality of property, lighting a crucial chain of signifying fires. Had the headline narrated her as nanny or babysitter, it would have partially infantilized her, relegating her status to the realm of children. But as housekeeper, she gains access to the privileges associated with holding responsibility for *other* people's property; she is implicitly celebrated for having defended that property. This position is further underscored by América's status here as subject of the sentence. Her locale as subject of this sentence may be guaranteed by her responsibility for property, subtly reminding readers that the concept of the knowing subject emerged along with the idea of private property.[19]

The shift from maid to lover in the subsequent headline, a shift underscored by their differing positions within the economy of the sentence, doubly demotes América. Now she is identified as a maid, a category of strict subservience, one that does not indicate the responsibilities and access associated with housekeeper, nor one with the sanctioned intimacy of a nanny; she has also lost her status as subject and become the object of the sentence. The copula shifts the crime from one of property theft, to one of melodrama, and subtly underscores a patriarchal narrative, where the "intruder," now (male) "lover" becomes the main signifier. In addition to shifting the valence of Correa's death from defense against a thief to a lover's quarrel, thus from one of self-defense to manslaughter, the headline also underscores a distinct status—one more clearly aligned with the supposed shenanigans of illicit love attributed to the working classes—to maids. Similarly, Correa's status as lover rather than say, "estranged lover," tormentor, or "batterer," reestablishes his patriarchal dominance over América even in death.

Recovering in the hospital, América receives a visit from Karen Leverett who brings her final paycheck. América tearfully apologizes and Karen scolds her, "You should have told me; we would have helped you" (323). Odd as América's apology may seem, Karen's reply underscores that while América has had detailed knowledge of the most intimate aspects of the Leverett's life, they've known virtually nothing about her life. Replicating other aspects of the system of uneven valuation, the Leverett's disinterest enhances Karen's power and produces something like an affective gated community, interiorizing the concept of the suburban enclave. Thus what América may finally be apologizing for is that the fullness of her otherness crashed the gates, making the enclave's dependence, its relationship to a network of socio-spatialities, slightly more obvious.

The novel's curious conjunction of allegory with bildungsroman bears further scrutiny. The use of the allegorical mode is not fully surprising given Caribbean literature's long tradition of equating the nation with the island and the island as the primary, or exclusive locus of enunciation for all discourses of Caribbean identity.[20] For if it's the case as Thomas Scanlon argues, that "colonial activity would seem to encourage allegorical writing," or, as Christopher Lane argues, "that a nation's organization derives from its use of allegory," then to utilize the allegorical is to take up the very discursive terms entangling Puerto Rican/Boricuan literature.[21] Yet it is that very figuring that makes *América's Dream* surprising if not disturbing. What might even be called paradigms—nation as woman; Caribbean nation as eroticized woman available for multiple forms of conquest—inform this allegory at every turn. Of course allegory's flexibility of meaning, its play with discursive or interpretive "communities," its seeming dependence upon a recognizable interpretive key or index, its temporalizing of the figural, its capaciousness when meaning seems out of reach (or, as in the case of the post-empirical moment of Puerto Rico, disarticulated) would suggest that allegory is the shifty form necessary if Puerto Rico is neither precisely nation nor precisely colony, seemingly unrepresentable in terms of the political economy. Thus, allegory functions where the contingency of the gap between signifier and signified seems most especially arbitrary. Given this ambivalent matrix, the allegorical turn the novel offers, Puerto Rico not as eroticized woman, but as battered, frightened, laboring woman, highlights the context in which the United States imagines itself as the center of global change, as a "mind country" demanding the labor of "body countries."[22] Furthermore, by tropicalizing the allegory and the bildungsroman, the novel seems to suggest that the second mode answers the first's heuristic demands. That is to say, neither mode, in and of itself, provides an adequate framework for a tale of the Commonwealth of Puerto Rico, an entity that lies outside of the political representational system of nation-colony and of a woman, a servant, whose life lies far askew the angles of subjectivity. But its tropicalized resolution remains disturbing. For the suggestion of the text is that América's education only really begins when she leaves the island and comes in contact with her mainland family and the network of empleadas at the playgrounds. What does it imply about Puerto Rico?

América's blossoming at the close of the novel leaves her working again as a maid at a hotel, albeit for better wages, with benefits, a stronger relationship with her daughter, and a new sense of self. Such a conclusion may be "realistic," a bitter and ironic critique of American triumphalism, of the coming-of-age novel's relationship to bourgeois individualism, and of the cynical means by which the "American dream" serves as a means to lure laborers to the United States. Published in 1996, this conclusion also weirdly predicts that América's fate is also Vieques's fate. The bombing may have stopped, but Vieques is now a newly designated tourist site with major luxury hotels structuring the island anew.

Maybe this "bildungory"—the maneuvering the novel asks readers to perform between formal modes—prompts readers to consider the service narrative forms provide in a context of being served, within the context of the structures of a U.S. economy that conditions the possibilities of intellectual knowledge production, about among other things, global change. Here the novel's analytical contribution may be to ask readers to look at service awry, to see maids and readers as embricated in the structures of defense of the homeland as much as generals and laser guided bombs. The new imaginaries feminist economists have called for may precisely begin with the doubt, "So your social is real?" This doubt suggests that the real may be contoured to provide very different "socials" and very different realities, all intermeshed in nested hierarchies.

If América's tragic encounter with Correa demystifies the tacitly acknowledged affective gated community that shields suburban employers from the complexity of their employees' lives and helps them remain immune to the violent effects of their participation in the global labor economy, it does so only partially and temporarily. For Leverett's encounter with América's private life does not radically dispel the widely held anxiety about the affective economy structuring those who do intimate work for pay and their employers' suspicion of the authenticity of their sentiments. As Jean Paul Sartre argued more than fifty years ago:

> Fake submission, fake tenderness, fake respect, fake gratitude. Their entire behavior is a lie. We are led to believe that this falsifying comes from their false relationships with their mistress . . . their truth is always elsewhere; in the presence of the masters, the truth of a domestic is to be a fake domestic and to mask the man he is under a guise of servility; but in their absence, the man does not manifest himself

either, for the truth of the domestic in solitude is to play at being master.[23]

While servants are expected to perform real care and concern, real sympathy, they are, in Sartre's estimation, embroiled in a systemic lie. Sartre here suggests that affective authenticity entails only the desire to be master, not servant and that indeed it is that framework that structures the service economy alone. In contrast, Denise Chávez suggests that rather than understanding service work only within a feudal or neofeudal narrative of subjectivity, one ought to understand service as a form a labor, not the creator of identity.

In her very funny novel *Face of an Angel* (1994), one that similarly utilizes the allegorical mode,[24] Chávez offers a slippery meditation on the formation of Chicana femininity and family values and tells the story of Soveida DosAmantes—a woman who survives incest, abusive husbands, and a family structure meant to withhold critique of male violence. Soveida finds solace and meaning in her work as a server in a Las Cruces, New Mexico restaurant called El Farol. Chávez deploys a technique that links her longish novel to *Moby Dick* and *Almanac of the Dead*—that is, she writes a book within a book. In the novel, Soveida dosAmantes writes what she titles "The Book of Service," an instruction manual on how to be a good server that Soveida gives to a newer employee named Dedea. The short chapters of "The Book of Service" are interspersed throughout the narrative in a contrapuntal shift from the action of the novel—Soveida's search for love, stability, and an understanding of her traumatic childhood. The Service passages offer comic relief as well as a glimpse of Soveida's interiority and sense of personal authority.

The tone of "The Book of Service," like the novel as a whole, slips from the ironic to the earnest, from the satirical to the self-righteous. Here is the opening passage: "As a child, I was imbued with the idea that the purpose of life was service. Service to God. Country. Men. Not necessarily in that order but lumped together like that. For God is a family man" (171).

That shift from Catholic piety to sardonic distance is characteristic of "The Book of Service." Soveida's choice to describe herself as impregnated with the ideal of service links her to an ongoing understanding of the ways Chicana subject formation entails a kind of sacrificial modality and that such a linkage gains its authority by reference to a Catholic God. But her playful comment, "For God is a family man" helps to disentangle that essentializing mythos even as

Soveida will continue her effort to elevate her labor's status. Soveida gives Dedea instructions on techniques for waiting tables, on the problem of stray hairs and appropriate hair styles, on how to deal with flirtatious customers, and why to choose sensible shoes and uniforms.

> To some extent this Book of Service is an etiquette manual, a guide to the middle-class manners that a proper, and properly ambitious server might display. Yet each chapter is also laced with Soveida's meditations on the philosophy of service and these meditations repeatedly call for sincerity of purpose, for taking pleasure in service work rather than seeing it as subservient and demeaning.

Soveida Dosamantes does not want to assume that servants strive to become masters as if there were no greater state of humanity outside of being master. The Book of Service is her effort to construct an alternate sense of meaning and purpose to that dominant structure. Its slyly simplistic tone works to undermine assumptions about the insincerity behind service, but it also argues for a broader dignity to any kind of labor. In this sense it eschews social hierarchies underpinned by economic structures. And in that sense, like "California Fashion Slaves" and *América's Dream*, the novel participates in the larger effort of Latina feminists to offer an alternative account of labor and class structures.

In a relatively short period, global restructuring has almost naturalized the massive economic transformations currently underway. The rapid flow of capital increasingly relies on differential spaces for the management of people with unprotected identities of workers neither aquí, nor acá, neither here, nor there, working in the interstices of economic and legal structures. Cultural work that brings service workers into focus must in this context be seen as a crucial intervention. For by changing the subject so to speak, artists such as Alma López, as well as novelists such as Esmeralda Santiago and Denise Chávez shift the terms by which we understand the work of culture and the culture of working. In this manner, their work can play a vital role in nurturing and sustaining social change by offering new identities and stances apart from the real with a circumscribed "social." What is perhaps most admirable about all of this work is that through such a rehearsal, between the folds of parody and fantasy lies the possibility of moving beyond doubling strategies and allegories, where, too often, at the end of the day we are left only with critique.

Notes

I am especially grateful for the work of Mary Romero, whose extraordinary research has laid the foundation for my analysis. This essay is respectfully dedicated to her. I would also like to thank audiences at University of California, Santa Barbara, Penn State University, Princeton University, and the University of Southern California for their helpful comments on earlier drafts of this essay.

1. Saskia Sassen, *Globalization and Its Discontents* (New York: The New Press, 1998).
2. Benjamin Alire Sáenz, *The House of Forgetting* (New York: Harper Collins, 1991). For a useful discussion of African American domestic workers' activism, see Cecilia Maria Rio, " 'This job has no end': African American Domestic Workers and Class Becoming," in J.K. Gibson-Graham et al. (eds.), *Class and Its Others* (Minneapolis: University of Minnesota Press, 1998), 23–46; Deborah McDowell, *Leaving Pipe Shop: Memories of Kin* (New York: Scribners, 1996); for another set of imaginative reconsiderations of domestic labor, see Barbara Neely's series of mysteries featuring "Blanche White," a domestic-worker--detective. For a transnational discussion of domestic work, see Bridget Anderson, *Doing the Dirty Work? The Global Politics of Domestic Labour* (London: Zed Press, 2000).
3. Alma López provides a wonderful internet site that includes images of her work. See www.almalopez.net.
4. Alejandro Morales, *The Brick People* (Houston: Arte Publico Press, 1992).
5. Yolanda López, "Portrait Of My Grandmother." *Connexions* 2 (Fall, 1981).
6. Janet Abu-Lughod, *New York, Chicago, Los Angeles: America's Global Cities* (Minneapolis: University of Minnesota Press, 1999).
7. Esmeralda Santiago, *América's Dream* (New York: Harper Perennial, 1996).
8. For a compelling discussion of the commodification of the "American Dream" see Jimmy Breslin, *The Short Sweet Dream of Eduardo Gutierrez* (New York: Crown Publishers, 2002).
9. Jaime E. Benson-Arias, "Puerto Rico: The Myth of the National Economy," in Frances Negrón-Muntaner and Ramón Grosfoguel (eds.), *Puerto Rican Jam: Essays on Culture and Politics* (Minneapolis: University of Minnesota Press, 1997), 77–94.
10. See María Josefina Saldaña-Portillo, "Developmentalism's Irresistible Seduction—Rural Subjectivity Under Sandinista Agricultural Policy," in Lisa Lowe and David Lloyd (eds.), *The Politics of Cultures in the Shadow of Capital* (Durham: Duke University Press, 1997), 132–172.
11. Kimberly Chang and L.H.M. Ling, "Globalization and its intimate Other: Filipina Domestic Workers in Hong Kong," in Marianne

Marchand and Anne Sisson Runyan (eds.), *Gender and Global Restructuring* (New York: Routledge, 2000), 27–43.

12. Barbara Ehrenreich, *Nickel and Dimed: On (Not) Getting by in America* (New York: Metropolitan Books, 2001); Emma McLaughlin and Nicola Kraus, *The Nanny Diaries: A Novel* (New York: St. Martin's Press, 2002). Wayne Wang, *Maid in Manhattan* (Columbia Tristar) 2002.

13. See Grace Chang, *Disposable Domestics: Imigrant Women Workers in the Global Economy* (Boston: South End Press, 2000); Rhacel Parreñas, *Servants of Globalization: Women, Migration and Domestic Work* (Stanford: Stanford University Press, 2001); Barbara Ehrenreich and Arlie Hochschild, *Global Woman: Nannies, Mades and Sex Worers in the New Economy* (New York: Metropolitan Books, 2003); Rosana Ertz and Nacy L. Marshall, eds., *Working Families: The Transformation of the American Home* (Berkeley: University of California Press, 2001). See also Martin Manalansan, "Queer Intersections: Sexuality and Gender in Migration Studies" in *The International Migration Review* Spring 2006: 224–249.

14. Chang, 18.

15. Pierette Hondagneu-Sotelo, *Doméstica: Immigrant Workers Cleaning and Caring in the Shadows of Affluence* (Berkeley: UC Press, 2001), xiv.

16. See Jorge Duany, "Nation, Migration, Identity: The Case of Puerto Ricans" for a very helpful analysis of how Puerto Ricans navigate shifts in legal and social status between the Island and the mainland. *Latino Studies* 1 (2003): 424–444.

17. See, Charle R. Venator Santiago, "From the Insular Cases to Camp X-Ray: Agamben's State of Excedption and United States Territorial Law" in *Studies in Law, Politics and Society* 39 (2006): 15–55. See also, Bartholomew Sparrow, *The Insular Cases and the Emergence of American Empire* (Lawrence, Kansas: University Press of Kansas, 2006); Christina Duffy Burnett and Burke Marshall, eds., *Foreign in a Domestic Sense: Puerto Rico, American Expansion, and the Constitution* (Durham: Duke University Press, 2001); Frances Negrón-Muntaner, ed., *None of the Above: Puerto Ricans in the Global Era* (New York: Palgrave Macmillan, 2007).

18. My thanks to Charles R. Venator Santiago for discussions of this case.

19. Walter Mignolo, *Local Histories/Global Designs: Coloniality, Subaltern Knowledges and Border Thinking* (Princeton: Princeton University Press, 2000), 212.

20. Dara Goldman, "Out of Place: The Demarcation of Hispanic Caribbean Cultural Spaces in the Diaspora." *Latino Studies* 1 (2003): 405.

21. Thomas Scanlan, *Colonial Writing and the New World, 1583–1671: Allegories of Desire* (Cambridge: Cambridge University Press, 1999), 3; Christopher Lane, *The Ruling Passing: British Colonial Allegory and the Paradox of Homosexual Desire* (Durham: Duke University Press, 1995), 3; Jenny Sharpe, *Allegories of Empire: The Figure of Woman in the Colonial Text* (Minneapolis: University of Minnesota Press, 1993);

Aijaz Ahmad, "Jameson's Rhetoric of Otherness and the 'National Allegory.'" *Social Text* 17 (1987): 3–25. See also, Sangeeta Ray's discussion of Jameson, *En-Gendering India: Woman and Nation in Colonial and Postcolonial Narratives* (Durham: Duke University Press, 2000).

22. Joseph Stiglitz uses this distinction in *Globalization and its Discontents* (New York: W.W. Norton, 2002).

23. Quoted in Mary Romero, "Nanny Diaries and Other Stories: Imagining Immigrant Women's Labor in the Social Reproduction of American Families" *DePaul Law Review* (Spring 2003): 823.

24. Denise Chávez, *Face of an Angel* (New York: Warner Books, 1994).

CHAPTER 10

Oscar Hijuelos: Writer of Work

Rodrigo Lazo

In January 2005, Oscar Hijuelos published "Lunch at the Biltmore,"[1] a short nonfiction piece about a period, as the opening phrase tells us, "[i]n the autumn of 1959" when he suffered from the physical travails of a kidney infection and his father grappled with the aftershocks of a heart attack. The piece includes the standard fare for which Hijuelos is known. Starting with the opening reference to 1959, "Lunch at the Biltmore" provides a glimpse into Hijuelos's engagement with Cuba and the influence of Cuban culture on his family.

He remembers eating "suckling pig (*lechón*)" and "a journey I'd made to Cuba." The Spanish language regularly enters the descriptions: "A quiet man, *un tipo muy callado*, he said little to me." The recurrent invocation of Cuba in Hijuelos's oeuvre accounts for the way he has been represented in academic literary studies. Most critical work about Hijuelos's fiction focuses on Cuban American culture, raises questions about the influence of television and music in U.S. constructions of Cubanness, and positions his fiction within debates about Latino identity-formation.[2] Karen Christian, for example, argues that the mambo performance in *The Mambo Kings Play Songs of Love*[3] unravels essentialist and fixed notions of nationality and gender. "The hyper-masculinity and hyper-femininity of these characters (their excess) makes them resemble drag performers whose objective is to perform convincing gender illusions," Christian writes.[4] But to focus on ethnic or gender identity without considering the socially symbolic and material function of economic conditions, particularly occupations, is to gloss over an important dimension of Hijuelos's fiction, which constantly reminds us that people spend more time working and thinking about work than they do debating ethnic and gender labels.

Readers of Hijuelos's novels should not have been surprised that "Lunch at the Biltmore" also contained numerous references to labor, both organized and in references to occupations. "Restaurant and Bar Workers Union, Local No. 7," we are told, guaranteed the elder Hijuelos's paycheck while he recuperated from the heart attack. Hijuelos's father "was a cook" who "worked the breakfast shift," and "never made very much money, even with overtime, but he did have an arrangement with the butchers and the baker in the hotel which allowed him to bring home all kinds of food that he could not otherwise have afforded." Thus Hijuelos lets us into the economy of his household, offering an account of his father's work. Even the title of this memoiristic fragment calls attention to the difference between customers and the Hijueloses, who are "at a table in the back, where the cooks and waiters ate their meals." This is in keeping with a writer whose fiction offers a sustained contemplation of how work influences the lives of his characters.

In much of his fiction, Hijuelos is meticulous in documenting the type of work that a person does and how that work fits into the character's daily life. Work provides a way for wage laborers, professionals, and even producers of popular culture to think about themselves. The type of work that a person does often defines him or her, a point that "Lunch at the Biltmore" echoes by referring to Hijuelos's father's friends as "Mr. Martínez, a superintendent, and a sallow-faced Puerto Rican whom we knew simply as Frankie the Exterminator." The direct connection between name and occupation is most reminiscent of passages from *Empress of the Splendid Season*,[5] a novel about an immigrant from Cuba who becomes a cleaning woman after her waiter–husband collapses (like Hijuelos's father) with a heart attack. The connection between Lydia's husband and Hijuelos's father helps us situate *Empress* and its author within an immigrant working-class context in the New York of the 1950s and 1960s. The focus on work paves the way for reading the texture of Hijuelos's novels, which do not rely overtly on plot twists and conflicts but rather capture a series of episodes, sometimes repetitive ones, in the lives of people who have to earn money while attempting to overcome their economic and psychological limitations.

Empress of the Splendid Season points us back to a tradition of immigrant novels such as Abraham Cahan's *The Rise of David Levinsky*,[6] whose protagonist punctures the ideology of the American dream when economic success leaves him tragically alone. In an important critical intervention, Paula Moya writes the following about Helena María Viramontes's *Under the Feet of Jesus*[7]: "I contend that this novel should be placed within the tradition of American social realism, and that it is more usefully compared to novels like William Faulkner's *The Sound and the Fury*, John Steinbeck's *The Grapes of Wrath*, and Tomás Rivera's . . . *y no se lo tragó la tierra*, among others, than to works by other Chicana writers such as Sandra Cisneros, Gloria Anzaldúa, or Ana Castillo."[8] Moya's use of the phrase "more usefully compared" shifts critical emphasis away from gender and ethnicity toward a literary history that is primarily concerned with socioeconomic conditions. The *gran marchas* of 2006, rallies in which working immigrants called on the U.S. government to recognize an important labor force, did not raise ethnicity and gender to the level of a "chain of equivalents," to quote Ernesto Laclau and Chantal Mouffe, that imposes a symmetrical relationship among various identifying factors in movements for a radical plural democracy.[9]

Although various categories constitute subjects in contemporary society, the overuse of intersection (race, class, and gender) can mystify the economic conditions that lead to the exploitation of people of Latin American descent in the United States, particularly immigrants. Along this line, Antonia Darder and Rodolfo Torres have called on Latino studies to move beyond analyses that are "overwhelmingly rooted in a politics of identity—an approach that is founded on parochial notions of 'race' and representation, which ignore the imperatives of capitalist accumulation and the existence of class division within Latino communities."[10] Darder and Torres argue against an "intersection" by which class is "merely one of a multiplicity of (equally valid) perspectives."[11] On the other hand, class is also a category whose economic foundation is in need of revision, given increased neo-imperial economic relationships in the Americas and other parts of the world. "Class" is not in and of itself a panacea for a lack of attention to the economic dimensions of racial and ethnic formations.

Without disregarding the concerns of class-based analysis, I propose *work* as a concept and process that is both physical and mental, both material and literary, and is an important dimension of many contemporary novels by writers who are identified as Latinos and Latinas. Work, as I use it here, functions in multiple ways. First, it is a reference to the labor process, the actions and events through which people create different forms of use value. "Work" also refers to a variety of occupations that identify people and constitute social and economic roles. In its potential form—as in "a job"—it also refers to labor-power, a commodity that sells on the open market as a potential for production. Finally, work is the material result of mental and physical production—the work of a writer. This is not a reversal of the Barthesian call for a move from work to text; in other words, it is not an attempt to return to the author's intended creation as opposed to the play of the signifier that Barthes associates with "text."[12] Rather, I call a novel a work in recognition that it was produced in part by mental labor and is connected by readers, the publishing industry, and academics to a writer.

Three works by Hijuelos—*Mambo Kings, Empress,* and *A Simple Habana Melody*[13]—conspicuously emphasize the importance of work in the daily lives of characters. Pessimistic in their treatment of characters' aspirations for improved living conditions, the novels present people caught in the churning of labor, whether nationally in the United States or globally, in the case of *Habana Melody.* Usually, characters remain in one type of occupation for their lives with little or no change, although ethnic labor does present a site for building community in terms of personal and private relationships (the cleaning women in *Empress*). But the novels refuse to offer either a political or personal panacea for the brutalities of the workday, even though the workplace in its many forms can become a site of pleasure. The novels hold up two stereotypes, the Hispanic cleaning woman and the Latin lover, and thus develop a dialectical tension between the representative power of ethnic fantasy and materialist conditions that feed and challenge those fantasies. Rather than offer a celebratory conclusion, Hijuelos takes a pessimistic turn in which daily struggles lead only to an ongoing demand for toil from one generation to the next.

"THE SPANISH CLEANING LADY": HOW WORK WORKS

Not many pages into *Empress of the Splendid Season* it becomes clear that the word "work" will appear unrelentingly throughout the novel. A chronicle of the thoughts and activities of Lydia España, a Cuban immigrant turned cleaning woman in New York City, the novel focuses on her quotidian experience as she enters the homes of professionals and multimillionaires, then returns home to care for her husband and two children. Lydia carries the double burden of cleaning other people's houses as well as her own, but has faith that hard work "was at the root of all that was good in the world" (81). The opening sentences encapsulate the book's focus on the way economic necessity affects Lydia's choices and actions:

> In 1957 when her beloved husband, Raul, had fallen ill, Lydia España went to work, cleaning the apartments of New Yorkers much better off than herself. She took up that occupation because Raul, with jobs in two restaurants, had waited on so many tables, for so many hours, and had snuck so many drinks from the bar and smoked so many cigarettes, that his taut heart had nearly burst, half killing him one night at the age of forty-one. (3)

Raul is described as "the kind of Cuban who lived mainly for work" (10), while various workplaces provide many of the settings for the book. Lydia and Raul, for example, meet while he is on the job: "It was 1949 and Lydia, working in the sewing factory at the time, had been dragged to the party by friends. Raul had gone there to work, waiting tables, and as he poured some of the 'table rum' into her glass of Coca-Cola, a conversation had started up between them: about Cuba" (19).

Lydia's transition into U.S. society is accompanied by a corresponding shift in class. In Cuba, Lydia had come of age as a spoiled and vain teenager, cared for by maids, with a closet of fine dresses. She is surrounded by poverty yet "[i]n a time when most Cuban children were shoeless, she was hardly aware that others suffered in this life" (47). The bourgeois house is sustained by an unforgiving patriarch who banishes Lydia after she has casual sex with an orchestra leader. Throwing her out is her father's benevolent alternative to "killing her or sending her for life into a nunnery" (51). The "princess of Cuba" (51) makes her way to New York, where she learns "how life really works for people without money and connections" (52). She takes up a job as a seamstress in "one of those nonunion shops" (52) and then moves through a series of "jobs for the poor" (6) before marrying Raul. Lydia is attracted to Raul because she reads in his eyes "*work ethic* and *decency*" (italics in the original; 20). A man "who'd known only work from early childhood" (10), he wants her to stay home to care for the children. But when Raul has a heart attack, she is forced to support the family and sets "woefully about doing something which, in her youth, she could never have imagined, being someone else's servant" (15–16).

Lydia's entrance into the workforce offers a lesson on how ethnic identity in the United States is created in part through certain occupations. In chapter subheads, Lydia is described as "Lydia, the Cuban Cleaning Woman" (15) and then as "The Spanish Cleaning Lady" (16). Cleaning is the common denominator from one phrase to the next, implying that the type of labor she does is what produces the change from an initial national identification to a more general ethnic label without a proper name. (That job also ages her into "lady.") "Spanish," a term that one might hear on the streets of New York, functions as a metonym for the homogenous ethnic label "Hispanic." Like all ethnic labels that encompass numerous ethnicities and nation-alities, Spanish is a misnomer that circulates in everyday usage. It is a street form that differs from the academically correct or governmen-tally sanctioned labels Latino or Hispanic.[14] In *Empress*, it also points ironically to the last name España and Lydia's self-perception as an upper-class Cuban, an attitude that is reminiscent of people who claim to be Spanish to distance themselves from indigenous populations.

The rhythmically trochaic "Spanish cleaning lady" is a convenient term for "American" employers, who do not know she is born in Cuba (23). But the description of Lydia as a cleaning lady is at odds with the way she perceives herself, as a stunning "empress" who must dress down to do her daily work. Society's ability to define her by occupation comes as a surprise: "Quite simply, she had turned around to find that Lydia España, from Cuba, the Empress of the Splendid Season as her husband once thought of her, had somehow become Lydia the Spanish cleaning lady" (18). In other words, she is ushered into a U.S.-based definition that effaces her particular experiences yet situates her within an economic context marked by changing demo-graphics in the late twentieth century.

Lydia's progression from Cuban to Spanish, in the novel's terms, depicts the importance of ethnically typed occupations in the creation of ethnic U.S. subjects. The emergence of the Hispanic cleaning woman, both in the labor force and in cultural representation, is at once a reminder that Chicanas have a long history of doing domestic work but also that the last two decades have brought an increase in the num-ber of immigrants from Latin America taking on such jobs.[15] Among novels, films, and television shows that recently have featured cleaning women of Latin American descent are Esmeralda Santiago's *America's Dream*,[16] which opens with the imperialist context of Vieques (infa-mous as a site for U.S. military maneuvers) and recounts the troubles of a woman who takes a job on Long Island to escape and abusive man; the movie *Spanglish*,[17] a tantalizing objectification of a live-in Mexican domestic worker who is rarely shown cleaning a house but regularly portrayed giving psychological comfort to her wealthy employers; the politically inspired film *Bread and Roses*,[18] which focuses on two sisters in the Los Angeles janitorial workforce who, respectively, participate in and reject a union campaign; and the box-office stomper Cinderalla-story, *Maid in Manhattan*.[19] Usually objects of sexual attention (from Hispanic men and Anglo employers), the cleaning women in these movies are figures through which a wide segment of the U.S. population attempts to make sense of hemispheric migration, demographic changes, and the cultural conflicts prompted by immigration.[20] In the most ludicrous Hollywood productions (e.g., *Maid in Manhattan* and *Spanglish*), a focus on the woman's allure overshadows conditions that feed migration, including unemployment in Latin American countries and hemispheric political conflicts such as the wars in Central America in the 1980s.[21] Both the narratives themselves and the cultural overproduction of a character type leave intact the notion of an ethnically typed job. If Lydia turns around to find herself a Spanish cleaning lady it is because both employers *and* employees increasingly assume that the cleaning lady will be Hispanic.

On the one hand, labor-power becomes ethnic under the auspices of supply and demand. As that which is sold by workers before the actual labor process takes place, labor-power sells on the not-so-open market. "By labour-power or capacity for labour," Marx writes, "is to be understood the aggregate of those mental and physical capabilities existing in a human being, which he exercises whenever he produces a use-value of any description."[22] Thus Marx draws a distinction between the work done to produce value and labor-power, which is a potential for future work. As such, labor-power is a commodity, albeit an intangible one, that sells on the market as a capacity and ability to produce goods or do certain tasks. How much is an employer willing to pay for labor-power and how much is an employee willing to accept for the work? That question crosses the border, as certain employers know too well. Immigration, whether legal or not, affects the price of labor-power.[23]

Cleaning work, for one, is plagued by attitudes that devalue housework. As feminist scholars have pointed out for some time, because people view domestic work as less important than work outside the home, wages for domestic work are usually lower than those for other types of jobs. As the cases of "Nanny-gate" involving presidential appointments have shown, some people even view domestic work as something other than employment. For example, Linda Chavez, nominated by George W. Bush as labor secretary in 2001, went so far as to claim that she failed to pay Social Security and adequate wages for her live-in undocumented employee because the domestic worker was a companion benefiting from Chavez's charity.[24] As such, Chavez reiterated the line that domestic work is not a form of work that circulates on the open market while taking advantage of her employee's lack of immigration papers. Thus we see that domestic work is devalued socially at the same time that it is susceptible to a supply-and-demand flow that operates outside of governmental regulations regarding wages and Social Security. That is not to say that the women workers devalue domestic service or other types of cleaning jobs. In *Maid in the U.S.A.*, a book based in part on interviews with twenty-five Chicana domestic workers, Mary Romero writes, "In the discussions, I began to understand the paradox of domestic service: on the one hand, cleaning houses is degrading and embarrassing; on the other, domestic service can be higher paying, more autonomous, and less dehumanizing than other low-status, low-skilled occupations."[25] And therein lies a contradiction: whatever comforts the home space provides also creates attitudes that bring down wages.

History, literary and otherwise, instructs us that labor markets are willing to incorporate whatever groups of people can bring down the price of labor-power in a given context. In the early twentieth century, segregation in U.S. society contributed to a climate that ushered black women into the cleaning workforce. More than half a century before *Empress of the Splendid Season* appeared in print, Ann Petry's *The Street* featured another woman in New York City who is forced to take up a job as a domestic worker. Lutie Johnson concludes, "It must be hate that made them wrap all Negroes up in a neat package labeled 'colored'; a package that called for certain kinds of jobs and a special kind of treatment."[26] But wheter "hate" is a factor or not, the labor market, which will wrap any group into a package if it leads to cheap labor. That is one of the lessons of Upton Sinclair's *The Jungle*,[27] in which the stockyards feed off a succession of immigrant groups from Europe: "The Poles, who had come by tens of thousands, had been driven to the wall by the Lithuanians; and now the Lithuanians were giving way to the Slovaks" (57). In the system of the jungle, Packingtown turned to new immigrant groups from different countries to maintain low wages and long hours while precluding labor strikes (57–58). In this process, the churning of immigrants creates ethnic labor-power, even as the specific ethnicities change. Hijuelos's Lydia becomes a Spanish cleaning lady because she does not have other options and must help support her family. "Spanish" and "lady" are identity tags that are added by a socially symbolic process that interconnects ethnicity and gender with certain occupations.

"A Supernatural Emanation": The Work of Fantasy

The fantasy of the cleaning woman emerges in several ways in *Empress of the Splendid Season*. First, it is Lydia's fantasy that she will move out of her job and into her own wealthy domestic space. Second, it is also the fantasy of readers or movie viewers who place themselves in the cleaning worker's position, wishing a rich, handsome man will take her (and them) away. Certainly, a reader of *Empress* awaits the moment when Lydia and one of her wealthy employers will form a romantic bond or at least an interlude. This, after all, is the fantasy of films such as *Maid in Manhattan*, in which romance leads the cleaning worker into the position of spouse. Men who wish to marry a woman who will clean for them are also susceptible to the fantasy of "the Spanish cleaning lady." This is a circular effect by which the labor of the cleaning worker functions as a commodity that affects social relations in the household at the same time that the worker's fantasy life is affected by the commodity fetishism of the homes she cleans.

Lydia does not view herself as someone exploited by the capitalist system or even working class. She distinguishes between "people without money who had class and refinement and those who did not."[28] For someone who grew up with status as an important dimension of self-formation, class is more than an economic relation. "Liking to think of herself as upper lower class," Lydia separates herself from people in other low-paying occupations, considering it a fluke or a strange destiny that someone of her family ends up cleaning houses.[29] Her children view her (and themselves) more directly through her occupation. Thinking of their mother as a woman who gets on her knees to clean, "There was something the kids could not get out of their minds—which they were of the 'lower' classes" (35). In other words, Lydia's work is not in synch with her consciousness. For Lydia and other characters in Hijuelos's novels, poor working conditions are sweetened by the ideology of upward mobility. And for Lydia, domestic work even facilitates the types of fantasies that nurture a sense of self outside the cleaning labor force.

Luxury items usher Lydia into a realm of fantasy, a process most clearly seen when she visits her most regular client at a lavish house on New York's Upper East Side. "Mr. Osprey," a multimillionaire "aristocratic attorney in the practice of international business law" (37) with a "magnificent" home, appeals to Lydia's self-perception as an upper-class woman. Osprey's home represents for Lydia a multifaceted ideology of class, replete with books that display an elite education,

Osprey's "tremendously cordial and courtly" behavior (37), and decorations that included "several small Florentine portraits from the school of Piero di Lorenzo" (41). "The trappings of his worldly success," the narrative tells us, "worked on her psyche like a nearly supernatural emanation" (36–37). The Osprey house inspires Lydia to envy his possessions and consider their relation to a world far outside her immediate life: "Cleaning his carpets (Chinese, art deco, Persian Kirmans), she fantasized about the history of mankind, the curvy rug weaves reminding her of epic desert flicks and ancient palaces in Hollywood movies" (41). Over two decades Lydia at times allows her desire for wealth to mutate into a desire for Osprey himself. "[W]hile sorting through his laundry, she had conjured the image of his large bony hands caressing her breasts and touching her under her dress" (64). Even on her last day cleaning his home, past retirement age, the narrative tells us that "while vacuuming his Baghdad carpets, bored in the middle of the day, she dreamed he had fallen in love with her, as in those soap operas with which she so often amused herself" (333).

Lydia's intertextual fantasy about Osprey places her within the romantic configurations of soap operas, "the cleaning woman's staple" (64). In *Maid in Manhattan*, for example, the "maid" ends up with a senator on the front pages of glamour magazines, with all the celebration of romantic comedy. But Lydia draws from another, more sinister source, fantasizing about herself in relation to "the plots of the dime-store plantation novels she sometimes read, books about master-slave love" (64). Such a fantasy entails ownership, not only Osprey's ownership of her body but also her own possession of the Osprey house. She sees herself as the "*dueña* of Osprey's *casa*," cashing in on educational opportunities for her children, who would attend private schools and learn French (64). Positioning herself as the owner of the house (*dueña*) Lydia betrays a desire to invert the master–slave relationship. Slavery here is a metaphor for the "double burden" of caring for two homes. Feeling like "a cleaning lady in her private life" (60), Lydia at one point remembers something a friend said: "'*Soy una esclava*,' or, 'I'm a slave'" (202). The repetition of the line in Spanish and English emphasizes that the point "remained with Lydia" (202) and returned to her at those moments when it became clear she would neither be rich nor be swept into the middle class.[30]

It is the inability to rise out of working-class occupations—in contrast to characters' fantasy life—that make up the series of events in *Empress of the Splendid Season* and *The Mambo Kings Play Songs of Love*. *Empress* short-circuits the Cinderella fantasy: "Nothing ever happened between" Osprey and Lydia (64). Without a Lydia–Osprey love union, the novel refuses the kind of familial incorporation that readers come to expect from the cleaning woman narrative. At the end of the book, Osprey gives her a bonus and a hug and waves "to her as she made her way to the fancy cherrywood elevator and stepped inside" (334). Lydia and Osprey do indeed develop a relationship over the years, but one based on mutual admiration and trust. Osprey thinks about her regularly and worries about her health. "Her matter-of-fact approach to life had always amazed" him (329), and late in life he considers what he can "do for her" (330). Osprey extends his benevolence to the tune of twenty thousand dollars over two years "(to protect her from tax liabilities)" (330). As his concern with taxes indicates, *Empress of the Splendid Season* is unrelenting in marking economic difference, refusing a happily-ever-after conclusion.

While the commodities in Osprey's house work like a "supernatural emanation" that encourages fantasies of moving into the upper class, *Empress* as a novel refuses to consummate that fantasy. Like much of Hijuelos's writing, it punctures a hole in the hope that a person can romance or dance her way out of the working class. Instead, the novel calls attention to the everyday experiences that structure the lives of people who feed Latin stereotypes and ideological narratives such as the "American dream." *Empress* reminds readers of the daily lives of workers, and in that sense shares a narrative underpinning with *The Mambo Kings Play Songs of Love*.

The most compelling part of *Mambo Kings* is the second half, which provides a detailed account of the disintegration of Cesar Castillo. By contrast, the book has come to be known for its recreation of mambo culture. The publication of *Mambo Kings* and subsequent awarding of a Pulitzer Prize to Hijuelos was received with the kind of fanfare that the mambo kings would have reveled in (during their party phase). The book was hailed as a sign of a publishing boom for Latino literature and Hijuelos was called a "cross-over artist" in the vein of Gloria Estefan. Supposedly *The Mambo Kings* portrayed Cuban American culture in the heyday of the mambo, rumba, and cha-cha-cha in the United States of the 1940s and 1950s. The invocation of a cultural reality, signified through the recreation of a period and ample references in the text to musicians such as Tito Puente, Chano Pozo, and Celia Cruz, provided the kind of textual material that sustains ethnic literature, which presumably provides insight into the lived conditions of a particular group. By the time Hollywood released the movie, featuring Antonio Banderas and Armand Assante as the seductive Castillo brothers, the entire country could watch a club full of beautiful people dressed in bright outfits dancing with gusto. But the movie cut out the B side of the book, the part where Cesar becomes a building superintendent who eventually drinks himself to death.

The first half focuses on the Mambo Kings' hit record, an appearance on the *I Love Lucy* show, and minor financial success. What receives less attention is that by day the mambo kings take an assortment of jobs. At one point the fabulous Néstor Castillo is described working: "He would lift the side of the white fatted beef off the conveyor belt and hoist it onto the back of a freezer truck, wearing a long smock that was smeared with blood and a pair of rubber boots" (113). Hijuelos's use of the imperfect tense of "lift" echoes the type of repetitive labor process that is so common to wage labor. By night, the mambo kings perform a much different type of work. While playing music and chopping meat are vastly different forms of labor, both provide limited opportunities for advancement in the novel. Once the success of the hit record wears off, the mambo kings must return to working-class occupations. Pickled on alcohol, Cesar literally disintegrates, his body like so many slabs of meat that are processed at the plant; or, one could say that he becomes disposable, like the vinyl of his hit record.

One of the most intriguing aspects of Hijuelos's novels is the way that plots develop. The action does not look like an arc; it is more like a plateau created through a retrospective telling that shifts from a present at the edge of death to a youthful past. Events plod along, and at times the books seem to be devoid of conflict. In the end, these novels read like a succession of experiences over decades in the lives of characters, with scenes repeating like unshakable memories. If Cesar Castillo recalls nights with Vanna Vane dozens of times throughout the novel, it is because memories repeat like other things, including the mundane manual labor that makes up the workday:

> Down the stairs and into the basement, and following the hallway past the boiler and washing-machine rooms, he went. Then for the hundredth time—or was it the thousandth?—Cesar Castillo, ex-Mambo King and former star of the *I Love Lucy* show, found himself before the black bolt-studded fire door that was the entrance to his workroom. (233)

The ironic reference to *I Love Lucy* show emphasizes that the basement is the real workroom. If the mambo kings look like exaggerated stereotypes of the Latin lover, that's because Cesar's most common experiences are not playing on stage but living with the "the conga-drum pounding of the washroom dryer" (233). The rest, the life of mambo, is fantasy, facilitated by the day job and created in a narrative that is filtered through Cesar's delusions.

The different forms of labor (musician and superintendent) do have something in common. While the type of work that a person performs to write a song or sing on stage—"working joints" (256)— is not the same as turning screws in a basement, both cases involve the production of services and goods. The novel is not particularly senti- mental about cultural production in the sense that it does not grant it a value that is more permanent than other types of work. Mambo is actu- ally a commodity that is recreated each time a new record comes out: "Mambo Nocturne," "Jingle Bells Mambo," "My Cuban Mambo," and "Traffic Mambo." "By the mid-seventies," Cesar comes to see, "most of these records had vanished from the face of the earth" (15). One can assume that among the vanished records is "The Mambo Kings Play Songs of Love," a collection of love songs the Mambo Kings released as a thirty-three LP album. That the novel is named after a record reflects not only Hijuelos's engagement with popular culture but also a pessimism about the novel as a form. *The Mambo Kings Play Songs of Love* is particularly brutal in capturing how U.S. society consumes music, food, and people (and by association, novels) without much discernment, then discards these products.

It is this society of consumption that frames Cesar's treatment of women. If the Pulitzer-Prize-winning *Mambo Kings* periodically veers into the language of a second-rate bodice ripper, it is because Cesar has come to intertwine Cuban machismo with the meat market of New York's nightlife. Cesar remembers Vanna's "fine ass" and throw- ing her on the bed, "pumping her so wildly she felt as if she was being attacked by a beast of the forest" (17). Then he remembers it again and again. Hijuelos does not spare us details about body parts. When Cesar's body succumbs to systemic kidney failure, he feels "a heavy black rag being pulled out of you" (395). He dies holding a glass of whiskey in one hand and a piece of paper with song lyrics in the other. Like his nephew after him, Cesar hangs on to the fantasy until the end.

"Work Will Set You Free":
The Composer's End

It appears that the only certainty for Hijuelos's characters is the decomposition of the body. In response, characters remember specific experiences and fantasies to ward off bodily evisceration. In order to accomplish this, Hijuelos constructs novels that present the everyday actions of working-class people and producers of culture. If his biographical accounts periodically replicate the sweet aching of nostalgia, they more often valorize the repetition of mundane moments that add up to a lifetime, the very type of repetition that might be associated with a workday. These are the products of Hijuelos's work, ongoing attempts to hold off the inevitable conclusion that material labor leads to repetition. Work, we are led to see, is a trap.

In *A Simple Habana Melody*, the workaholic composer Israel Levis leaves his native Havana to tour New York and several European cities and oversee productions of his musical numbers. Trying to escape both political repression in Cuba and the discomforts of his massive weight and limited romantic life, Levis figures, "The heavier his schedule, the better, as he wanted to lose himself in his work" (199). A product of Havana's musical heyday of the 1920s and 1930s, Levis is best known for the ubiquitous rumba hit "*Rosas Puras*," which is popularized internationally by a mulatta Carmen-Miranda-type figure. As someone who traffics in tropical images of Cuba, Israel cuts an imposing figure in the music scene of many capitals. But when the Nazis overrun France, the devoutly Catholic Levis is rounded up as a result of his name. He is placed on a freight car to Ettersberg, an episode that, despite the context of the repression he had witnessed, sends Levis fantasizing about the town: "It had once played host to the likes of Schiller and Goethe—a place of such Alpine loveliness that it had been the source of much poetic inspiration" (297). Comparing a "Nordic myth" to his own myth, Havana, Levis sets up a parallel between himself and German artists who derive inspiration from their locations. The full irony of Levis' devotion to music (and myth) as an art form that can raise him above the troubles of his physical existence becomes clear when he enters the main gate of Buchenwald, which bears the inscription: "ARBEIT MACHT FREI ('WORK WILL SET YOU FREE')" (297). That is the composer's illusion, but it also turns out to be prophetic. Levis is forced to play piano for his captors, and this privilege ultimately helps him survive the camp.

Levis' work is the creation of Cuban national culture. A gifted composer whose music is absorbed and consumed in numerous societies and economic systems, Levis experiences a deflation of his energy after living in the concentration camp so that "the very idea of writing yet a single passage of music seemed to invoke a fear" (307). His condition calls to mind Theodor W. Adorno's famous dictum: "To write poetry after Auschwitz is barbaric."[31] The line comes from the essay "Cultural Criticism and Society," which focuses most directly on the cultural critic's efforts to judge "that to which he fancies himself superior."[32]

Adorno's statement is not so much about poetry *per se* but about culture's inextricable connection to sociopolitical conditions, regardless of attempts by artists and critics to raise culture above the failures of "civilization." In other words, to write something or produce art that seeks to evade and ignore the moral decrepitude in society is to collude with oppressive forces. Following that logic, Levis's composition of rumbas—a contradictory pop culture form that approximates tropical souvenirs—during years when the island suffered from devastating economic conditions and political repression is a manifestation of the artist's vanity and part of the barbarism on the island. In the early 1930s, Cuba was ruled by Gerardo Machado, whose secret police and death squads clamped down on the population so that, as the historian Louis Pérez has written, the island "assumed the appearance of an armed camp, and terror became the principal means of government."[33] Seeking to rise above conditions that are neither rosy nor pure, Levis attempts both through his music and his departure from Havana to escape political and social conditions on the island, in other words to get away from "the Cuba hidden under a mountain of risqué postcards, of maracas decorated with palm trees, of aromatic cigars, rumba bands, troubadours, handsome singers and spectacular female dancers—the Cuba that the world did not know" (186).

Levis settles in Paris, and when the Nazis rush into the city, he responds to the general panic by maintaining "his daily regimen before the piano" (262). Faced with rumors about the mass deportations of Jews, Levis prefers to think they are exaggerations: "And during that time the only concession that the Maestro made to this disheartening course of events was to cut short his work one morning and go to the bank" (263). "His rigidies and devotion to this work" (264) are such that when the Gestapo knocks on his door, Levis responds, "I am at work, please come back later" (293). Levis, of course, is the type of artist who sees himself as divinely inspired and believes "*that music and the noble motivations of the artist would shut out the bad of the world*" (281).

Hijuelos's characters have an impressive faith in the power of work, whether they are composing music or cleaning bathrooms. But the labor process, the actions that produce value for employers or for a market that consumes commodities, stifles characters' dreams of moving out of their situation and into a more fulfilling economic or metaphysical life. *Empress of the Splendid Season*, for example, ends with Lydia España's son, Rico, at work. Unlike his parents, Rico has attended an elite university and entered the professional world of Manhattan as a psychologist. In monetary terms, he has fulfilled the immigrant's dream of a better life for the second generation. But what does he have in life? Without a substantial relationship or friends, Rico is "set in his solitary hardworking ways" (294). He is uncomfortable with the "bourgeois life," but cannot connect again with the old neighborhood, nor does he have a spouse or partner. Even when he goes back home, the dishes prepared by his mother, "steaks and *chuletas* and platters of fried plantains and garlic-soaked *yuca*, and rice and black beans," are foods he "no longer ate, for they were unhealthful and cholesterol-rich" (266). In his loneliness and separation from culture and neighborhood, Rico is reminiscent of Abraham Cahan's David Levinsky, whose rise in the world of manufacturing leaves him a lonely man, separated from his inner world of Talmudic scholarship. "There are cases when success is a tragedy," Levinsky tells us.[34]

Ultimately, Hijuelos's characters are caught in a wheel of work, one that churns new workers like the stockyards in Jurgis Rudkus's Chicago. That is why toward the end of these novels, characters often see themselves reflected in a succeeding generation. In the case of the mambo kings, two new brothers arrive from Cuba. And on Lydia's last day of work, she rides the bus home, looking out the window and day-dreaming that she is again a young woman, dressed smartly and going to new addresses to take on jobs as a husband with a weakened heart and two children wait for her at home. "How it all seemed so difficult and wonderful at the same time, Lydia found herself thinking" (334–335). Lost in "some kind of sweet recollection of faded youth," Lydia sees, "a young cleaning woman, a beautiful *chica*, no more than twenty-two or twenty-three years old, her bag with a change of clothes and a pair of shoes beside her" (335). Before her is the grind of the working life, which replaces one cleaning worker with another.

But then the young woman looks over and smiles, leaving Lydia "much moved by the simple kindness of that transcendent gesture" (335). The smile is transcendent because Lydia sees in it the value of the moments that make up her own life. The grandiose future she once envisioned gives way to an encounter with a mundane exchange. Lydia's professionally unhappy son has not reached this understanding. He appears in the final scene listening to a lonely patient. day-dreaming about a night out with his mother when the family had seen someone who looked like the actor James Mason. "Wouldn't it have been nice," Rico thinks, to have someone like James Mason show up in the middle of a session "getting rid of the heartaches, the concerns about health, the bills, and the anxieties, and spreading before them the promise of a wondrous future" (342). Instead, Rico is susceptible to seeing himself most commonly in a meaningless existence, one in which "the promise of the future" becomes "fainter and fainter" (200). "*And there is death waiting for you, at the edge of the endless-seeming sea*" (italics in the original; 200).

And here a brief return to "Lunch at the Biltmore" proves informative. In one of the most revealing scenes, the elder Hijuelos comes home with packages of meat wrapped in butcher paper, the blood seeping through and leaving "runny red blotches on his clothes." Father and son are both bleeding out, with Oscar Hijuelos suffering from a kidney disease that has him "passing blood and bloated with enema." Still recuperating from his illness, the young Oscar was not allowed to eat anything other than potatoes and baked chicken. When his father feeds him a hamburger made from a "handful of filets mignons" Hijuelos offers something like a transcendent experience, relatively speaking: "[I]n that moment, all thoughts of illness and mortality seemed to have passed from his mind forever." From his father's mind, that is. If a heart attack reminded Hijuelos that the working body ultimately falls apart, a simple gesture, like making someone a hamburger, can seem to ward off the inevitable disintegration brought on by the workday.

Work simultaneously brings on the weight of mortality and offers fantasies of a better future. Striving under capitalism, the characters who populate Hijuelos's fiction look to the American dream, metaphysical redemption, and even fame and fortune to lift them above the daily grind. But one has to wonder whether even an impressive body of work, say six novels and many smaller pieces published between 1983 and 2002, can offer anything more than the transcendence of a smile on a bus. U.S. economic systems are always waiting for the next occupation, the next generation. Work calls out relentlessly. It is a necessity. But it is also a trap, a fantasy of freedom from daily labor. Work does indeed set you free—to go back to work. And in the novels of Oscar Hijuelos, work is inextricable from fantasies of a better future.

NOTES

1. Oscar Hijuelos, "Lunch at the Biltmore," *The New Yorker*, January 17, 2005: 50–53.
2. Paula W. Shirley argues that the novel incorporates Desi Arnaz and the *I Love Lucy* Show to explore how music and television frame the characters' sense of Cubanness. "While music brings César and Néstor Castillo together with Desi Arnaz, it is their identity as Cubans in a foreign land that is continually underscored in their relationship." See "Reading Desi Arnaz in *The Mambo Kings Play Songs of Love*,"

MELUS 20 (Fall 1995), 73. See also Gustavo Pérez Firmat, *Life on the Hyphen: The Cuban-American Way* (Austin: U of Texas P, 1994); and Richard F. Patteson, "Oscar Hijuelos: 'Eternal Homesickness' and the Music of Memory." *Critique* 44 (September 2002): 38–47.

3. Oscar Hijuelos, *The Mambo Kings Play Songs of Love* (New York: Farrar, Straus, Giroux, 1989).

4. Karen Christian, *Show and Tell: Identity as Performance in U.S. Latina/o Fiction* (Albuquerque: U of New Mexico P, 1997), 75.

5. Oscar Hijuelos, *Empress of the Splendid Season* (New York: Harper Flamingo, 1999).

6. Abraham Cahan, *The Rise of David Levinsky*, edited by Jules Chametzky (New York: Penguin, 1993).

7. Helena Maria Viramontes, *Under the Feet of Jesus* (New York: Penguin, 1995).

8. Paula M.L. Moya, *Learning from Experience: Minority Identities, Multicultural Struggles* (Berkeley: U of California P, 2002), 175–176. Moya notes that critics have discussed themes such as finding a voice, crossing borders, and making sexuality explicit as examples of Chicana criticism. She does not take issue with the interpretive concerns of Chicana and, more generally, feminist literary criticism; rather, she merely questions whether these are the most appropriate lenses for reading this novel. Moya then analyzes *Under the Feet of Jesus* in relation to how the main character gains a type of literacy that allows her to develop social consciousness; in turn, Moya places interpretation itself at the center.

9. Ernesto Laclau and Chantal Mouffe, *Hegemony and Socialist Strategy* (New York: Verso, 1985), 176.

10. Antonia Darder and Rodolfo D. Torres, "Mapping Latino Studies: Critical Reflections on Class and Social Theory." *Latino Studies* 1 (July 2003): 309.

11. Ibid., 309–310. As a category of analysis, class in the Americas calls for a rethinking in light of transnational flows and the imbalance in economic power between U.S. low-wage workers and Latin American people who are under- or unemployed.

12. Roland Barthes, "From Work to Text," in Philip Rice and Patricia Waugh (eds.), *Modern Literary Theory* (New York: Arnold, 1996), 166–171.

13. Oscar Hijuelos, *A Simple Habana Melody (From When the World Was Good)* (New York: HarperCollins, 2002).

14. For a discussion of ethnic labels as abstractions of social importance in U.S. society, see Suzanne Oboler, *Ethnic Labels, Latino Lives: Identity and the Politics of (Re)presentation in the United States* (Minneapolis: U of Minnesota P, 1995), xv–xviii.

15. Mary Romero, *Maid in the U.S.A*, 10th anniv. ed. (New York: Routledge, 2002); hereafter cited as MUSA; Pierrette Hondagneu-

Sotelo, *Doméstica: Immigrant Workers Cleaning and Caring in the Shadows of Affluence* (Berkeley: U of California P, 2001).

16. Esmeralda Santiago, *América's Dream* (New York: HarperCollins, 1996).

17. *Spanglish*, dir. James L. Brooks. Sony, 2004.

18. *Bread and Roses*, dir. Ken Loach, VHS. Lions Gate, 2000.

19. *Maid in Manhattan*, dir. Wayne Wang. Columbia, 2002. The most popular of recent films with cleaning workers as central characters, it made more than $93 million during its six-month run in theaters (boxofficeguru.com).

20. Pierrette Hondagneu-Sotelo has argued that several factors have created increased demand for domestic workers in recent decades: more women are working full time, families are looking for alternatives to institutional day care, and growing income inequality makes it possible for more families to hire domestic workers (*Doméstica*, 4–5). Hondagneu-Sotelo found that even people with modest incomes are employing domestic workers (ibid., 8–9).

21. In considering the politico-military-economic conditions that motivate migration, Grace Chang argues that "migrant women workers are effectively imported into the United States from the Third World and subsequently channeled into the service sector, specifically in care work or paid reproductive labor." See *Disposable Domestics: Immigrant Women Workers in the Global Economy* (Cambridge, MA: South End Press, 2000), 12.

22. Karl Marx, *Capital*, vol. 1 (New York: International Publishers, 1992), 164.

23. A person who has no legal right to work in the United States may not have legal standing in the courts or even expect the protection of U.S. laws such as minimum wage. The U.S. Supreme Court, for one, has ruled that illegal immigrants do not possess certain rights of the workplace. In *Hoffman Plastic Compounds, Inc v. National Labor Relations Board* (2002), the Court ruled that undocumented workers are criminals and thus not entitled to the same protections under labor law as U.S. citizens and permanent residents. The case involved José Castro, a Mexican national who had been fired by Hoffman for helping to organize a union. The Court ruled that he was not entitled to back pay, despite provisions in the National Labor Relations Act (NLRA) that protect organizing efforts, because he was not legally eligible for employment in the United States.

24. MUSA, 14–15.

25. MUSA, 42.

26. Ann Petry, *The Street* (Boston: Houghton Mifflin, 1946), 72.

27. Upton Sinclair, *The Jungle*, The Uncensored Original Edition (Tuczon: See Sharp P, 2003).

28. Hijuelos, *Empress*, 4.

29. Lydia's view of class and her inability to embrace something like a proletarian identification are influenced by the transnational conditions of her experience. She left Cuba not for economic reasons but because of familial conflict and gender oppression. The Cuban Revolution of 1959 skews her consideration of leftist politics. Having soaked up the political positions of many Cuban exiles, Lydia sees Castro and Marx behind efforts to defend workers' rights, "Marx having been indirectly responsible for the monthly pound of meat rations that her family in Cuba had to live with, for the Russian soldiers there, for the existence of the Committee for the Defense of the Revolution" (ibid., 149).

30. The invocation of slavery touches on the domestic worker figure's genealogical antecedent in literal slavery. As Paula Rabinowitz has shown, in the 1930s and 1940s novels by black writers and film noir revise "the image of the black domestic from mammy to maid, recasting a symbol of antebellum racial hierarchies into an urbanized form of labor." See *Black and White and Noir* (New York: Columbia University Press, 2002), 63.

31. Theodor W. Adorno, "Cultural Criticism and Society," in *Prisms*, trans. Samuel and Shierry Weber (London: Neville Spearman, 1967), 34.

32. Ibid., 19.

33. Louis A. Pérez, *Cuba: Between Reform and Revolution* (New York: Oxford UP, 1995), 256.

34. Abraham Cahan, *The Rise of David Levinsky*, edited by Jules Chametzky (New York: Penguin, 1993), 529.

CHAPTER 11

Mass Production of the Heartland: Cuban American Lesbian Camp in Achy Obejas's "Wrecks"

María DeGuzmán

When I told Lourdes, she suggested that if I know the accident is imminent, and that if having the accident is the only way out of this post-Sandra depression, then maybe I need to just get it over with and run over a newspaper boy, ram a mailbox, or hit a station wagon filled with suburbanites. She said that maybe by avoiding the accident I'm delaying the healing process, sidestepping the very idea that Sandra and I are as dead as disco.

—Achy Obejas, "Wrecks"

IDEOLOGICAL DIMENSION OF AN AESTHETICS

The last two lines of Achy Obejas's short story "Wrecks" punctuate the story with the question of assimilation as mainstreaming, "Finally it's just me and the cops on the ramp. They turn off their blue lights, flick on their turn signal, and wait for me to mainstream into traffic."[1] This scenario of officers of the law waiting for and expecting an individual driver to join other drivers moving in the same direction along a pre-charted road serves as a highly charged metaphor for the act of becoming and being part of a given society or social structure. The verb "to mainstream," which resonates with the noun and adjectival forms used interchangeably in common parlance to indicate the centrality of dominant culture and the relative position of everyone and everything not deemed to be in the "mainstream," raises the issue of the relation of this mainstreaming to assimilation and vice versa. This issue is central to the study of ethnicity and sexuality not merely in terms of sociology or demographics, categories of lived experience, or in narratives understood as reflections of lived experience, but also in a performative and aesthetic sense in as much as aesthetics involve tactics of representation and the types of cultural intervention these tactics effect.

This essay seeks to illuminate the political or ideological dimension of the aesthetics of contemporary Cuban American lesbian writer Achy Obejas's work of the 1990s, specifically a short story entitled "Wrecks" from her collection of stories *We Came All the Way from Cuba So You Could Dress Like This?* published in 1994. By political or ideological dimension of an aesthetics I mean the way in which, in this case, a text manipulates value and/or revalues cultural codes and values by repeating and recycling objects and signs of cultural production and experience. So as not to merely reduce the aesthetic to social and political issues, I view the project of illuminating the political or ideological dimension of a work's aesthetics as seeing ideology and aesthetics in dialectical relation to each other, a relation the "function" of which is the assignment of value, value that directly impinges upon concepts of citizenship and relations of desire, membership in and what is possible within a given society.[2] Obejas's "Wrecks," in the condensed but often experimental and risk-taking space of the short story, manages to intervene in the assignment of value that shapes such ideas of citizenship and relations of desire. As a text by a Latina and specifically a Cuban American, it defies many of the expectations that readers—particularly (though not exclusively) non-Latina/o readers—often place on Latina/o literary production. The general expectation on opening a book of stories by a Latina/o author is that one will encounter stories that convey the experience of living in the United States as a Latina—or, more specifically, as a person of Cuban, Puerto Rican, Mexican, Dominican, Guatemalan (etc.) heritage— who highlights her difference and comes bearing the gifts of her people's history. This often gets marketed, quite unashamedly, as Latin flavor or accent, not so much by the writers themselves or by Latina/o-centered publishing houses such as Arte Público Press or Editorial Bilingüe as by the mainstream New York and Boston presses, though every institution and producer of culture feels the identity-tourism pressures of the mass market. Part of that identity tourism entails an expectation of an auto-ethnography, that the writer will explain her/himself and her/his history or background. The story involves a kind of ethnographic accounting of oneself and those assumed to be like oneself.

"Wrecks" frustrates the expected auto-ethnographic project while at the same time conveying difference, but a difference that both results from and is performed as a complex and subtle intersection of ethnicity, sexuality, and gender communicated on the basis of repetitions, recyclings, and redefinitions. Such repetitions have been identified with camp and yet "Wrecks" takes the tactics of repetition and recycling that certain critics have identified with camp to create a resistant form of assimilation quite lethal to mainstreaming and that proves that despite the post-Stonewall disrepute of camp, camp can indeed be re-Stonewalled, stonewalling the action of mainstreaming even as it would seem to participate in it.

The society at stake for Achy Obejas's work to date is that of the United States in the 1990s/early twenty-first century, a time when the issue of whether this country has and is going to have a "genuinely" multicultural culture and not merely a mono-culturalized, Anglo-dominated, hetero-normative, patriarchal nominally "multiculture" has been explicitly foregrounded in debates between politicians, academics, and within the media at large. As "deterritorialized" Mexican-cum-Chicano cultural critic, activist, and performance artist Guillermo Gómez-Peña declared in 1989 in "The Multicultural Paradigm: An Open Letter to the National Arts Community," referencing what I would call the "Latin(american)ization" of the United States,

> The need for U.S. culture to come to terms with the Latino-American [and he might have also said "Latina-American"] "cultural other" has become a national debate. Everywhere I go, I meet people seriously interested in our ideas and cultural models. The art, film, and literary worlds are finally looking south.
>
> To look south means to remember; to capture one's historical self. For the United States, this historical self extends from the early Native American cultures to the most recent immigrations from Laos or Guatemala.[3]

With the mention of Laos and "Asian" immigration along with current Central American "Latino immigration" to the United States, Gómez-Peña opens up the possibility of the inclusion of Asians and other ethnicities and cultures within a rubric of "Latino/a(american)ization" of this country. The main point that I would like to emphasize, however, is his manifesto-like claim not only about

Latino cultural production, but also about a "Latino/ a(american)ized" one that "To look South means to remember; to capture one's historical self."

Achy Obejas—fiction writer, poet, translator, and journalist who has won awards for her coverage of the Chicago mayoral elections, who has been the Springer Lecturer at the University of Chicago since fall 2003 and Distinguished Writer-in-Residence at the University of Hawaii, fall 2005, who writes stories about "uprooted" people attempting to survive their ordeals of exile and displacement, and whose stories and first award-winning novel *Memory Mambo*[4] are taught in courses entitled "Contemporary Narratives by Latina Writers" listed several years ago on the Cornell University Latino Studies Program website[5]—captures a historical self that (unlike the narrator of her 2001 novel *Days of Awe*, an extended effort to connect to history through bloodlines) seldom reaches farther back than 1959, the eve of the Cuban Revolution, and that is cut off from Gómez-Peña's "South" by U.S. borders. Though that South exists within these borders, for Obejas being inside the continental United States involves a mode of existence that greatly problematizes, even suspends, this act of remembrance of which Gómez-Peña speaks and writes. In contrast to the later *Days of Awe* (with its references to Jewish life in Babylon and pre-Inquisition Sevilla and Toledo, to the Spanish Inquisition, to Columbus, and to Cuban history from the late 1700s to Cuba's "war of independence," to the 1930s, and onward[6]) and with the exception of a few ironic references to the "legendary" Bartolomé de las Casas and José Martí, the stories and the first novel do not "remember" past 1963 and even 1978 when as the twenty-four-year-old woman narrator of *Memory Mambo*, Juani Casas, tells readers at the outset of her tale, "My family and I came from Cuba to the U.S. by boat when I was six years old" (9), thus confirming her membership (like the author's) in what Cuban American writer and critic Gustavo Pérez Firmat has termed "the 1.5 generation"—a concept borrowed from Latino sociologist Rubén G. Rumbaut—of Cuban Americans.[7] Later, Gina, the narrator's Puerto Rican independentista lover, asks her, "Do you remember anything about your life in Cuba?" (133) and the narrator (again, in contrast to the narrator of *Days of Awe*, a genealogical saga about a Cuban's return to the island) realizes that she left "Cuba too young to remember anything but snatches of color and scattered words, like the cutout letters in a ransom note. And what little [she] could put together had since been forged and painted over by the fervor, malice and nostalgia of others" (133). In contradistinction to these "forged" memories, *Memory Mambo* explores its own experience-based and thus supposedly "authentic" memories of a love relationship between two women (imploded by horizontal violence) and memories of family violence and sexual abuse. These memories the narrator distinguishes from the nostalgic mythology of exile at the same time that the narrative intermixes them producing "Memory mambo . . . one step forward, two steps back" (194). The novel takes the mambo dance, originating with and appropriated from Afro-Caribbean slaves and popularized in Cuba and the United States in the 1950s and early 1960s by musicians celebrating Cuba's syncretic musical heritage, and turns it into a metaphor not so much of public, historical colonization of the Pearl of the Antilles by both Spain and the United States as of the private "historical" memory of internalized, intra-familial violence—a personal colonization by homophobia, misogyny, and competition between Latinas (a Puerto Rican independentista and an exiled Cuban) over who has suffered more and who is more effectively addressing her political oppression.

For many readers, Latinas/os and otherwise, the 1990s work of Achy Obejas might strike them at odds with Gómez-Peña's call to look South and his definition that "to look South means to remember; to capture one's historical self." Save for droll references to such "Cuban" heroes as Las Casas, Martí, and so on, and serious but briefly outlined references to the Cuban Revolution and *los Marielitos*,[8] looking South (and, in this case, South-East) is a question of looking "within"—both in the personal sense and in the national sense, the latter to the extent that the South or South-East has been displaced into a within demarcated by the geographical borders of the United States. Ironically, for Obejas's Cuban American and/or Latina immigrant narrators, the most "authentic" remembrances are those "confused" ones formed through lived experience within the United States, a geographical and cultural terrain that Gómez-Peña and other cultural critics have deservedly accused of being characterized by homogenization and amnesia. Other memories, those not garnered from lived experience here in the United States, those she has absorbed from other family members, though "fresh," "fantastic," and "detailed," feel improbable, "false" (*Memory Mambo*, 9).

This paradox of false distinctness and authentic confusion structuring the relation of memory to identity-construction strongly implies that the "historical self" to whom Gómez-Peña alludes is for many Cuban Americans also, or at least as much, a "fictional self." In other words, the historical self is as much about what is produced and performed in the moment (*en el momento de la verdad or, más bien, de la mentira*) as excavated from the past, distant both spatially and temporally. Looking South and remembering in Achy Obejas's 1990s work means representing or, perhaps more accurately, presenting a U.S.ian[9] a-historical self, a self or rather a mode of existence set adrift or exiled from an excavatable "history" (which Mexican Americans might invoke) and abducted and colonized by the relentlessly "a-historical" presentness and futuricity of "the American Way" of life in the United States. I should clarify that with the phrase "a-historical self" I do not mean to imply a negative evaluation of Obejas's earlier work. I am employing the phrase to underscore the lived or felt conditions of its production. If any negativity adheres to the phrase I ask readers to think of it in terms of an affect produced by historical conditions (for instance, the over forty-year history of a Cold War between the United States and Cuba, routine visa denials, and other such policies that split the Cuban American subject from tangible access to a past in the present). When Gómez-Peña, a Mexican/Chicano, calls artists, writers, performance artists, educators, arts administrators, and politicians to look south, to remember and capture a historical self, and in this way to make viable a truly multicultural border culture as an alternative to a false, Anglo-dominated, media-generated, meta-reality of monoculture, he would seem to speak from the certainty of having a history to know and even access in the flesh. This certainty about the true and the false, the real and the simulated, would seem to correlate with the construction of oneself as an inhabitant of a particular border zone, a border zone that, however de-territorialized, is the extension of the paradigm of borderlands located along the Rio Bravo or the Rio Grande and involving the centuries-old grounded encuentro between Native Americans, Spaniards, and Anglos (among others) within the territories of the Southwest.

Despite the postmodernity of Guillermo Gómez-Peña's work, one finds at the heart of its vision of history a spatio-temporal certainty born out of a strong sense of orientation, this Southward orientation toward the South American continent and Mexico in particular, however transculturated and de-territorialized. The temporal dimensions of this detectable spatio-temporal certainty are not just composed of a sense of continuity, however negative in many of its aspects (the history of war, border disputes, economic exploitation), between the past and the present, but between the present and the present as well as between the present and the future. As writer and the son of Mexican immigrant parents Richard Rodriguez points out in his speech/essay "Pocho Pioneer,"

[A]diós was never part of the Mexican-American or the Puerto Rican vocabulary. We didn't turn our backs on the past. We kept going back and forth, between past and future. After a few months of work in New York or Los Angeles, we would cross the border.[10]

Despite his brief comparison of Mexicans with "wandering Jews" in his 1992 *Days of Obligation*, "Mexicans had no true home but the tabernacle of memory,"[11] Rodriguez reinforces his "Pocho Pioneer" observation in his 2002 memoir *Brown: The Last Discovery of America* when he writes:

> Never did these Mexican men [workers] speak of having left the past behind . . . These Mexican men worked to sustain the past; they sent money to the past every Saturday. From the Mexican migrants' point of view, California was a commute.[12]

The fact that Mexicans or Mexican Americans and Puerto Ricans can routinely return to the country or territory of either their own "origin" or their families' origins makes possible more of a nexus of memory and experience rather than a severance between the two as has been the case with many Cubans/Cuban Americans during the continuing Cold War between Cuba and the United States. Rodriguez's equation of Mexican Americans and Puerto Ricans with regard to the practice of coming and going between the United States and the country from whence they or their relatives immigrated/emigrated helps to explain the role of the foil to the narrator that Gina, the Puerto Rican independentista, plays in the novel *Memory Mambo*. It lends definable characteristics to the cultural de-racination of Achy Obejas's Cuban American narrators more generally, including the relatively unmarked but potentially "autobiographical" one of the short story "Wrecks."

In contrast to the "cultural certainty" or, if "certainty" sounds too absolutist then "orientation," born of spatio-temporal continuities and geopolitical proximities potentially available to Mexican Americans and Puerto Ricans, the uncertainty of a history and the function of an imagined or mentally conjured memory in relation to the rescuing of one's history (national and personal) appears to be a manifestation of that "sea change" suffered by Cuban refugees fleeing the impositions of the Cuban Revolution only to be intercepted by the U.S. coast guard "just a few miles from Key West" (*Memory Mambo*, 10), forcibly "Americanized" in a confused and confusing hurry, and thrown upon the kindness of "cousins" living in Miami and other parts of the United States. Compounding the sense of alienation is the ironic equation (by non-Cubans as well as some Cubans themselves) of this "deracination" (*destierro*) with social mobility, of this "a-historicity" with advantage instead of its opposite.[13] For instance, in *Memory Mambo* Gina, the Puerto Rican independentista girlfriend of Juani, the Cuban American narrator with complex of gusana (traitor to the Revolution and to Cuba), thinks that because Juani is Cuban she is "automatically privileged" and Juani adds bitterly, "as if my family had ever been privileged, as if we were doing anything except trying desperately to stay afloat" (78). This brief scene of confrontation between Gina and Juani serves to link deracinated a-historicity with psychological stress and cultural alienation rather than with social and/or economic advantage.

This scene of confrontation between Gina, the independentista who is a closeted lesbian, and Juani, a more or less openly lesbian Cuban American, also reminds readers that more than one type of cultural conflict and "dis-orientation" is at stake for Latinas and that in the struggle to achieve visibility and representation, one aspect of identity is often pitted against another. For Gina, it would seem that her lesbian identity[14] must be sacrificed in favor of Puertoricanness. For Juani her Cubanicity or *cubanidad* puts her in a double-bind of being not "American" enough and yet also not "Latina" in the right ways because she is assumed to be more upwardly mobile than most other Latinas and cannot take pride in her family's country of origin across a whole spectrum of political issues from political orientation (Castro's Cuba being quite literally "banned" in the United States) to sexual orientation. The "revolutionary" regime was never fair to those whom it perceived to be gender or sexual traitors, "sexiles" to borrow a term that exists in many contexts for various kinds of sexual exiles but which has been appropriated by scholars such as Luis Aponte-Parés and others in reference to "Latino queers . . . migrating to el Norte . . . to escape oppressive environments where they felt threatened, or where they could not be 'themselves.'"[15]

In relation to the injunction to "look South . . . to remember . . . to capture one's historical self," Achy Obejas's fiction does more than associate the a-historical self with alienation. Rather, it leads the reader to view this a-historicism of personal existence as part of the immigrant's and especially the (s)exiled immigrant's experience in the United States. Nor, in its effects does the fiction stop there. What is perhaps an especially *Cuban American lesbian camp* aesthetics of deliberate repetition—nowhere more clearly visible than in the short story "Wrecks"—interrupts or intervalizes this a-historicity of life in the American Way and its expectations for the amnesiac propulsion of immigrants regardless of gender, sexual orientation, "race," ethnicity, or "origin" into a conformist assimilationist future. The intervalization of the a-historical resistantly slows down, drags on, the process variously described (depending on one's perspective) as accommodation, acculturation, or assimilation with a sense of the weight and form of each of the pieces composing the floating wreckage—*la balsa*—of a traumatic and complex cultural exile constituted of interrelated factors. The deployment of a particular camp aesthetics of deliberate repetition to intervalize the a-historical or the un-braking drive of the present into the future brings us directly to the question of the political or ideological dimension of an aesthetic tactic.

"Wrecks" and Repetition

Achy Obejas's short story "Wrecks" presents us with a challenging case for the exploration of a hypothesized relation between aesthetics and ideology. The story, unlike the novel *Memory Mambo*, contains no references to Cuba or to Cuba's relation to the United States or to anything else that readers might ordinarily regard as "political" or, for that matter, recognizably "ideological." "Wrecks" is the first in the collection of seven stories in *We Came All the Way from Cuba So You Could Dress Like This?* More significantly, it occupies a primary place for the way in which it foregrounds an aesthetic that governs most of the collection of camp—usually identified as "humor" or a comic vision by reviewers, the latter an evaluation with which Susan Sontag's 1964 "Notes on 'Camp'" would be in partial agreement.[16]

The story itself is simple. The narrator, unmarked in terms of identity coordinates except for being a self-declared "lesbian and a feminist" (15) and perhaps a thinly disguised version of the author herself (though the story yields no failsafe clues), has a best friend named "Lourdes" (20), is a Catholic, and, like a homesick coastal or island inhabitant, nostalgic for a place she has never quite been, spends most of her time hanging around Chicago's Montrose Harbor (20, 22) and on the "concrete circle that overlooks the lake" (20) akin to an ocean. Even though the narrator does not explicitly mark herself as Cuban American or as a Latina, Sandra, the "dark" and "jealous" (11) stereotype of a Latina lover of this potentially de facto Latina lesbian narrator, has just left her for another woman who lives in the queer Mecca of San Francisco, the historically Spanish city whose gay heart is Castro Street, an irony for any queer Cuban exile as Guillermo Cabrera Infante is wont to point out.[17] The narrator, whose tale of woe unfolds in a confessional mode, warns us that she always has an automobile accident after a breakup with a girlfriend.

Following this confession, the story repeatedly jumps back and forth in time "reconstructing" other breakups and subsequent car wrecks, but cruising all the while toward the "inevitable" denouement—the latest wreck, her "red and rusty" Volkswagen bug against a sleek, black BMW, with a dog lying under the latter's wheel.

The story is very concrete about many things, especially girlfriends' names and car models. It repeats and emphasizes through repetition certain place markers, identity markers, and habits. The word "Chicago" crops up numerous times, not only as the story's setting but possibly as a specific marker of the potentially Cuban American narrator's isolation. According to the census of the year 2000, Chicago's Cuban population was and still is notoriously small in relation to its Mexican and Puerto Rican populations. Another word that reappears numerous times is "lesbian." The narrator spends most of the story driving, grocery shopping, or mulling over broken relationships with various women whose choices conform to certain lesbian stereotypes—San-Francisco-bound, or vegetarian, or commune separatist, or *chicas con botas* (in this case, "little pointy boots" [16]), or even "straight-acting" to marry a rich man. She compares these broken relationships to dead-engine cars, claiming ignorance of how "the gears stopped working . . . the machinery went rusty . . . the motor simply wouldn't turn over" (17). However, this story, like "Cradleland" and "Man Oh Man," is also very unspecific about the first-person narrator's ethnicity and/or country of origin, which is striking because the title of the collection *We Came All the Way from Cuba So You Could Dress Like This?* raises expectations that *cubanidad* will be at the center of each of these stories. Yet, only the seventh tale with the same title as that of the collection foregrounds Cuban identity in the United States, though all of the tales save for "The Spouse" involve a first-person narrator. In two of the six first-person narratives the narrator is clearly not a Cuban American but instead, respectively, an Anglo gay man with AIDS and a Puerto Rican lesbian activist. The overall effect is to make cubanicity and particularly Cuban American status, at least for the 1.5 generation forward, a matter of absence rather than presence, of difference so "subtle" (19) one is compelled to ask what the difference in the difference is.

In the context of an a-historicity or dis-articulated history produced through exile and dislocation, repetition becomes a means to create, extemporaneously as it were, a history in the void. Of course, this void really isn't one but instead U.S. culture itself with its multiplicity of pressures compelling citizens or would-be citizens to conform. And, this culture, like others, is by and large patriarchal, hetero-normative, ethnocentric, and classist. The history created through the kinds of repetitions in "Wrecks"—on the most obvious level, breaking up with girlfriends and getting into car accidents—is a case history.

A case history is composed of the recording of recurring symptoms and illnesses. It is constructed on the basis of the recurrence of pathologies. "Wrecks" draws on this model of history constructed through repetition. The story begins with the question of insurance needed to cushion the narrator from the consequences of her own actions (11). The narrator presents herself as a distraught lover sifting through telltale signs of a failing relationship, trying to figure out where the trouble began that led to collapse. She mentions habits, repeating behaviors, that contributed to irritation and alienation between herself and her successive girlfriends. She charts behaviors into pre- and post-relationship phases (13). She mulls over the rise and fall of each relationship as if in search of the etiology of an illness. The equation of love with sickness—the construct "love-sickness"—is as old as chivalric romances, if not older. Obejas's story exploits the formula and "lesbianizes" it just the way she "'lesbianize[s]' high school necking experiences" (21) in her VW at Montrose Harbor. Such moments of "lesbianization" specifically inflect the camp recycling of high and low culture, of a whole gamut of codes and objects understood in relation to these codes. It is a crucial part of the difference in this redoing, or repetition, with a difference. One might be tempted to view this lesbianization as a kind of pathetic role-playing, a second-hand version of a macho code of behavior that includes frequent breakups with girlfriends and car wrecks. Insurance companies actually take into account the latter in the cost of insurance policies for males under the age of twenty-five. As for the lesbianization of a usually macho code of behavior, the story itself literally suspends the promise of its effectiveness in quotation marks, as if to indicate "nice try" to this trying-again or repetition. But, it is precisely through these types of repetitions and suspensions that the story invokes the codes of dominant culture to rob them, commit an act of theft that steals their power through the introduction of difference within the repetition. In José Esteban Muñoz's terms one might say that the narrator of "Wrecks" disidentifies with a macho Anglo-American Beat code of the road, changing the code by inhabiting it in ways that signify quite antithetically or at least resistantly to a hetero-normative, patriarchal system.[18]

Repetition's capacity to rob rather than reinforce may come as a surprise to some readers and critics. In *Difference and Repetition* (first published in 1968), however, philosopher Gilles Deleuze insists that repetition belongs to an economy of "theft and gift."[19] And about repetition under the rubric of theft, Deleuze notes, "if repetition is possible, it is as much opposed to moral law as it is to natural law . . . Repetition belongs to humor and irony; it is by nature transgression" (5). It is a theft and a transgression because each repetition usurps the place of and displaces that which it repeats; it interrupts the repeated thing with difference, self-same difference. Thus, repetition may be said to give rise to difference, not sameness, in the mind of the contemplator, viewer, or reader (70). At the very least, it aides and abets it: "Difference inhabits repetition" and it also "lies between two repetitions" (76)—all the more so when repetition occurs within a framework of a differential, of self-conscious loss. This loss, this difference as differential, has the simultaneous status of a concept and an emotion. In "Wrecks" the difference between one repetition and the next, one relationship and another (and the trashed repetition of each failing relationship in the form of a car wreck followed by another car wreck) is measured in the feeling of that which falls "short," fails to live up to promises—disillusionment. To clarify through example, each successive relationship is supposed to make up for the pain of the previous failed one and yet it brings "more" pain by bringing more or less the same pain. The effect involves an involution of Marx's observation, which Deleuze cites, about the relationship between history and repetition: "all great events and historical personages occur, as it were, twice . . . the first time as tragedy, the second as farce" (92). In Obejas's story, the last breakup (with Sandra) is the most tragic because it is the most farcical. It was supposed to make up for the pain of the previous relationships and instead it repeats the pain, returning, in the aftermath wreckage of its crack-up, irradiated with the farce (a different kind of force) of tragedy.

"WRECKS" AND CUBAN AMERICAN LESBIAN CAMP

Why choose the word "camp" to describe the sort of serialization as repetition and repetition as recycling that occurs in this story? After all, repetition can be described in many ways and has been, as the work of Deleuze, among others, testifies (not that Deleuze's theorization of repetition and difference and discussions of camp are mutually exclusive, quite the contrary). Furthermore, camp per se is not descriptive enough. The numerous definitional essays in the reader *Camp: Queer Aesthetics and the Performing Subject* edited by

Fabio Cleto show that camp is not one thing (in fact, according to Esther Newton, not a thing at all but a relationship between things, an activity of transformation) nor does it have a known and certain origin despite understandings and manifestations of it as a gay or queer sensibility. There are different kinds of camp. As a category, camp is inclusive, therefore elusive. In his "Introduction: Queering the Camp," Cleto compares camp to a diamond, a multiuse, multifaceted crystal that resists attempts to crystallize it even while critics circle around, but cannot settle on, the identification of recurring yet also competing understandings of camp: as exaggeration and flamboyance, as irony, as parody, as witty incongruity, as relishing in a conscious indulgence of the vulgar, as a coded language or lingo (presumed to have originated within Anglophone British homosexual subcultures), as a mode of perception, as a mode of performance, as semiotic ambiguity (a movement from place to place, quite literally a "camping"), as a series of repetitive and stylized acts, as a crisis of codes and signs that undoes culturally sanctioned binarisms and differentiations between the genuine and the simulated, as self-expression, as a strategy of invisibility or passing, and so on. Cleto adds that, politically speaking, camp has been associated with both elitist (aristocratic) and democratic impulses (Sontag's 1964 essay does both without resolving the contradiction); practiced and read as both conservative and progressive, assimilationalist or accomodationist, and subversive or resistant.[20] He suggests that camp, like queer, can only be understood "in the mobile or transversal relation" of such polarities, opting for both/and rather than either/or logic (23). But even after one has admitted that camp in its many manifestations defies neat polarization and that such is most definitely the case in a survivalist, depressively upbeat (affectively picaresque?) story entitled "Wrecks," one is still left with the task of determining the suitability of invoking the term camp in relation to Obejas's story and, having deployed the term, of exploring it in this instance, as a particular practice or kind of performance to illuminate the dialectic between aesthetics and politics in this work.

Furthermore, establishing the suitability of the elusive term camp to "Wrecks" is only part of the task. Without falling into the trap of essentialism, of producing the impression that there exists one kind of Cuban American lesbian camp and that "Wrecks" is its representative text, the other and more ideologically significant part of the task lies in demonstrating how the story "Cuban Americanizes" and lesbianizes a camping out generally assumed to be the province of a white, gay, male, upper-class subject and/or a culturally "knowing" dominant bourgeois subjectivity. As a matter of fact, Sontag's "Notes on 'Camp'" explicitly describes camp as a "badge of identity among small urban cliques" (275) and flags the "peculiar relation between Camp taste and homosexuality" arguing that "[w]hile it's not true that Camp taste is homosexual taste, there is no doubt a peculiar affinity and overlap" (290). Throughout her essay sketch she refers to and/or quotes the most famous of white British and homosexual dandies, Oscar Wilde. Not once does Sontag associate camp with a lesbian woman, and her exclusions as well as her ambivalent inclusions— "I am strongly drawn to Camp, and almost as strongly offended by it" (276)—have earned her essay and persona as public intellectual more than a modicum of irritation from scholars in the area of gay & lesbian and queer studies. Having said that, it is important to emphasize that "Wrecks" is not simply a particular example of camp by a Cuban American lesbian writer. If that were so, there would be little point in exploring the "Cuban American lesbian rubric" or suggesting, as I wish to do, that the story "Wrecks" proceeds out of and performs a curious cross-hatching between "Cuban American" as a deracinated and "wrecked" Latina sensibility and lesbian as both a nomadic and abjected one (cast away and downcast) within U.S. hetero-normative patriarchal commodity culture. If the joystick macho car culture has been and is a characteristic manifestation of a hetero-normative patri-archal commodity culture in which the car is used as a means by which boy gets girl and men show off their chrome equivalent of money and sexual potency, Obejas's story "Wrecks" puts quite a dent—actually many dents—in this vehicular confidence. Moreover, and here is one of the places where the "lesbian" and "feminist" (15) inflection of the story makes itself apparent, the narrator holds responsible not only heterosexual men, but potentially homosexual men complicit in the rebellion-containing mystification that is the "American Way" in the form of the "patriotic as hell" (18) machismo of the open road:

> I'm no fool, though. I know all this romantic posturing about wide-open spaces, the adventurous South, and on-the-road possibilities; all these images and metaphors for freedom are inspired by men, jaded men like Jack Kerouac—that repressed homosexual who never really found love and died a pathetic mess of a human being. It's all a cover-up for just one thing: desperation. (14–15)

In this way, the narrator delivers several blows to dreams of free-dom and independence, the treasured staple of a masculinist Anglo-American ideology of manifest destiny. She also knocks the activity most stereotypically associated with gay men in Western cultures and that is the transmutation of restriction and pain into beauty and perfection, into dreams of romantic possibility. The phrases "pathetic mess" and "desperation" resonate with homophobia turned into exaggerated critique, presenting not so much the "truth" as the cliché of the ugly truth beneath the glittering surface, the restrictive mundaneness under the already commodified joystick sweetness of "a tall, cool take-out Coke" the narrator gingerly secures between her legs while "pressing down on the accelerator" (25) in one of the story's many self-parodying mock-phallic moments. In the context of "Wrecks" this critique is emptied of self-righteousness. The difference between her sensibility and that of the macho dominant culture and those "repressed homosexual[s]" who repress not so much their sexuality per se as their emotional pain in a homophobic society is that she portrays herself as a castaway and a downcast—a lesbian melancholic on the move, going nowhere fast—and, in the process, "recuperates" pain, disillusionment, and abjection in the form of a simultaneously subtle and searing critique of the American Way.

This double movement keeps the camp from coming off as merely "self-hating complicity with the status quo" and pushes it more toward what Eve Sedgwick describes as "reparative" in *Novel Gazing: Queer Reading in Fiction*:

> The desire of a reparative impulse . . . is additive and accretive. Its fear, a realistic one, is that the culture surrounding it is inadequate or inimical to its nurture; it wants to assemble and confer plenitude on an object that will then have resources to offer to an inchoate self. To view camp, as among other things, the communal, historically dense exploration of a variety of reparative practices is to be able to do better justice to many of the defining elements of classic camp performance . . .[21]

Obejas's "Wrecks" is more mischievous than the therapeutic term reparative would suggest, and so reparative does not quite describe its tactics either as the story seems invested in breaking things up and setting them off! But, then, perhaps neither is it "classic" camp. It is hardly Anglo-centric in contrast to the list of writers and performance artists that Sedgwick names: "Ronald Firbank, Djuna Barnes, Joseph Cornell, Kenneth Anger, Charles Ludlam, Jack Smith, John Waters, Holly Hughes" (28). The difference between Obejas's camp in "Wrecks" and that described by Sedgwick or Sontag, for that matter, resonates, not surprisingly, with José Esteban Muñoz's exploration in *Disidentifications* of what he terms "*cubana* dyke camp" (125). In chapter five entitled "Sister Acts: Ela Troyano and Carmelita Tropicana" of *Disidentifications*, he introduces what he describes as a distinctly Cuban and Cuban American aesthetics of camp in the form of *choteo*:

> I propose choteo as another optic, one that is perhaps aligned with a camp reading and, at other times, perhaps out of sync with such a hermeneutic, in order to decipher Carmelita's performances and production. Choteo is like camp in that it can be a fierce send-up of dominant cultural formations. Choteo, again, like camp, can be a style of colonial mimicry that is simultaneously a form of resemblance and menace. (135–136)

He emphasizes the "cubanidad" of *choteo* as opposed to the more culturally unspecific or perhaps more Anglo-inflected sensibilities of camp (as discussed by Sontag, Sedgwick, and other critics) and cites Cuban anthropologist and ethnographer Fernando Ortiz's definition of *choteo* as a practice imported to Cuba and a term derived from "African culture" and involving "a range of activities that include tearing, talking, throwing, maligning, spying, and playing. All these verbs help to partially translate the practice of *choteo*" (135). *Choteo* does not exactly match up with camp nor camp with *choteo*, and yet they are so intertwined in the practice of Ela Troyano and Carmelita Tropicana that he concludes by asserting their practice as one of cultural hybridity. I see no reason to abdicate the term camp in relation to Obejas's story. However, Muñoz's discussion of *choteo* underscores and reminds readers of the menacingly mischievous quality of camp in "*cubana* dyke camp" (125). This quality is certainly apparent in Obejas's "Wrecks," and the story constitutes a significant contribution to and short-story-based elaboration of Cuban American lesbian camp.

Let us consider the suitability of the term camp in approaching the culturally inflected—the (s)exilic—aesthetic tactics of "Wrecks." Andrew Ross's culturalist definition of camp helps to approach and approximate these tactics. In his well-known essay "Uses of Camp," Ross argues that camp, more than the remembrance of things past, is "the re-creation of surplus value from forgotten forms of labor."[22] His emphasis on "labor" in particular indicates an attempt to politicize camp or its uses at least in contrast to Sontag's de-politicization of it in her 1964 essay in which camp is dissociated from "content," "seriousness," or "morality" (another term for ethics?). For him, camp sensibility manifests itself as an implicit knowledge about culture in relation to history, to the passing of time—that is, about the way in which cultural icons and forms lose, rather than gain, commodity value over time, regaining it only when, as "history's waste," they are "irradiated . . . with glamour" (66–67). Ross situates camp in relation to the past and to the "ragbag" revival, knowing and often ironic (not merely nostalgic) of the past. While it is true that much of camp sensibility would seem to "rescue" and feed off of the past and many of the references found in "Wrecks" are to things strongly associated with the 1950s, such as "a 1956 vanilla-colored Porsche 356" (14), as well as the 1960s and 1970s (for instance, a VW bug, "one of the original Beetles" [13] and disco), this theory of camp does not account for the bricolage of features from the past and from the very present everyday, a bricolage in which modes and objects of present or ongoing existence are taken up with the same irony and bittersweet ludicrousness classically associated with camp revival.

The camp of "Wrecks" can be defined as a tactics of reiteration, reenactment, and repetition that is not so much irradiated with glamour as suffused with pain, with the anguished melancholy of a broken-hearted lesbian for whom mourning is problematic because, among other reasons, society does not take her pain seriously. As a lesbian and a potential member of the 1.5 generation of Cuban Americans, the narrator cannot count on hetero-normative Anglo-dominant, Cuban, or specifically conservative Cuban American cultures to be sympathetic toward or respectful of her grief for the loss of her girlfriend. In this country, as in many countries around the world, far too many people find it inconceivable that a "lesbian" or "gay" person might be in a profound state of shock and grief at the loss of a partner. As women in patriarchal cultures, lesbians face the added exclusion of not being taken seriously or granted respect. It is no accident that lesbians typically have gained the most visibility as stand-up comedians. That is a role for which patriarchal culture makes some allowance, although usually in a highly circumscribed form. The humor must not be too biting, lest it seem castrating, which explains why many lesbian stand-up comics do their best to threaten phallogocentrism in all its forms. As the narrator of "Wrecks" jokes darkly, deconstructing the hetero-sexual marriage industry trading in notions of the proper paths for consummation and consumption, "I . . . forgave myself for the temporary insanity that let me forget . . . that lesbians can only have, at best, a pseudo-marriage. I told the girl I was pseudo-separated, and surely headed for pseudo-divorce" (22).

Furthermore, as a whole, Cuban Americans in the United States, partly because of the political reactions of Cuban American communities in Miami, are routinely portrayed in the media, like women themselves, as hysterical and out of control. Those who are not rightwing are rendered invisible. Arguably, perhaps in reaction to this kind of general dismissal or the privileging of the feelings of certain sexual, ethnic, and political groups over others, the operation of camp repetition in "Wrecks" picks up on the return of the Freudian repressed (consider the narrator's seemingly involuntary penchant for post-relationship car wrecks) and hitches it to a calculated, contrived (though seemingly "natural") return of the very objects and commodified figurations of identity and identification. Camp as a tactic or repetition that brings back or up certain cultural objects, signs, icons, and so on, suffused with pain, not glamour, can be understood as a means to make spaces, *lacunae*, for the grief of a minoritarian subject, the minoritarian subject whose grief is discounted on numerous levels, in terms of ethnicity, sexuality, and gender.

THE AGENCY OF CAMP IN "WRECKS"

Although this type of camp repetition shares the action of "returning" with the workings of the unconscious and the irruption of the unconscious into consciousness, it is distinguishable from the merely involuntary and spontaneous generations of the unconscious by its intentionality. If the agent of the unconscious is an impersonal "drive," the agent of this kind of camp (which has been designated, variously, by critics from Sontag onward as deliberate, active, or performative) is a person who underscores her involvement in repetition—is self-conscious about it.[23] This is so even when the repetitions occur involuntarily. The narrator of "Wrecks" is self-conscious about her involuntariness and self-conscious in a way that pokes fun at the therapy model of cathartic expression of an unexpressed or unresolved conflict:

> When I told Lourdes, she suggested that if I know the accident is imminent, and that if having the accident is the only way out of this post-Sandra depression, then maybe I need to just get it over with and run over a newspaper boy, ram a mailbox, or hit a station wagon filled with suburbanites. She said that maybe by avoiding the accident I'm delaying the healing process, sidestepping the very idea that Sandra and I are as dead as disco. (23)

At every opportunity, the narrator not only confesses her own dysfunctionality but does so in a way that exposes the absurdist or irrational "functionality" of the society around her, proliferating with cars, mailboxes, cigarettes, Coke machines, 7-Elevens, pimp shoes, radios, televisions, phone and fax machines, and stray dogs, unwanted or discarded pets (akin to other kinds of Significant Others) soon to become roadkill or the like. Despite critical disagreement over the validity of the category of "intentionality" with regards to camp, the narrator of "Wrecks" is such an agent, if not as performer in the narrative then most definitely as observer and commentator upon her own actions, however involuntary those are represented to be.

According to the intentionality argument, camp as noun and verb both imply the consciously contrived or stylized gesture, that which is purposely mannered or obviously coded. More than conscious production, camp, according to this argument, entails self-consciously intended production and perception. Intentional agency is also what distinguishes camp from kitsch. Kitsch applies to objects that repeat without intention and without self-consciousness—mechanistically— like Campbells soup cans and car wrecks and "crazy wind-up toys" that are "too wound up" and "careen[ ] off into the furniture" (15) even though these items, as everyday living items as well as "damaged goods," might be classified as schlock according to the explanation of these aesthetic categories set forth by Ross.[24] Furthermore, the narrative drive of "Wrecks" toward disaster subjects what could be classified and/or experienced as "kitsch" to seemingly irrecoverable demotion, loss of what little worth it might have had. Kitsch becomes schlock when it does not work well, when it breaks down, when it lies inert and "dead as disco" (23), well, up to a point. When kitsch corrodes or decays beyond a containing general category such as schlock, when, to borrow from Obejas's story "Wrecks," "the gears stopped working for us . . . the machinery went rusty without our knowing, and one day the motor simply wouldn't turn over" (17) or worse, the dog's body reveals itself to be upon closer inspection a "colossal, mangled heap" under a BMW's wheel, "one eye like blue glass, the other black with blood from the ruptured sclera" (27) it, that is, what was kitsch, can no longer provide what Obejas's "Wrecks," referring to cars, describes as a "very cool, very American answer to pain" (14). Kitsch, broken and decaying beyond the boundaries of its own metal, plastic, or integumentary containerization (in the case of roadkill), becomes something else. It becomes, to employ a phrase from "Wrecks," "shrapnel of guilt and regret" (21), sharp, bloody, and potentially wounding bits and pieces of thwarted desire. It no longer serves to sedate or numb pain. Moreover, as roadkill, it "lies" bleeding outside of the bounds of culture and culture's concerns with ordering and stratifying its own productions. It cannot serve to mark status in social terms. It represents the abolishment of all such lines of demarcation. Camp, kitsch, and even schlock—to the extent that they are aesthetic categories inscribed within a discourse of class distinction wherein camp connotes social mobility (i.e., consider the implications of the metaphor of the diamond to explain its functioning) or a kind of arch recycling versus kitsch and schlock, stasis (despite aspirations) and lack of status—generally affirm, like comedy, the triumph of the social order as an ordering of matter and identity.[25] Wrecks and roadkill, however, belong to what Julia Kristeva has theorized as the realm of the abject,[26] that which in one fell blow, like a tragic flaw (but this time in the service of a game of chance and probability), annihilates status and the limits upon which it depends, reducing symbol-making creatures, human beings, to our "condition" in its most untouchable forms—blood, guts, putrefaction, rust, and slime.

A ruptured, rupturing de-containerized, de-borderized kitsch together with the calculated repetition of iconic fragments of "American culture" attests to the operations of a tragicomic camp sensibility running through Obejas's collection of stories *We Came All the Way from Cuba So That You Could Dress Like This?* in subtle contrast to Sontag's claim that "camp proposes a comic vision of the world" (288). This particular camp sensibility deliberately combines what is mechanistically manufactured by the culture at large with the flotsam and jetsam of unrequited and unrewarded desire. It shows up how desires for love, acceptance, and belonging have been colonized by a very U.S. world of consumerist mass production—so much so that the mechanistically repeated and the return of the unconscious (its drives) are inseparable, not only for this sensibility but within it. The effect is both amusing and painful, if not lethal, as with the broken bits of kitsch that are its material or with the "reckless macho men or women" who, in their wretchedness, inflict misery "on an innocent bystander whose only desire was love, or comfort, or maybe even something as simple as fun" (21).

Heart-Br(e)aking the "Mainstreaming into Traffic"

In relation to this story of relentless breakups and car wrecks cruising to its inevitable and heavily foreshadowed denouement, the phrase with which I began "mainstream into traffic" is a loaded and key directive. How brilliantly campy to end this tale of the brittle shrapnel of attraction and desire with so slick an image. "Mainstreaming" originally coined to describe the action of tributaries in relation to larger bodies of water, means to join the dominant course or flow. Curiously and perhaps significantly it evokes images of water. Obejas actually wrote a short story entitled "Waters" about a Cuban American lesbian who returns to Cuba on what might seem like a reverse-direction national project to mainstream with a pre-Castro Cuba of memory though the story's currents drag on any such nostalgic attempt.[27] This story is filled with images of water, oceans, showers, rain, sweat, and so on. Water in that story is, among other things, an extended metaphor for desire between women. But streaming in "Wrecks" has quite a different signification, harnessed as it is to the containing, majoritarian "main" and yet dropped almost as a bad joke, following in the wake of streaming green antifreeze from crushed cars and blood from a slaughtered dog. In a story about the adventures of a narrator–protagonist so fixated on cars and driving—as she tells us, "I can't stay away from cars when I'm heartbroken" (13)—the phrase "mainstreaming into traffic" ostensibly points to the action of rejoining the flow of traffic after the interruption occasioned by the accident. But, of course, as an act of closure (and the mention of the act does bring the story to a close), it not only conforms with, but perfectly represents the operation of camp in Obejas's stories. What would appear at first merely as closure is in fact repetition or deliberate reiteration. In this case, what is reduplicated like a gesture no longer original or innocent is textuality itself and specifically the workings of metaphor that may be conceived as functioning according to the components of tenor (the concept) and vehicle (the means by which the concept is conveyed).

Beyond textuality, the phrase "mainstreaming into traffic" reduplicates in miniature the streamlining pull of the dominant culture upon so-called (I reluctantly invoke these phrases[28]) subcultural or minority subjects. In cultural terms, for instance, we might ask ourselves what it means for a Latina, possibly Cuban American, lesbian who has crashed into the car of a non-Latino family man with a "perfect haircut" (26) and wearing a "trench coat" (27) to mainstream into the traffic on a U.S. highway. On the one hand, many details indicate the narrator's desire to fit in with dominant, English-speaking, Anglo-American U.S. culture—references to Coke machines (11), various U.S.-made cars such as a Dodge Valiant (12) and an "old Chevy van" (13), "all American" pop icons Jimmy Dean and Jack Kerouac, 7-Elevens and "American flags" (24), freeways, Country and Western music, and the patriotism of renting a speedy sports car and "driving at night, very fast, sure, in a car that does absolutely everything you want it to" (18). On the other hand, the cities invoked in the course of the story—Chicago, Los Angeles, San Francisco, Washington, D.C., New Orleans, Miami, and Santa Fe—all have high non-Anglo, and in many cases, specifically Latina/o populations. The map or cultural topography "Wrecks" conjures of the United States reinforces rather than erases cultural heritages alternative to a dominantly "Anglo" and hetero-normative one. "Wrecks" does present a few glimpses of nuclear-family heterosexuality (12, 26) and concentrates on various more or less long-term couple relationships between lesbians with a butch-femme dynamic camping typical "straight" relationships. However, the story is ultimately about the experiences of a "heart-broken" Latina (and potentially Cuban American) lesbian on the loose who, behind a wheel, becomes more of a (s)exile than ever, an outlaw, a "criminal" (27), a "menace" to herself and possibly to others. This driver's education version of the "lavender menace" would seem to be playing with the heterosexual fear of "the homosexual exception" that is the subject of Michael Bronski's 1998 book *The Pleasure Principle: Sex, Backlash, and the Struggle for Gay Freedom.*[29] The narrator's outlaw-with-a-broken-heart stance, a female James Dean, defies the mass production and codification of identification through consumer citizenship at the same time that it participates in it—for what is this stance but the campy repetition of resistance toward the mainstream, the dominant culture's values?

The painful and painfully "funny" camp sensibility in Obejas's stories turns repetition into a mode of deferral and loss, and resistance through such stalling, serial wreckage. The familiar image of cops "waiting" for a driver to mainstream back into traffic introduces, at the story's end, the possibility that this particular driver may not mainstream even though she is expected to do so. Ironically, the story closes with an action that has not happened and yet is more or less inevitable. To drive, the narrator must mainstream into traffic. However, the mainstreaming will neither succeed in erasing the memory of the breakdown and the sensation of feeling "like a criminal caught in some horrible act" (27), nor does it insure progress once the motor has started again. A potential traffic jam and further collisions (*or choque de coches*) lie ahead, not swift and painless assimilation or "getaways" (14) on the "open road." No wonder the story concludes with having the cops "wait" for our Latina lesbian narrator to mainstream into traffic.

In terms of cultural citizenship or membership within the larger social order, the end of the story underscores the operation of camp sensibility in Obejas's work. The reiteration of the coded gesture, the recognizable cultural icon, the stereotype, the cliché is as much if not more about stepping on the brakes and breaking, halting, the streamline than about pledging allegiance to the flow of the dominant culture. Thus, although the text references icons and products that inhabitants of the United States consume voraciously (according to their respective means) to prove themselves American and part of the dominant culture—Coke, cars, American Express credit cards, Hollywood films, popular magazines such as *Time, Popular Mechanics,* and *Penthouse,* Country, Western, and hard Rock & Roll music, and insurance—it does not, at any point along the way and certainly not in the end, deliver the goods but hijacks them (even from its antiheroine narrator). Within the framework of "Wrecks," these goods are a long-term relationship that continues to work—as the narrator puts it, analogizing the relationship to a cross-country car trip, a relationship in which "I didn't ever really know where we were going, but we were going, and it was steady, and it mattered" (19).

Lest one misconstrue a "long-term relationship" as merely a personal affair of the heart, it is important to note that, unlike Lourdes, the narrator's best friend, little and sometimes nothing designates the women with whom the narrator attempts to make a go of it as Latinas. Sandra, Loretta, and Doris appear generic, undifferentiated from the U.S. mainstream except with regard, perhaps, to their sexuality. Unlike the narrator, they do not collect Mexican rugs, drop references to "the domino theory" (13), or contemplate buying *santería* "materials for a hex to cause California to fall off the earth and thus eliminate all chances of happiness for Sandra and her new babe" (20). Thus, the narrator's quest to make a long-term relationship work entails surviving and negotiating the *choque de coche,* the one long car crash composed of an expanding series of car crashes, that is, culture clash between herself and her lovers and between her own life and that of the dominant culture.

Actually, "Wrecks" as a text is an exercise in the assimilation of colliding bits and pieces of culture(s)—from *santería* to Cuisinarts and Metallica, from Philip Glass tapes to Mexican rugs. Implicitly, the story juxtaposes this helter-skelter model of assimilation against mainstreaming or the dominant culture's model of assimilation as homogenization in which the crazy disjunctures, cracks, and crashes between things no longer show. "Wrecks," like the narrator, "assimilates" all manner of things "from" the dominant culture and especially products such as cars in the U.S. heartland on a desperate quest for romantic happiness and fulfillment. However, the cars, those literal and metaphorical "vehicles" of Obejas's short story, repeatedly mentioned and that collide together—a VW and a BMW—are not U.S. models such as a Dodge or a Chevy, but foreign ones, specifically German. The presence of German cars cuts in several directions, not least of which is an ironic comment, within the framework of concerns about assimilation as homogenization versus assimilation as hybridity, on the long-standing emulation of German culture by Anglo culture and vice versa. The repeated mention of German cars in the Midwest, the supposed center of manufacturing of American cars, wedges a split between assimilation as homogenized conformity to an American standard and assimilation as cultural hybridity and the transformation of the familiar by the foreign. German products are usually associated with power, efficiency, and transcendence of mundane limitations, almost as if the product were to have captured a bit of German idealism, though, generally, such philosophical matters have no household recognition in the United States. The story "Wrecks," however, works against any transcendence, philosophical or otherwise, by wrecking such promise every time. The transcendence of romantic happiness and fulfillment elude the narrator; instead, she is left with mangled mass productions and a broken heart. This state of affairs might be described as the incongruity between having and holding. In the world of "Wrecks" the narrator consumes—repeatedly proving herself a socially mobile, good consumer citizen or a dupe of commodity capitalism depending on the reader's perspective—but she cannot hold the one thing she wants most. To make matters worse, her ongoing quest has resulted in the creation of her own little assembly line production—a string of wrecked relationships metamorphosing from camp to kitsch to "shrapnel of guilt and regret" with each successive failure. Readers are encouraged to view the landscape of her heart (and of the U.S. heartland) as one of rusting metal scrappage, a reiterative twist on the familiar phrase "the rust belt" deployed to describe an economically depressed postindustrial Midwest where manufacturing plants have closed to reopen overseas with cheaper sources of labor.

In "Wrecks" a model of assimilation or integration as crack-up and failure in the context of a campy being-in-the-know about and reiteration of various cultural codes to no avail manifests itself in a postcolonial lesbianly and Cuban Americanly inflected resistance to the "progress" that the authoritarian law (represented here by the cops) of mainstream culture expects. If camp reiterates in Obejas's stories to deliberately combine what is mechanistically manufactured by the culture at large (including stereotypes of identity and identification) with the flotsam and jetsam of unrewarded desire, this assimilative repeating combination manages to transform repetition into a mode of deferral or postponement while it cruises toward (and even at the very moment of) narrative denouement. Although the narrator, who never uses a word of Spanish except for the term "*santería*" comes across as an assimilated Latina, and although none of the stories in the volume of stories *We Came All the Way from Cuba So You Could Dress Like This?* treat the reader to the linguistic code-switching and trans-linguistic wordplay in which some Cuban American writers such as Cristina Garcia and Eliana Rivero and performance artists Coco Fusco and Alina Troyano (alias, Carmelita Tropicana) engage, the code reduplication, including the suspended image of mainstreaming into traffic, resists or stonewalls. It stonewalls (one might claim even jinxes) the American Way that immigrants and exiles are ideally supposed to experience—"a new world" (to quote from the story with the same title as the collection's) and beginning "anew" on a new road. I invoke the term "stonewall" to summarize the story's campy strike against "the American Dream" and to signal that this Cuban American les-bian camp repetition is linked to breakdown and even death, *real* wreckage, not to mere devaluation over historical time and subse-quent re-glamorizing recuperation. The actual 1969 historical event now referred to as Stonewall began in the wake of a literal death—gay icon Judy Garland's, from what the coroner's verdict pronounced an accidental overdose of sleeping pills (one repetition too many). On the evening of Garland's funeral, the New York City Vice Squad police descended on the gay and lesbian patrons of the Stonewall Inn bar on Christopher Street. When, in the usual manner, the police tried to heckle and arrest these patrons, they, who in their grief were in no mood for this "game" of routine harassment, refused to budge and instead set their bar on fire and assailed the police with bottles, cans, stones, and whatever else was at hand. Rather than compliance, the police were greeted with rage. If the patrons burned their own bar—their own yellow brick road or life line "garland" to pleasure and momentary happiness in an oppressive world—so be it. Like Judy they had had enough and were unwilling or simply could not be made any longer to dance and sing at the end of a rope. Similarly, the camp of "Wrecks" attempts to resist colonization by mollifying promises. The narrator spins her wheels in the heartland, mass producing begin-nings and endings, over and over, stripping the gears of American experience of their purported authenticity even while the accidents attract cop cars with their all-American red, white, and blue lights revolving and flashing like disco strobes or exploding like fireworks in the frightened narrator's face: "There are lights everywhere: red and terrible white lights from all the cars, blue lights threatening epileptic seizures . . ." (26).

For a story structured around so many car-crashes, one might expect it to be called "Crashes" in homage (however parodic) to J.G. Ballard's 1973 novel or David Cronenberg's 1996 film entitled "Crash." But unlike the premise of the novel and film about people turned on by such crashes, "Wrecks" does not offer this sort of demented catharsis. In fact, its ontology is quite different from the very notion of a crash measured in units of maximum impact though impacts do occur in the story. The word "Wrecks" refers as much to shipwrecks as to car crashes, a fact that may not seem significant at first until one considers that this is after all a story by a Cuban American writer and that "wrecks" carries the burden of factual allusion to the wreckage of so many *balsas* or rafts from Cuba to Miami or to other parts of the continental United States. As factual allusion, it also resonates more broadly as a metaphor for Cuban exilic experience, in this case Cuban American. The story inflects that exile with one of being a lesbian looking for a relationship that will not wreck and instead making "one false start after another" (15) largely because these women are carrying too much cultural baggage with them. One of the heaviest items on these rafts adrift in the heartland and continually splintering apart is the burden of desire for the next thing, some place and someone better than what they know. At least two of the narrator's ex-girlfriends succumb to the lure of a westward horizon and leave the "heartland" of Chicago for "Los Angeles" (12) and "San Francisco" (14), somewhere West from the East, and not Southward. This repeating pattern may be "Wrecks" ultimate implosive camp repetition of the American Way and its heartless effects. The story does not imply that such dysfunction is particular to lesbian women or Cuban American women or, for that matter, to Cuban American lesbians. Neither the narrator nor any of her ex-girlfriends is marked as Cuban. Someone by the name of "Doris" would seem to be Anglo. When I say "these women," I mean all the women in the story. The cultural baggage they are carrying are the promises and expectations generated by the American Way. However, in the case of those who, like the author and even the narrator, may be of the 1.5 Cuban American generation, the burden of a compounded odyssey (west across the United States in search of happiness after already having drifted westward from Cuba on a raft that wrecked) was and is especially crushing. "Wrecks" employs this crushing burden of a compounded odyssey to crush the promise of somewhere else or elsewhere into a devastated and devastating here and now.

Obejas's 1996 novel *Memory Mambo* ends with the image of a blue fly smashing itself against a windowpane immediately after having been released from a puddle of water by the narrator and central protagonist Juani Casas. One might read the puddle of water in terms of an island such as Cuba and the windowpane in terms of a country such as the United States or a continent such as North America. Repetition and repeated wrecks govern this pathetic little scene from *Memory Mambo*. The story "Wrecks" concludes with a stray dog crushed under the wheels of a BMW. The dog signals a wanderer or a beast fable version of a (s)exile unwanted and potentially mistreated in any nation (whether Cuba or the United States or both). At first referred to by the narrator as a "he" (27), the dog becomes a "she" when the narrator claims her as "irreplaceable" (27). This s/he dog (a sacrificial substitute for or representative of the narrator herself as much as of her ex-girlfriends) is no longer a voyager but instead literally stopped dead in her tracks, reduced to the here and now or, reversing and compacting that phrase, to a nowhere abjectly resistant to that to-be-manifested-destiny of a *somewhere over the rainbow* trumpeted as the reward for mainstreaming. This abject resistance to an elsewhere cuts in at least two directions simultaneously. While showing up what Emilio Bejel refers to as "the enormous pull of American consumerism and mass culture,"[30] it most definitely plays "dead" on the American Way. But, it also refuses nostalgic notions of conscription into a Cuban nationalist project (pre-Castro, *castrista*, or post-Castro) that can be divorced from queer lesbian–feminist experiences of history and desires for the present and the future.

NOTES

1. Achy Obejas, "Wrecks," in *We Came All the Way from Cuba So You Could Dress Like This?* (San Francisco, CA: Cleiss Press 1994), 28; hereafter cited in parentheses in the text.
2. Janet Wolff, "The Sociological Critique of Aesthetics," in *Aesthetics and the Sociology of Art*, 2nd ed. (London: The Macmillan Press Ltd., 1993), 11–26.
3. Guillermo Gómez-Peña, "The Multicultural Paradigm: An Open Letter to the National Arts Community," in *Warrior for Gringostroika: Essays, Performance Texts, and Poetry* (Saint Paul, MN: Graywolf Press, 1993), 45.
4. Achy Obejas, *Memory Mambo* (San Francisco, CA: Cleiss Press, 1996); hereafter cited in parentheses in the text.
5. February 20, 2002. *http://latino.lsp.cornell.edu/98spring.htm.*

6. Achy Obejas, *Days of Awe* (New York: Ballantine Books, 2001), 32–44, 91.

7. Gustavo Pérez Firmat, *Life on the Hyphen: The Cuban-American Way* (Austin, TX: University of Texas Press, 1994). According to Isabel Alvarez Borland in her book *Cuban-American Literature of Exile: From Person to Persona* (Charlottesville, VA: University of Virginia Press, 1998), Gustavo Pérez Firmat was "the first critic to popularize this rubric in his Life on the Hyphen" that cited the findings of Rubén Rumbaut about the one-and-a-half generation's having to "'cope with two crisis-producing and identity-defining transitions: (1) adolescence and the task of managing the transition from childhood to adulthood, and (2) acculturation and the task of managing the transition from one socio-cultural environment to another'" (7, Borland quoting Pérez Firmat).

8. According to the glossary at the back of *Memory Mambo*, this term is applied sometimes pejoratively, sometimes affectionately (depending on context) to those Cuban exiles who came to the United States through the port of Mariel in 1980 as part of a mass exodus used by the Cuban government for propaganda purposes. According to official Cuban broadcasts, those who left were "social scum." Many were young men, dark-skinned, and/or gay, lesbian, or bisexual people against whom the government discriminated and who encountered further prejudice in the United States and yet who managed to survive and establish themselves in the face of these odds.

9. I do not know who first coined the term "United Statesian." February 2002, I found it employed in Chicano scholar and writer Alejandro Morales's 1992 novel *The Rag Doll Plagues* (Houston, TX: Arte Público Press) in the following sentence: "Mutual respect endured between the Mexicans, Canadians and United Statesians, but there still persisted an attitude of apprehension" (144). However, I would like to thank my students from the expository writing courses I taught on Latina/o literature at Harvard University, fall 97–spring 99 for being the first of my classes to experiment with the term "United Statesian" as a more geo-culturally precise term than "American." The latter was, after all, first used to designate the Caribbean and South America, not the United States, and technically refers to the Americas as a whole, not just the United States. I have condensed the slightly unwieldy term "United Statesian" to U.S.ian. It has a somewhat sci-fi sound to it, but perhaps that is most appropriate for a country that vacillates between imagining itself to be the world and imagining itself to be another world, another planet within or "off" this one. I am not sure that U.S.ian presents a more progressive identity concept for the United States in relation to other countries of the world even though it does serve to check the grandiosity of assuming unproblematically that the United States is "America."

10. Richard Rodriguez, "Pocho Pioneer," in Bobby Byrd and Susannah Mississippi Byrd (eds.), *The Late Great Mexican Border* (El Paso, TX: Cinco Puntos Press, 1996), 217.

11. Richard Rodriguez, *Days of Obligation: An Argument with My Mexican Father* (New York: Penguin Books, 1992), 48.

12. Richard Rodriguez, *Brown: The Last Discovery of America*, paperback ed. (New York: Penguin, 2003), 155.

13. *Days of Awe* describes deracination as "destierro" in the following terms: "In English, destierro always converts to exile. But it is not quite the same thing. Exile is exilio, a state of asylum. But destierro is something else entirely: its banishment, with all its accompanying and impotent anguish. Literally it means to be uprooted, to be violently torn from the earth" (309).

14. I have employed the phrase "lesbian identity" rather than "lesbianism." The latter has been used in a pathologizing, essentializing manner. In fact, one might argue that in the United States the suffix "-ism" automatically gives rise to a phobic response in as much as it is associated either with disease (a syndrome) or ideology or both. Ideology is frequently pathologized as something to be abjected from the body politic rather than acknowledged and claimed.

15. September 20, 2001. http://www.historyproject.org/projects/aeintro.html.

16. Susan Sontag, "Notes on 'Camp'" in *Against Interpretation and Other Essays* (New York: Farrar, Straus and Giroux, 1964); hereafter cited in parentheses in the text. According to Sontag's sketch, "Camp proposes a comic vision of the world. But not a bitter or polemical comedy; if tragedy is an experience of hyper-involvement, comedy is an experience of under-involvement, of detachment" (288).

17. Guillermo Cabrera Infante, *Mea Cuba*, trans. Kenneth Hall (New York: The Noonday Press, 1995), 71.

18. See José Esteban Muñoz, *Disidentifications: Queers of Color and the Performance of Politics* (Minneapolis, MN: University of Minnesota Press, 1999), 25–27; hereafter cited in parentheses in the text. Muñoz's definition of "disidentification" as a technology of self and a political strategy is indebted to "anti-assimilationist thought" in which the subaltern or minoritarian subject receives, decodes, and recodes elements of/from majoritarian or dominant culture.

19. Gilles Deleuze, *Difference and Repetition*, trans. Paul Patton (New York: Columbia University Press, 1994), 1; hereafter cited in parentheses in the text.

20. Fabio Cleto, *Camp: Queer Aesthetics and the Performing Subject* (Ann Arbor, MI: The University of Michigan Press, 1999), 1–42; hereafter cited in parentheses in the text.

21. Eve Sedgwick, "Paranoid Reading and Reparative Reading; Or, You're So Paranoid, You Probably Think This Introduction is About

You," in *Novel Gazing: Queer Readings in Fiction* (Durham, NC: Duke University Press, 1997), 27–28.

22. Andrew Ross, "Uses of Camp," in David Bergman (ed.), *Camp Grounds: Style and Homosexuality* (Amherst, MA: University of Massachusetts Press, 1993), 67; hereafter cited in parentheses in the text.

23. Cleto, *Camp*, 23.

24. Ross, "Uses of Camp," 145.

25. As is evident from my discussion of camp, kitsch, and schlock, I wish to shift further downward Ross's associations of kitsch with "the class aspirations and upper mobility of a middlebrow audience, insufficient in cultural capital to guarantee access to legitimate culture" (Ibid., 145). I would argue that "kitsch" is the failure of such middlebrow ambitions, a failure marked by "clichéd" taste that does not have the campy wits to recognize itself as such. Ross does observe, however, that "kitsch is no more a fixed category than either schlock or camp" (145). It would seem that for intellectuals (that aristocracy of the mind?) to participate in kitsch is taboo. One may "camp about" or admit to having produced or read "schlocky work." But "kitsching about" is unheard of and no one would be likely to approvingly describe her or his own work or even someone else's as "kitschy."

26. On the collapse of categorical borders and the social order threatened by what lies outside or beyond it, see Julia Kristeva, *Powers of Horror: An Essay on Abjection*, trans. Leon S. Roudiez (New York: Columbia University Press, 1982), 53–55, 71.

27. See Achy Obejas, "Waters," in Naomi Holoch and Joan Nestle (eds.), *The Vintage Book of International Lesbian Fiction* (New York: Vintage Books, 1999). I am indebted to Patience Vanderbush for pointing me to this story.

28. I reluctantly invoke the widely used phrases "minority" or "subcultural" because while they do accomplish the task of marking difference from hegemonic culture, they have a way of reinforcing perceptions of those cultures or groups of people to which they refer as indeed "minority" when in fact such a designation may be outdated or only possible from a hegemonic ethno-geo-centric perspective. Specifically, "Latinas/os" may be described as a minority group within the geographical borders of the United States, but not within "America" or the Americas in a hemispheric sense. From this latter perspective, Anglos could be described in terms of a minority.

29. Michael Bronski, *The Pleasure Principle: Sex, Backlash, and the Struggle for Gay Freedom*, 1st ed. (New York: St. Martin's Press, 1998).

30. Emilio Bejel, *Gay Cuban Nation* (Chicago: The University of Chicago Press, 2001), 211.

INDEX

(Please note that page numbers in *italics* indicate end notes.)